GOLF'S
GREATEST
EIGHTEEN

GOLF'S GREATEST EIGHTEEN

TODAY'S TOP GOLF WRITERS DEBATE AND RANK THE SPORT'S GREATEST CHAMPIONS

EDITED BY DAVID MACKINTOSH
WITH "NEW MONEY" STATISTICS BY JOEY KANEY

Contemporary Books

Chicago   New York   San Francisco   Lisbon   London   Madrid   Mexico City
Milan   New Delhi   San Juan   Seoul   Singapore   Sydney   Toronto

Library of Congress Cataloging-in-Publication Data

Mackintosh, David.
  Golf's greatest eighteen : today's top golf writers debate and rank the sport's greatest
champions / edited by David Mackintosh ; statistics by Joey Kaney.
    p. cm.
   ISBN 0-07-141366-9
    1. Golfers—Rating of. 2. Golfers—Statistics. 3. Mackintosh, David.
 I. Kaney, Joey. II. Title.

  GV964.A1G64 2003
  796.352'092'2—dc21   2002041489

Illustrations by Paul Szep

1 2 3 4 5 6 7 8 9 0 AGM/AGM 2 1 0 9 8 7 6 5 4 3

ISBN 0-07-141366-9

McGraw-Hill books are available at special quantity discounts to use as premiums and sales
promotions, or for use in corporate training programs. For more information, please write to the
Director of Special Sales, Professional Publishing, McGraw-Hill, Two Penn Plaza, New York, NY
10121-2298. Or contact your local bookstore.

This book is printed on acid-free paper.

To my wife, Susana, for her incomparable belief, exceptional good humor, and understanding. Without her constant encouragement this book could not have become a reality.

Also to Joey, best numbers man in the business.

Contents

Foreword

There is endless animated debate in famous clubhouses—at Augusta during the Masters, St. Andrews during Royal and Ancient Golf Club meetings, indeed at all major championship venues: if a foursome of Bobby Jones, Ben Hogan, Jack Nicklaus, and Tiger Woods were to play today, who would be the champion of champions? The proposition would be even more intriguing were they to compete on the same terms of modern, wonderfully conditioned courses, using the latest aerodynamic golf balls and rocket-shafted titanium clubs.

A fantasy, of course, but David Mackintosh has come close to answering this intriguing question with actuarial acumen.

Indeed, the intrepid compiler of this book has gone much further than just one match, pitting the best of the twentieth century, all against all, in the most fascinating analysis ever. Applying a logic that the most constant factor in professional golf over the years has been competition for prize money, David has given every great player in his *Golf's Greatest Eighteen* a fascinating opportunity—playing on today's world tour for the same rewards to see who comes out on top.

This remarkable feat of accurately balancing many thousands of events over ninety years reveals some remarkable and previously unconsidered aspects of the game's all-time heroes. So who really was the greatest of all time? In the spirit of the challenge, the author simply provides the facts, many thousands of them, neatly arranged to put these glorious champions in perspective, each reader then the final judge.

Additionally, chapter after chapter, vivid word portraits capture these great figures at the pinnacle of their time on center stage—their spirits as well as their crucial swings. James Dodson on Sam Snead in southern hillbilly vernacular is splendidly authentic; Stanford man John Garrity on Stanford champion Tom Watson, both with midwestern values, is arrow-straight. Kay Kessler has the ultimate inside track on Jack Nicklaus, following his every footstep from schoolboy Ohio days to the present. Jaime Diaz on the determined, disciplined, and shot-making perfectionist Ben Hogan is splendid stuff as indeed is each and every contribution.

I have had the great privilege to play with some of the men portrayed here or at least stood in awe in the presence of Bobby Jones, Ben Hogan, and others. And I know all these writers and admire their passion for our game's great history—passion obvious in each turn of phrase, each word of praise. No false flattery here. The authors of the eighteen essays here know their men and their times. Past greatness simply flows from their pens, chapter after chapter, leaving the warm afterglow of having met excellence, in its own time.

I hope you will savor the treats presented within the covers of this outstanding compilation as much as I did.

Enjoy!

Robert Trent Jones, Jr.
Palo Alto, California, March 2003

Introduction

The concept that gave rise to this book is really quite simple—the search for an unbiased standard by which to compare the greatest players of the modern age of golf.

The methodology was equally straightforward, even if achieving the summary-numbers required several thousand hours of research and computing time! What we've done within these pages is put golf's greatest eighteen players on the same course, playing for the same prize money. Hypothetical money, obviously, but an entirely realistic treatment of the theme.

Rather than a meaningless application of monetary inflation over the period since 1914, we've built an entirely revolutionary "New Money" model that incorporates factors such as present-day values of past tournaments combined with a mathematically precise evaluation of events no longer in existence but, in their time, tournaments of significance.

In effect what we've done is build our new-money model to ensure every event, even if no longer on the Tour schedule, has been assigned a hierarchical value, particularly taking account of field quality and the perceived importance of the event by the players themselves. For instance, from its inception in 1899 up to World War II, the Western Open was considered a major championship by all players. In addition, high-level events of yesteryear no longer in existence, such as the Miami Open, the North and South, the Metropolitan, and the Southern Spring Open, have been restored to former glory.

Clearly the major championships stand apart, although it is fair to say that the current "Big Four" became true heavyweights only after World War II. Prior to that time, although winners of the U.S. Open and PGA gained maximum public attention, the prize money allocated for these titles was frequently less than for other zone titles or even exhibition matches. Indeed, delving into the past reveals that on more than one occasion a major title-holder decided to forgo the following-year tournament in favor of better cash available elsewhere.

Established in 1934, the Masters Tournament became a major only after a considerable incubation period, with the Western Open retreating to regional status. The PGA Championship moved to a higher plane when it adopted the stroke-play mode in 1958, and the venerable British Open, although the 1860 granddaddy of them all, was in desperate need of inter-national resuscitation until 1960. Simply, the glorious evolution of the game of golf is comprehensively acknowledged in the New Ranking calculations.

The "New Money" numbers in this book, while taking note of some of the eccentricities of the early days, wholeheartedly recognizes the current "Big Four" major championship structure and the major championship ranking tables are entirely based on results from the Masters, the U. S. Open, the British Open, and the PGA. Thus, sadly, Walter Hagen receives no *major* credit for his five Western Open victories—but then again, nei-ther does Bill Casper, who won the event on four separate occasions.

Hagen was past his best by the time the Masters began and although Gene Sarazen won the championship in 1935 with that glorious double-eagle, his best years were also well behind him.

This quirk noted, applying our "New Money" formula to the *current* major championship structure presents an entirely fresh perspective on the all-time rankings, adding significance to what increasingly has become a confusion between simple win-totals and real value. No longer, however, can anyone claim to have passed Sam Snead's lifetime earnings in one event—or Sarazen's during a lucrative afternoon!

Initially, readers may question why this book does not include senior-circuit earnings in the overall-money section. There may be a case for doing so elsewhere, but to be included within this structure we'd also have had to find a way to incorporate the early years' exhibition-match earnings of Hagen, Sarazen, and others who were dependent on such income for survival—long before the advent of competitive golf for the over-fifties. It should also be noted that to balance past and present (in the early days sometimes even tenth-place paid zero cash) New-Money calculations are based on first through twenty-fifth places and ties, with wins-only in the international section.

It would be wonderful to be able to bring back Ben Hogan, Gene Sarazen, and Walter Hagen, playing with modern equipment on today's beautifully manicured courses against Jack Nicklaus and Arnold Palmer in their prime or today's Tiger Woods. Even the authors of this anthology cannot conjure up that miracle. This book, however, is the most realistic level-playing field constructed to pit all against all.

Because the one constant, whether yesterday, today, tomorrow, or next century is this—professional golfers will always play for money.

It's what they do!

Choosing the Greatest Eighteen Ever

Why eighteen? More than a couple of centuries ago some Scotsmen in Fife thought it was the number best suited to golf, so why change a winning formula?

Which eighteen? Perhaps the hardest choices are whom to leave out. There is a small and very select group that automatically selects itself—Ben Hogan and Jack Nicklaus probably the most obvious. Maybe even the secondary list, let's say the Greatest Ten, would not be too difficult to assemble, although numbers nine and eleven would probably be as hard to choose as numbers eighteen or twenty-one.

So we set one standard. Those eligible for inclusion must have captured more than one modern-day major championship, that is, more than one title—not just two U.S. Opens or PGAs. So what's Greg Norman doing there, you ask? In defense, could anyone imagine leaving the Great White Shark off the list of modern greats? Fortunately book editors, unlike golf referees, are able to bend the rules from time to time. Which brings us to another exception.

Robert Tyre Jones, Jr.? An amateur in a money-rankings book? Hypothetical money, of course! Could we honestly have ranked twentieth-century major championships and excluded Bobby Jones? Although he never banked one professional cent from his victories, RTJ is a noble exception.

The Other Greatest? Arguably the contributing authors to this anthology, but among the wonderfully talented golfers excluded yet not ignored are Roberto De Vicenzo, Henry Cotton, Arthur D'Arcy Locke, Peter Thomson, Flory Van Donck, Jimmy Demaret, Tom Kite, Johnny Miller, James Braid, Doug Saunders, Bernhard Langer, Harold Hilton, Bob Charles, Julius Boros, Tony Jacklin, Tom Weiskopf, Tommy Armour, and many, many more. Frankly, we'd love to do another book on these guys as well.

Individual New-Money Career Records

At the end of each chapter you will find individual New-Money career records for the player discussed. These records have been collected painstakingly, event by event, year by year, from a multitude of public-domain and contributed sources to provide the most comprehensive career records ever assembled on the players who make up Golf's Greatest Eighteen. Each year of each player's tournament life is here, an analysis that has incorporated approximately eighteen thousand event appearances. Taking account of each and every player's Top 25 finishes over his career has meant sifting around 450,000 items of data.

In addition, although charting international wins was a tiny exercise by comparison, simply finding ways to capture and analyze the data, then transform it into meaningful 2002 U.S. dollars, was a fascinating and occasionally bizarre exchange-rate paper chase.

What we discovered during these last nine months is that composite ready-reference books on player winnings, or indeed comprehensive major championship money records, simply did not exist—until now.

New-Money Rankings of Golf's Greatest Eighteen

Before we turn to the individual giants of the game, let's take a look at where things stand through the end of the 2002 season.

First, let's review the total career wins used in our analysis, bearing in mind that we have incorporated certain wins that were in subsequent years categorized as unofficial:

WHO'S WON WHAT

	Total Wins	Major Wins	Non-Major Wins
Gary Player	124	9	115
Jack Nicklaus	86	18	68
Sam Snead	84	7	77
Greg Norman	74	2	72
Arnold Palmer	71	7	64
Seve Ballesteros	69	5	64
Ben Hogan	57	9	48
Billy Casper	57	3	54
Byron Nelson	51	5	46
Walter Hagen	45	11	34
Tom Watson	44	8	36
Tiger Woods	41	8	33
Gene Sarazen	40	7	33
Nick Faldo	38	6	32
Lee Trevino	35	6	29
Hale Irwin	28	3	25
Ray Floyd	25	4	21
Bobby Jones	7	7	N/A

Now let's review total New Money for each of the individual major championships:

INDIVIDUAL MAJOR CHAMPIONSHIPS

	Masters	U.S. Open	British Open	PGA
Jack Nicklaus	$11,017,207	$7,618,651	$9,906,731	$9,301,551
Sam Snead	7,689,127	4,450,252	1,418,229	7,498,276
Gary Player	6,621,272	3,799,923	5,660,590	4,292,200
Tom Watson	5,942,160	4,018,072	6,858,000	2,619,630
Walter Hagen	361,200	6,043,434	5,918,750	6,662,941
Arnold Palmer	7,068,600	5,349,147	3,812,297	2,560,433
Ben Hogan	6,918,287	7,155,568	1,106,140	2,921,875
Gene Sarazen	2,231,740	5,986,745	3,069,801	6,554,694
Nick Faldo	3,576,133	1,737,425	6,234,853	1,657,632
Ray Floyd	4,791,467	2,603,528	1,660,474	4,009,648
Byron Nelson	5,819,660	2,020,009	252,832	4,715,459
Lee Trevino	733,872	3,458,304	4,356,193	3,601,216
Greg Norman	3,498,240	1,844,551	4,179,063	2,427,810
Seve Ballesteros	4,452,867	1,052,015	4,665,539	625,900
Billy Casper	3,496,780	3,403,900	603,636	3,085,684
Tiger Woods	3,477,824	2,569,830	1,771,930	2,711,500
Bobby Jones	258,907	6,728,682	3,318,419	0
Hale Irwin	1,847,000	4,335,260	1,115,423	1,146,888

That gives us the following New Money totals:

TOTAL—MAJOR CHAMPIONSHIPS

	Total Majors
Jack Nicklaus	$37,844,140
Sam Snead	21,055,884
Gary Player	20,373,985
Tom Watson	19,437,862
Walter Hagen	18,986,325
Arnold Palmer	18,790,477
Ben Hogan	18,101,870
Gene Sarazen	17,842,980
Nick Faldo	13,206,043
Ray Floyd	13,065,117
Byron Nelson	12,807,960
Lee Trevino	12,149,585
Greg Norman	11,949,664
Seve Ballesteros	10,796,321
Billy Casper	10,590,000
Tiger Woods	10,531,084
Bobby Jones	10,306,008
Hale Irwin	8,444,571

Now we'll add all nonmajors to the package to reach the final, overall New Money totals:

NEW MONEY FINAL RANKINGS
UP TO END-SEASON 2002

	Total New Money	Majors New Money	Non-Majors New Money
Jack Nicklaus	$128,054,968	$37,844,140	$90,210,828
Sam Snead	123,362,693	21,055,884	102,306,809
Arnold Palmer	98,389,720	18,790,477	79,599,243
Billy Casper	88,814,588	10,590,000	78,224,588
Ben Hogan	85,993,150	18,101,870	67,891,280
Tom Watson	79,892,441	19,437,862	60,454,579
Gary Player	75,484,122	20,373,985	55,110,137
Byron Nelson	73,622,091	12,807,960	60,814,131
Gene Sarazen	66,254,136	17,842,980	48,411,156
Lee Trevino	65,843,558	12,149,585	53,693,973
Greg Norman	63,039,268	11,949,664	51,089,604
Walter Hagen	62,349,220	18,986,325	43,362,895
Ray Floyd	59,126,977	13,065,117	46,061,860
Hale Irwin	54,822,395	8,444,571	46,377,824
Nick Faldo	50,406,547	13,206,043	37,200,504
Seve Ballesteros	50,082,127	10,796,321	39,285,806
Tiger Woods	45,207,924	10,531,084	34,676,840
Bobby Jones	10,306,008	10,306,008	N/A

Of course, as the following eighteen stories confirm, there are many measures used to evaluate greatness, and who knows what money number or final rating Tiger Woods will achieve when he reaches Jack Nicklaus's age? However that may work out in the future, here's a new and different way of summing up the fabulous achievements of golf's greatest heroes for the twentieth century and beyond—as well as a means for each and every reader to reach a personal decision on who really was or is the *Greatest Player of All Time.*

PART ONE

Front Nine

Tom Watson

John Garrity

A couple hundred spectators surrounded him on that flat little seventeenth tee at the Pebble Beach Golf Links. Others milled about and chattered on the road behind him, creating a buzz like that at a cocktail party. Behind a big green hedge, a portable generator throbbed. Tom Watson, undistracted, took a couple of brisk waggles, slashed at his ball, and watched intently as it soared out toward the Pacific Ocean, hung in the air with the seagulls . . . and then plunged into a greenside bunker.

It was not the summer of 1982. It was not the final round of the U.S. Open, and Watson was not about to deflate Jack Nicklaus by chipping in for a birdie from the thick rough by the seventeenth green. No, this was some years later, a Saturday afternoon in February, and Watson, past his prime, was trying to survive the fifty-four-hole cut at the AT&T Pebble Beach National Pro-Am.

To do so, he now needed to get up and down from the sand—something he had done with monotonous regularity in the late seventies and early eighties, when he was the best player in the world.

"And then Tom did something I'd never seen him do," recalls former USGA president Sandy Tatum, Watson's longtime friend, mentor, and amateur playing partner. "He chunked it in the bunker, took a double bogey. Missed the cut."

An hour later Watson joined Tatum for lunch at the nearby Cypress Point Club. "I think any other man, having been what Tom Watson had been, wouldn't have been much fun," Tatum says. "Not Tom. He was a joy. We had a delightful lunch." As they left the club, Watson looked at his watch. "It's 4:30," he said. "We've got time to play nine holes."

"You've got to be kidding," Tatum said.

"I'm not kidding. We can play nine."

Tatum looked around. "You don't have any clubs."

"We can borrow some."

"How about shoes?"

"Can't you get me a pair of shoes? And a sweater?"

A quick search of the clubhouse turned up some shoes, a sweater, and Cypress Point member Hank Ketchum, a golf nut and creator of the "Dennis the Menace" cartoon strip. Within minutes the three men were out in the gloaming, hitting golf shots past deer grazing on turf grass. "We played with Hank's clubs, and I can't remember having more fun," says Tatum. "There was a dimension to Tom that I found almost unique, a deep, abiding love for the game. He still played for the sheer joy of playing."

There was, of course, another side to Tom Watson. He could be overearnest, obsessed with decorum, judgmental, even preachy. (Envious tour rivals used to call him "Carnac" because he had all the answers.) When he denounced comedian Bill Murray for his slapstick antics at the 1993 Pebble Beach Pro-Am, Watson looked stuffy. When he wrote a letter to Masters chairman Hord Hardin asking that wisecracking commentator Gary McCord be taken off that tournament's telecast, Watson appeared meddlesome. When he declined to autograph a program for Scotland's Sam Torrance at a 1993 Ryder Cup dinner, Watson—long admired for his impeccable manners—came off as rude.

But none of those missteps occurred when Watson had a golf club in his hand. The game brought out the best in him—the inspired competitor, the affable midwesterner, the supportive friend. Golf was his enduring link to innocence and wonder, and he fought to maintain that link, knowing its value. "When you mature, when you lose the dreams you had as a kid, you're no longer capable of playing a sport to its best," he once said. "Money has a lot to do with that. Abundance dilutes the desire."

It was a typical Watson remark—intelligent, on point, and tinged with self-reproach.

His was always the examined life. Watson was born on September 4, 1949, the second of three brothers, and driven home to a prosperous, leafy neighborhood in Kansas City, Missouri. His father, Ray Watson, was an insurance broker, a prominent amateur golfer, and a man for whom games represented moral instruction. "All the people who played golf with my dad were serious golfers," Tom says. "Serious meaning they loved the game, and every time they hit a golf shot they were there for one purpose only, and that was to hit it the best that they could."

By his midteens Tom played regularly with these grown-ups at the exclusive Kansas City Country Club. In the summers he entered the city and state amateur championships, drawing smiles with his short pants and droopy white socks—until suddenly he was wearing long pants and taking home the trophies. He had a boyish, gap-toothed grin, but he was an old soul, eagerly absorbing the tall tales and instruction of men three times his age. At Stanford University, where he played well but not brilliantly for the golf team, he would be remembered as an independent thinker who flirted with the antiestablishment views of the day, only to return in the end to the bourgeois sensibilities of his parents. "I was somewhat of a fish out of water at Stanford," he admits.

It was not until he graduated in 1971 that Watson decided to try professional golf, and the game he took out on tour was ragged. He didn't trust his swing—how could he, playing as often as he did from trees and ankle-high grass?—but his scrambling skills were extraordinary, and he chipped and putted as if he'd had a nerve bypass. The tour's Andy Bean said, "When you drive into the left rough, hack your second out into a greenside bunker, come out within six feet of the hole, and sink the slippery putt—when you do that, you've made a Watson par."

Watson was not, however, a winner. Tournaments slipped away from him on Sundays, and halfway into his third tour season players and reporters were beginning to whisper the C-word. Yes, Watson admitted—to himself, if not to others—he choked (although, as he would point out a few years later, "A lot of guys who have never choked have never been in the position to do so"). His most painful failure came in the 1974 U.S. Open at Winged Foot Golf Club. Leading by a stroke after three rounds, Watson wandered home with a final-round 79 and finished tied for fifth, five strokes behind his playing partner, Hale Irwin. In the locker room afterward, golf legend Byron Nelson approached a disconsolate Watson and said, "I know how you feel, son. I've thrown away tournaments, too." Nelson added: "If you ever want to talk about your game, call me."

Thus began one of the most significant friendships in golf history. Watson seized the opportunity to work with Nelson, and the old champion soon became another of those seasoned guides that he trusted. On the lesson tee in Texas, Nelson watched Watson hit balls, making an occasional suggestion and bolstering his confidence. Watson then watched Nelson hit balls, looking for elements he could incorporate into his own swing. "I always marveled at how Byron's club went through the impact area," Watson said. "If you drew a perfect arc, he was on it time after time. He never hit a wild shot. I was just sitting there, a boy with a man. He could play rings around me."

With Nelson and Kansas City Country Club pro Stan Thirsk monitoring his swing, Watson quickly dispelled the notion that he lacked heart. He got his first tour win, the Western Open, in the summer of '74. A year later, at Carnoustie, Scotland, he won the British Open, beating Australian Jack Newton in a play-off. During the next decade Watson exceeded his childhood dreams. Between 1977 and 1984 he won twenty-nine more PGA Tour events, including two Masters titles and the '82 U.S. Open, and won the British Open four more times, endearing himself to British golf fans. He also won three Vardon Trophies (for low scoring average), five PGA Tour money titles, and six PGA of America Player of the Year awards.

The most memorable Watson victories came at the expense of Jack Nicklaus, the greatest player of all time. The Missourian first baited the Golden Bear in the spring of 1977, firing a final-round 67 at the Masters to beat Nicklaus by two. A few months later the two Americans staged their famous "Duel in the Sun" at Turnberry, Scotland, in what was arguably the most dramatic final round in major championship history. Far ahead of the rest of the field, Watson and Nicklaus locked horns in a titanic test of wills, each topping the other with inventive shot making and pressure putting. "I don't believe I have ever before seen two golfers hole so many long putts . . . on fast, breaking, glossy greens," wrote Herbert Warren Wind. "They were also doing such extraordinary things from tee to green that it was hard to believe what you were seeing."

On the final hole, Nicklaus, trailing by a stroke, hit a miracle eight-iron from an almost unplayable lie at the foot of a gorse bush. He then rammed in a thirty-five-foot putt for birdie. Watson, having hit his seven-iron approach to within two feet of the cup, calmly rolled his putt in for the win. With his final-round 65, Watson finished at 268, smashing the British Open tournament record by eight strokes. Nicklaus walked off the green with his arm around Watson's shoulder, and both men smiled like winners.

Five years later, when the U.S. Open returned to Pebble Beach, Watson thwarted Nicklaus again. This time, though, the Bear had finished his round and was off the course when Watson delivered the coup de grâce. Any golf fan can replay the moment in his head: Watson with an impossible downhill chip from the deep rough just left of the seventeenth green . . . the aggressive chop with a sand wedge, the ball popping onto the green and picking up speed . . . the ball smacking the flagstick and diving into the hole for birdie . . . Watson running in a delirious loop, his arms raised above his head. That night, while having a celebratory drink with Watson, Sandy Tatum said, "You know, I never saw you look at the leader board."

"Yes, I did," Watson said. "I looked at it once, when I was walking from sixteen to seventeen. I looked at that leader board, and I said to myself, 'It's just me and Jack, and I beat him every time.'"

So good was Watson in his decade of dominance that observers scoffed when he predicted that family life would eventually undermine his commitment to tournament golf. The only thing that could bring down Watson, they argued, was his tendency to overanalyze his game. He treated his swing like a dirty carburetor, taking it apart and putting it together so many times that other pros said there had to be leftover parts on the garage floor. "I'm stubborn," he explained, "and I still don't know how to swing the golf club very well." His obsession with improving his swing was mocked by many; but—funny thing—his swing improved. Watson, in his forties, hit the ball better from tee to green than he had in his glory years. He found fairways. He moved the ball around at will: high or low, left to right, right to left, with spin or without spin. Unfortunately, his ability to putt and chip deserted him at the same time.

Suddenly he was the anti-Watson, a ball-striking machine with the short game of a weekend golfer. Asked if he had the dreaded yips, Watson would sigh and shake his head. "My problem is simply making a good, consistent short stroke. When I'm under pressure, the club goes straight inside. Closed and inside." Sympathetic fans sent him putting tips. And putters.

Watson's last great year was 1984, when he won three times in the United States and led the money list for a final time. He continued to play fifteen or sixteen tournaments a year, and he contended in several majors, playing with a kind of grim fatalism that struck some as heroic and others as masochistic. Few understood that Watson had always been steeled to failure; it went with his pursuit of perfection. Bruce Edwards, his caddie for close to three decades, told how his boss, striving for victory at Pebble Beach during a Bing Crosby Pro-Am, hooked his approach shot on the eighteenth hole into the Pacific. Another golfer might have hurled his club or turned away in disgust, but Watson watched the flight of his ball from impact to splashdown, his lips pressed together. "Why didn't you react?" Edwards asked afterward. Watson's reply: "Because that's my punishment."

To Watson, the ball in the drink was as instructive as the ball in the hole. He won five British Opens, but there was a poignant luminosity to the ones that got away, like the 1984 Open at St. Andrews, where he came to grief against the old stone wall behind the Road Hole. He won two green jackets, but he would forever be haunted by his final tee shot at the 1991 Masters, which darted into the trees on the right and left him without hope. "I don't make excuses," he said. "You make excuses, you're not fooling anybody."

There was still life in Watson's game. In 1996, after nine seasons without a victory, he shot a final-round 70 to edge David Duval at the Memorial Tournament. "I was looking for keys, secrets to perfection, the Holy Grail," Watson said, uncertain how to explain his return to form. "Then finally the lightbulb went on. I ironed out a few basics, and golf became fun again." Two years later, at forty-eight, he replaced Ben Hogan as the oldest player to win the MasterCard Colonial. The span between his first tournament victory and his last was the third longest in Tour history—twenty-three years, eleven months, and twenty-four days.

Watson accepted these late triumphs graciously and without hubris. "I don't put myself in the class of Nicklaus and Hogan," he said. "I'm not the golfer that they were." Perhaps not, but Watson's course management skills rivaled those of Nicklaus, and he was Hoganesque in his practice regimen and his insistence that a golfer's private life was not a matter of public interest. For a fair appraisal of Watson, the man, one had to go to his father, to Nelson, to Thirsk, or to Tatum, the men who had shaped his views on golf and life.

Tatum was the most voluble, employing his lawyer's mastery of language to describe a Watson more nurturing and playful than the one the public saw. ("Sandy uses words with which I'm not familiar," Watson said, reworking the old Bobby Jones line about Nicklaus. "He loves the game with a passion, and I love being around people who are like that.")

We go back to Tatum, then, for the last word on Watson. "I took Tom on a trip to Ireland one year," his old friend begins, "because I'd been kidding him about the fact that he had won three British Opens by that time, but he didn't have the slightest idea what playing golf in that part of the world was like." Tatum wrote ahead, advising the secretary of the Ballybunion Golf Club that Watson would be traveling incognito and didn't expect any hoopla. Ballybunion's members, respecting Watson's wishes, shared the secret with only a couple of close friends each. When he and Tatum arrived, Watson was greeted at the fabled links by two thousand spectators, some of whom had come from as far away as Belfast: "It was an absolute madhouse," Tatum recalls, "and a simply wonderful day."

At the fourteenth green someone had set up a table with Irish linen, Waterford crystal, and two large bottles of Irish whiskey. Watson and Tatum each downed a slug or two before moving to the fifteenth tee, where Watson drank in the view of towering dunes before sizing up his shot to the emerald green.

"How far is this hole, Tatum?"

"It's 227 yards, Watson."

Watson reached into his bag. "Watch me rip a one-iron."

"And rip a one-iron he did," Tatum says with an appreciative chuckle. "Finished about two feet from the hole, an absolutely glorious stroke."

After Ballybunion the two tourists drove to Dublin to play Portmarnock. From there they flew to Scotland for a round at quirky little Prestwick and another round just up the road at Royal Troon, where Watson would soon win his fourth Open Championship. The trip ended at Royal Dornoch Golf Club, in the far north of Scotland, where another crowd came to pay homage to the latest in a distinguished line of Open champions named Tom. "It was raining, the wind was blowing, huge crowd," says Tatum. "Coming up to the eighteenth green, at about a quarter to six, Tom said, 'Hey, why don't we send the caddies home and then come back when all these people are gone and play again?'"

The caddies, delighted to be part of the ruse, made a show of leaving but returned in an hour. "Now it was just the two of us with our caddies. We were walking along the third hole, and the wind was really whipping our rain pants, the rain was sliding off our faces."

The champion suddenly stopped. Tatum, looking back, said, "What is it, Watson?"

And Watson said, "I just want you to know this is more fun than I've ever had in my whole life in golf."

They played on in the North Sea gale, enjoying that blissful state that golfers know, where punishment is indistinguishable from reward.

TOM WATSON

	Total New Money	Wins	Top10s	Top25s
Majors	$19,437,862	8	45	65
Other Official Tournaments (and International Wins)	60,454,579	36	187	300
TOTALS	**$79,892,441**	**44**	**232**	**365**

MAJOR CHAMPIONSHIPS

	New Money	Wins
Masters	$5,942,160	2
U.S. Open	4,018,072	1
British Open	6,858,000	5
PGA	2,619,630	0

BEST OTHER EVENTS

	New Money	Wins
Byron Nelson	$6,112,257	4
New Orleans	4,107,675	2
World Series of Golf	3,837,020	1
Western Open	3,531,579	3

Year	New Money	Total Wins	Top 10s	Top 25s	Majors	Other Events
1972	$ 643,071	0	1	7	$ 0	$ 643,071
1973	1,394,985	0	7	12	104,500	1,290,485
1974	2,740,541	1	10	20	301,593	2,438,948
1975	5,409,743	3	14	24	1,565,960	3,843,783
1976	2,389,478	0	11	15	250,653	2,138,825
1977	7,217,945	5	19	22	2,441,709	4,776,236
1978	6,272,376	5	15	22	1,134,088	5,138,288
1979	6,581,709	5	15	18	604,175	5,977,534
1980	8,464,727	8	18	24	1,637,872	6,826,855
1981	4,707,949	3	10	17	1,112,346	3,595,603
1982	5,469,013	4	13	18	2,461,940	3,007,073
1983	3,634,799	1	11	15	1,937,540	1,697,259
1984	4,785,707	4	11	17	1,235,454	3,550,253
1985	1,693,915	1	7	11	312,463	1,381,453
1986	1,866,299	1	9	13	321,430	1,544,869
1987	2,561,016	1	6	13	1,028,334	1,532,682
1988	1,455,149	1	6	11	156,800	1,298,349
1989	1,060,990	1	3	8	562,540	498,450
1990	838,781	0	5	9	219,338	619,443
1991	1,411,652	0	6	10	355,585	1,056,067
1992	1,117,838	0	6	8	0	1,117,838
1993	1,092,742	0	5	10	419,187	673,555
1994	1,210,850	0	5	10	509,786	701,064
1995	737,296	0	3	7	100,800	636,496
1996	1,858,479	0	4	7	174,479	1,684,000
1997	1,262,342	0	6	9	357,291	905,050
1998	1,673,000	0	4	5	0	1,673,000
1999	64,000	0	0	1	0	64,000
2000	132,000	0	1	1	132,000	0
2001	0	0	0	0	0	0
2002	144,050	0	1	1	0	144,050

Byron Nelson

Dave Hackenberg

Byron Nelson had befriended Bing Crosby during World War II, when the pair would often team up at Red Cross and other war effort benefits, so Nelson wasn't particularly surprised to see the famed crooner standing near the first tee at Riviera Country Club during the first round of the Los Angeles Open, the season's inaugural PGA Tour event in 1945.

"You going to go with me some?" Nelson asked Crosby.

"I'm going to follow you till I feel you've made a bad shot," the singer replied. It wasn't until the twenty-ninth hole, number eleven in the second round, that Crosby gave Nelson a wave and walked off to watch some of the other action. It was a thin six-iron approach that landed short and in a greenside bunker that sent Crosby on his way.

Good thing, too. If Nelson hadn't hit that shot, Crosby might have had to follow him from city to city, course to course, tournament to tournament, from January until around mid-October. Byron Nelson, you see, didn't hit many bad shots in 1945.

With 61 career victories, 52 of them in PGA-sanctioned events, five major championships, two Ryder Cup appearances (he was selected for two others that were not played during World War II), and a streak that began in early 1941 and saw him finish "in the money" in 113 consecutive PGA events, a record to this day, "Lord Byron" can hold his own with any and all of the great players in golf history.

When the subject is 1945, though, none can even come close. Nelson won eighteen tournaments that year, eleven of them in succession. The previous record for consecutive wins? Four. The best since? Six—by Ben Hogan in 1948 . . . the same by Tiger Woods in 2000.

Nelson finished second seven times and had 100 subpar rounds out of 112 played, highlighted by a 62. He set records for the lowest tournament score (21-under-par 259) and lowest single-season stroke average (68.34). The former stood for a decade, the latter for fifty-five years, until Woods bested it.

The best golfer of all time? Probably not. His career lasted, for all intents and purposes, for just eleven full seasons. It wasn't until 1935 that Nelson played in more than five tour events during one year, and 1943 hardly counted with only three official events on the then-Tour schedule.

At the end of the 1946 season, just one year removed from his record-setting campaign, Nelson retired without a career grand slam and with only two money titles. Sam Snead, Jack Nicklaus, Ben Hogan, and Arnold Palmer all won more tournaments.

So, no, not even computer wizardry can elevate him to the status of all-time best. But when it comes to a single season, no one has done it better, before or since. Three major titles in the same year by Hogan in 1953 and Woods in 2000 are certainly large blips on the radar screen, and some fans might put them in the same category as Nelson in 1945. But eighteen single-season wins, eleven of them in a row, one after another after another and so forth, well, these are numbers that will never, ever be touched.

Any discussion of Nelson's season in '45 must begin in 1944, his last of five years as head professional at storied Inverness Club in Toledo, Ohio. He finished sixth or better in all twenty-one PGA events he entered, winning eight times, averaging 69.67 strokes per round, and banking Tour-high earnings of $38,000, combining cash and war bonds ($8.78 million in New Money). But he wasn't satisfied. "I kept a record of every round, and when I went back at the end of the year I saw too many references to poor chipping and just plain careless shots," Nelson recalled recently. "I really wanted to set records like scoring average and for the lowest tournament score, records that might stand awhile."

Nelson had another motivation as well, one that only he and his wife, Louise, knew about. Leaving Inverness at the end of 1944 allowed him to concentrate solely on tour golf, but he didn't intend to do it for long. He dreamed of owning a ranch, of making that his life, but neither he nor Louise, both products of the Depression, wanted to borrow the money. It had to be a cash purchase, and his accomplishments of 1944 led him to believe his dream could be realized with one or two more great seasons.

"My game had gotten so good and so dependable that there were times when I actually would get bored playing," Nelson wrote in his autobiography, *How I Played the Game*. "I'd hit it in the fairway, on the green, make birdie or par, and go to the next hole.

"The press even said it was monotonous to watch me—but having the extra incentive of buying a ranch one day made things a lot more interesting. Each drive, each iron, each chip, each putt was aimed at the goal of getting that ranch. And each win meant another cow, another acre, another ten acres, another part of the down payment."

Beginning with a runner-up finish to Sam Snead at Los Angeles, Nelson posted three victories and five seconds in his first eight events of 1945. His ninth tournament was a different story, a sixth-place finish behind Snead in Jacksonville, who won for the fourth time in the still-young season. "I played terribly," Nelson said of the Jacksonville tournament. "I guess I got a little steamed." How steamed? The next event, the Miami Four Ball, was played March 8–11. Nelson teamed with his close friend Harold (Jug) McSpaden to win that, and the Texan would not taste defeat again until August 19, when he finished tied for fourth, six shots behind amateur Fred Haas, Jr., at the Memphis Invitational.

In eleven straight tournaments over a period of more than five months, Nelson poured it on, winning five times by seven or more strokes. He played the nine stroke-play events in 109 under par. He won the PGA Championship, a match-play event in those days, by finishing seventeen-up in five matches. For the record, he played 204 holes en route to that major title at Moraine Country Club in Dayton, Ohio, in thirty-seven under par.

Of course, as is often the case with streaks, this one hardly got started before someone threatened to end it. And that someone was Sam Snead, no mild threat, who seemingly had the Charlotte (N.C.) Open won, not once but twice.

One week after winning with McSpaden in Miami, Nelson found himself number seventeen when his second shot flew over the green and out-of-bounds markers behind it only to hit a car and carom back into play. "Slamming Sam" was able to save par there, but not on the eighteenth hole, where his approach was short and he three-putted from a distant fifty feet.

That bogey forced an eighteen-hole play-off the following day, and Snead again lost a late lead, this to a Nelson birdie, producing another dead heat. Another eighteen holes were called for but almost didn't take place. In a bizarre development, a Charlotte newspaper columnist wrote of rumors that Snead had deliberately bogeyed the seventy-second hole of regulation so that a play-off would be required and he would be able to claim a share of the extra day's gate receipts. Snead was incensed by the report, at first threatened not to play, and was obviously distracted en route to a round of 73. After reading the morning paper, fewer than two thousand fans bothered to attend as Nelson shot a 69 for a four-shot victory. From there on Lord Byron was rarely challenged, winning twice more in North Carolina before cashing winner's checks in Atlanta, Montreal, Philadelphia (where he rallied with a final-round 63), and Chicago.

Even the nation's top courses fell into some state of disrepair during the war years, and the 1940s Tour rarely made those stops. Nelson instead won at courses called Myers Park, Starmount Forest, Hope Valley, and Capital City—mostly ragged courses, fairways often a mix of hardpan and unattended weeds—to the extent that many events were played using "winter rules," allowing competitors to move the ball a few inches into playable lies.

Nelson handled the quality courses equally well, however, surviving a second-round scare in the PGA Championship at Moraine Country Club—Mike Turnesa was two up with four holes to play, but Nelson finished birdie-birdie-eagle-par for victory—before scoring his largest win (by an eleven-stroke margin) in the biggest-money event of the year at Tam O'Shanter Country Club in Chicago and then making it eleven straight victories at the Thornhill Country Club, near Toronto, in the Canadian Open.

Nelson admitted years later that the pressure was "really getting to me" and that he was battling both mental and physical fatigue when he arrived at the Memphis Invitational. His concentration was wavering and with a second-round 73 putting him behind the eight ball, Nelson said he was genuinely relieved when Fred Haas won to end his incredible streak.

But it didn't put an end to the winning. Nelson scored again by ten shots in his next tournament at Knoxville, captured a seven-stroke win at the Esmeralda Open, and won his last two events of the year, in Seattle and Fort Worth, by a combined twenty-one shots. Prior to that strong finish, Nelson finished a distant second behind Hogan in Portland as the latter set a new all-time, 72-hole scoring record of 261.

"I remember some writers asked me how long Ben's score would hold up," Nelson said. "I told them it could be forever or it could last a week."

Close. It was two weeks later that Lord Byron won in Seattle with rounds of 62-68-63-66 for a new record, 259.

So he had his records, his incredibly low stroke average—another money title. He had, simply, the greatest single season ever authored by a golfer, one so incredible that it has quite appropriately reached mythical proportions through the years.

Something else has happened through the years, too. Critics, for one reason or another, have tried to cheapen Nelson's accomplishments in 1945 by suggesting that World War II allowed him to feast on weak fields and easy courses. Nelson was excused from military duty because of a blood condition, but Hogan, Snead, Horton Smith, Jimmy Demaret, and others were in uniform at one time or another, although most never saw overseas duty and spent considerable time on military-base golf courses. Regardless, many were back on tour in time for considerable portions of the '45 season. Snead played in twenty-six tournaments, winning six times, and Hogan played in sixteen events, winning twice. Among the most formidable of opponents was Nelson's close friend Jug McSpaden, who also set another tour record that year by finishing second thirteen times. At the time Nelson and McSpaden were nicknamed "the Gold Dust Twins," and for good reason.

"I think some people have a hard time now believing the numbers," Nelson said. "Maybe it's easier to believe them if they also believe no one else was playing."

Jack Burke, Jr., who won four tournaments in a row during the 1952 season, has no difficulty appreciating Nelson's accomplishment. "I don't care if he was playing against orangutans," Burke said. "Winning eleven straight is amazing."

Golf legends always seem to come in threes. Jones, Hagen, and Sarazen. Nicklaus, Palmer, and Player. At the dawn of the 1940s it was Nelson,

Hogan, and Snead, certainly good company, although only Nelson had won a major championship by then. The three couldn't have been more different. Snead was a rough-edged hillbilly from Virginia—considered crude by many, despite a graceful swing that would produce eighty-one PGA Tour victories and a bunch more not incorporated into today's official records, more than any other player in history.

Hogan was cool and distant, opening himself up to only a select few friends, working at the game harder than anyone before or since, most likely, and playing with what the great writer Herbert Warren Wind called "the burning frigidity of dry ice."

Nelson was a seven-day Christian, a tall man who seemingly had no enemies, someone who always said he hoped he would be remembered as much for being a kindly gentleman, an ambassador of the game, as for his playing record.

Nelson and Hogan were both sons of Texas, and their career-long rivalry dated to the earliest of days, when both were caddies at Glen Garden Country Club in Fort Worth. They faced off for the first time in the 1927 caddie championship, and Byron narrowly won, a trend that would continue for most of the next two decades.

Less than three years after that caddie match, while still in his teens, Hogan turned professional. Nelson was not quick to follow. Instead, young Byron dropped out of high school, worked a series of jobs, and played a lot of golf. He mowed the greens at Glen Garden, worked as a file clerk for the Fort Worth–Denver City Railroad, then took a position that he described as both flunky and gofer for a banking magazine. Meanwhile, Nelson found plenty of opportunity to hit the links. Jack Grout, later a famous teaching pro who became Jack Nicklaus' coach, was the assistant pro at Glen Garden, and he and Nelson teamed up to win just about every pro-am event within driving distance.

His success in those competitions as well as numerous amateur tournaments in Texas helped Nelson realize that while he might not have the background or skills for a business career, especially during the Depression, he did indeed have a flair for the game of golf. So, after being invited to play in an open tournament for both professionals and amateurs in Texarcana, Texas, in November of 1932, Nelson got off the bus dragging a suitcase and his golf bag and asked the tournament organizers how one went about becoming a professional. Turned out it was pretty simple. No tour schools, no qualifying tournaments. Plunk down a $5 entry fee, state your intentions, and you were considered a pro. Nelson did just that, finished third, and won $75. Just that quickly, he was on his way.

By the midway point of the 1938 season, Nelson had seven professional victories, including the '37 Masters, and had earned a Ryder Cup berth. Hogan had won nothing and had yet to be invited to Augusta National. Away from the tour, Nelson had landed a sound and lucrative club-pro job at Reading (Pennsylvania) Country Club, making around $4,000. Hogan, on the other hand, was glad to take the assistant pro's position at Century Country Club in White Plains, New York, earning just $500 a year.

In 1939, when Nelson signed a contract to move to Inverness the following spring, the president of the Inverness Club sat down to write a letter informing the other finalist of the club's decision. It began: "Dear Mr. Hogan."

Less than a week after signing the contract, Nelson traveled to Philadelphia and won the '39 U.S. Open. How did the Inverness folks react to having an Open champion in their immediate future?

"They were happy for me, but they didn't renegotiate," Nelson recalled, laughing. Actually, they did. At the next board meeting the governors approved a recommendation made by the club president that increased Nelson's fixed compensation by $1,000 and eliminated charges for meals. It bumped Nelson's salary over the initial seven-month contract period to $4,600, plus all pro shop and lesson proceeds. Ironically, Nelson returned to Inverness days later to team with Jug McSpaden in the Inverness Four Ball. One local newspaper heralded his arrival with a banner headline, and another wrote: "Although the 1939 golf season has yet to scratch the surface, Inverness officials are already taking bows on the stroke of mastery which will bring Byron Nelson here as head professional."

The Gold Dust Twins tied for first at Inverness but lost in a play-off to Henry Picard and Johnny Revolta. But Nelson won the next week at the Massachusetts Open and would add the prestigious Western Open title later in the year.

During his five years at Inverness (1940–44), Nelson won twenty PGA Tour events, among these the '40 PGA and the '42 Masters, and five other regional and local events that were not tour sanctioned. His earnings from competition during those years amounted to $53,192 in cash prizes and nearly another $20,000 in war bonds. Big money back then, and truly staggering if stated in New Money terms: $68.2 million between 1934 and 1946.

Nelson made no secret of his belief that playing the Inverness course, which by then had hosted two Opens, and against the club's best golfing members, was a key ingredient to the success he enjoyed on tour. Most of those members held a certain measure of awe for their head professional, but there was one cocky young lad who responded differently.

The very finest local player at Inverness Club was Frank Stranahan, in his late teens when Nelson arrived at Inverness but soon to emerge as the best amateur golfer in the United States, if not the world, during a decade-long span that began in the mid-1940s.

Stranahan and Nelson, who was enlisted by Frank's father to give the youngster lessons, never exactly saw eye to eye. Stranahan would occasionally challenge Nelson to a match, but the club pro, busy with his own tournament and teaching schedules plus his club-shop duties, was frequently unable to fit young Frank into his hectic schedule. All that changed in one day, the moment Nelson read more than a simple challenge in Stranahan's request for a head-to-head match.

"He was with a couple of the boys he usually played with, and he made it clear he wanted to play me, but there was something in the way he said it that made me feel he thought I was afraid to play him," Nelson recalled more than fifty years later. "I guess he got under my skin, because I got hot and I said, 'OK, Frankie, not only will I play you, but your two buddies can come along, and I'll play all three of you, your best ball against mine.' I was nicely steamed up and shot a 63, a new course record, beat Frankie and his friends, and Frankie never bothered me again." Years later Stranahan said his memory of that round was hazy. But he did praise Nelson as being "the best of his era, during the war years."

Stranahan's recall was clearer on another issue. "There was a professional named Henry Picard, who worked at a club in Cleveland and then in Florida at Seminole. Hogan complained to him once that he practiced all the time, really worked so hard at his game.

"Then Byron would hit town, somebody would pick him up at the train station, drop him at the course, then he'd head right to the first tee without practicing very much and he'd beat Hogan every time. Picard told him not to let it bother him, to keep working as hard as always, and soon he'd be the best. And Picard was right. Hogan was the next great player." True. But not until after 1945 and, perhaps, not without an assist from Nelson, who walked away from competitive golf after a six-win season at the end of 1946.

Lord Byron was a meticulous record keeper who could tell you his bank statement down to the penny. When he earned $152.50 for a thirteenth-place tie at the Pensacola Open early in '46, he knew it gave him the final bit of escrow money he needed for a 630-acre plot of land he wanted in Roanoke, Texas, a crossroads some twenty miles outside Fort Worth. He and Louise named it "Fairway Ranch," and once he had it, Byron Nelson, then just thirty-four years old, wanted for little else. "I finally had to admit I'd accomplished everything I'd set out to do in golf," he said. "It was time to move on. I wasn't sick, and I wasn't scared of the pressure like some speculated. I was just tired. And I'd achieved my goal. Once we'd given them the money and signed the papers and the ranch belonged to us, nothing else really mattered."

Although retired from competitive golf, Nelson never really left the game. He made infrequent appearances at tournaments over the next two decades, winning his old friend Bing Crosby's pro-am in 1951, two years after Hogan's only win in the event and one year after Snead tied for the last of his four Crosby titles. Nelson's last hurrah came on foreign soil, winning the 1955 French Open at the age of forty-three, although he continued to compete at the Masters for another decade. The gentle Texan also became the first superstar to mentor promising young golfers, most notably Ken Venturi, Harvie Ward, and Tom Watson. He was the first pro to regularly do live television golf commentary, and he and Chris Schenkel went on to became the game's first famous golf-broadcast tandem.

In 1968, Nelson became the first and, to date, only pro golfer for whom a PGA Tour event is named when the Dallas Open became the Byron Nelson Golf Classic. His name is still on the event.

No, Byron Nelson, gentleman farmer, with the emphasis on *gentleman*, never completely walked away from the game. And he didn't completely stop playing it until the morning of April 5, 2001.

The day dawned crisp and sunny, the dew just starting to burn off the emerald fairways, when Lord Byron walked to the first tee at Augusta

National Golf Club for the final time after twenty years of service as a ceremonial starter at the Masters.

"OK, little ball, one more time," the eighty-nine-year-old legend muttered before taking that same pretty, solid, streamlined swing one final time.

The ball didn't go too far, but it landed in the fairway and, for just an instant, as the crowd roared and Lord Byron's well-creased face broke into that warm, affable smile, it could have been 1945 again, when he authored a season against which all others will be measured until they no longer play the game.

BYRON NELSON

	Total New Money	Wins	Top10s	Top25s
Majors	$12,807,960	5	28	37
Other Official Tournaments (and International Wins)	60,814,131	46	177	213
TOTALS	**$73,622,091**	**51**	**205**	**250**

MAJOR CHAMPIONSHIPS

	New Money	Wins
Masters	$5,819,660	2
U.S. Open	2,020,009	1
British Open	252,832	2
PGA	4,715,459	0

BEST OTHER EVENTS

	New Money	Wins
Tam O'Shanter Open	$3,420,000	4
New Orleans	2,630,250	2
Texas Open	2,342,667	1
North & South Open	2,082,633	1

Year	New Money	Total Wins	Top10s	Top25s	Majors	Other Events
1933	$ 343,200	0	2	3	$ 0	$ 343,200
1934	1,020,432	0	3	7	54,897	965,535
1935	2,783,672	1	12	16	156,800	2,626,872
1936	4,157,849	1	18	23	123,200	4,034,649
1937	3,821,044	2	11	17	1,525,476	2,295,568
1938	3,240,316	2	11	14	616,375	2,623,941
1939	5,989,160	4	18	20	1,781,600	4,207,560
1940	5,019,983	3	13	14	1,551,395	3,468,588
1941	5,841,998	3	18	20	1,287,986	4,554,012
1942	4,597,254	3	13	15	1,327,000	3,270,254
1943	375,600	0	2	2	0	375,600
1944	8,782,092	7*	20	20	594,000	8,188,092
1945	15,556,092	17*	29	29	990,000	14,566,092
1946	7,043,433	6	18	19	841,470	6,201,963
1947	604,800	0	1	1	604,800	0
1948	317,200	0	2	2	162,400	154,800
1949	350,400	0	2	2	168,000	182,400
1950	246,400	0	1	1	246,400	0
1951	1,060,133	1	3	3	162,400	897,733
1952	679,743	0	3	5	64,960	614,783
1953	274,100	0	1	4	0	274,100
1954	449,200	0	2	3	134,400	314,800
1955	644,756	1	2	4	151,200	493,556
1956	0	0	0	0	0	0
1957	95,200	0	0	1	95,200	0
1958	81,200	0	0	1	81,200	0
1959	37,840	0	0	1	0	37,840
1962	122,193	0	0	2	0	122,193
1965	86,800	0	0	1	86,800	0

*Excludes Miami Four-Ball

Sam Snead

James Dodson

Maybe the funniest—and most astute—thing anybody ever said about Samuel Jackson Snead was that he would probably be considered the greatest player who ever lived—if he'd only had Ben Hogan's brain.

Indisputably, Slammin' Sam, the Peckerwood Kid and pride of Hot Springs, Virginny, a Blue Ridge hamlet no bigger than the hips on a corn snake, won more tournaments in golf than anybody—he claims 180 in all, but the PGA Tour places the official total at 81—and was the only player to win tournaments in six different decades, the first to shoot 59 in competition, the oldest player to win a PGA Tour event (at Greensboro; he was fifty-two at the time), and the youngest player to shoot his age (a 66 at Quad Cities in 1979). He played on seven Ryder Cup teams and captained two more, scored thirty-four aces in competition, and undoubtedly plucked more "pigeons" in his legendary money matches than any who played the game.

The combination of his spectacular ability to drive the ball prodigious lengths off the tee and his engagingly unrefined "hillbilly" personality—partly real, partly the creation of his brilliant manager and Tour impresario Fred Corcoran—made Sam a true media phenom, the sport's first major star to emerge since the retirement of Bobby Jones, attracting thousands of new fans and igniting unprecedented popular interest in golf at a time when the pro game was seriously languishing. Armed with the most graceful "natural" swing ever seen in golf and clothes that looked as if they'd been tailored for him, it was "Slammin' Sammy Snead," (a nickname he actually disliked, placed on him by the irrepressible Corcoran) who along with Byron Nelson and Ben Hogan consistently drove Tour scoring into the sixties and went on to capture seven major golf titles—three Masters, three PGAs, and the 1946 British Open. Decades later, when his colleagues were long gone from active competition, it was the ageless Sam Snead who was still chasing Old Man Par and helping to organize the U.S. Senior Tour.

History loves winners, and the fans simply couldn't get enough of the golfing exploits and homespun antics of Sam Snead in his prime. Upon seeing his swing, Bob Jones said he couldn't understand how Snead ever shot above 70, while big-city reporters loitered at his elbow, waiting to jot down the amusingly unrefined things that came out of his mouth—often as crude as they were insightful. A product of the Great Depression, Sam spoke of loathing banks and preferring to keep his tour winnings in a tomato can buried in his backyard. Regaling scribes about how he used to play golf barefoot back home in hills that were so narrow "a dog had to wag his tail up and down," and egged on by the publicity-minded Corcoran, Sam slipped off his shoes and played two of Augusta National's toughest holes barefoot, earning a couple of birdies, national headlines, and Gene Sarazen's indignant wrath. Upon winning his first tournament in Oakland, California, in January 1937, Snead saw his photograph in a New York paper and dryly asked his manager, "How'd they get my picture, Fred? I've never even been to New York." Sam meant it as a joke, but Corcoran passed it off for years as an example of his client's backwoods innocence.

Unfortunately, over the long haul of his unparalleled playing career, it's what Snead failed to accomplish on the golf course that makes many, including the man himself, pause and wonder what greater glories might have been. "I figured out once that if I'd only kept my head and shot 69 in the final round," he told me one sunny autumn afternoon during a round at the Greenbrier's famous Old White Course, where Snead first went to work as a shabbily dressed assistant pro in the mid-1930s and for seventy years served as pro emeritus, until his death in 2002; "I'd have won nine, maybe even ten, National Opens and probably a couple more Masters and PGAs. Frankly, it's the Opens I let slip away that hurt the most. Not a day goes by when I don't think about that, I reckon."

As USGA historian Bob Sommers has noted, though Snead never attained the most coveted and difficult prize in golf, no one meant more to the U.S. Open than Sam Snead—or broke as many hearts attempting to claim a tournament he probably should have won several times. Beginning with a spectacular finish in his first Open at Oakland Hills during his rookie year in 1937, Snead all but had his massive country-boy hands wrapped around the tournament's hardware when drab Ralph Guldahl came out of nowhere to take the trophy, the first of a series of major disappointments for the lanky Peckerwood Kid.

Two years later, at Spring Mill in Philadelphia, in only his third full year on the Tour, all Snead had to do was finish the seventy-second hole with a relatively easy par five, and the national championship he hungered for would be his. Instead, misinformed by someone in the gallery and believing he needed to make birdie, he committed his own number-one sin in competition—"Thinking instead of acting"—lost his celebrated tempo and focus, topped his tee ball, and then compounded the problem by putting his second shot in the face of a steep fairway bunker. Six shots later he staggered off the green with a humiliating triple-bogey eight, presenting the tournament to Byron Nelson. As he walked toward the clubhouse, Sommers recounts, "Women's eyes watered and men patted him on the back. Other players turned away to save him embarrassment." That tournament would forever be thought of as the Open Sam Snead "threw away."

But he was far from through blowing National Opens. In 1947, at St. Louis CC, rattled by the unexpected intrusion of USGA rulesman Ike Grainger, who was summoned by the Slammer's playing partner Lew Worsham to measure the length of their final putts—both of which lay about two and a half feet from the cup—Snead stepped back from his ball. Moments later, granted the right to proceed but visibly fuming, he missed the putt and presented the championship to Worsham—an incident Snead stewed about for decades.

As if to simply add insult to injury, two years later at Medinah, seemingly cruising to the championship at last, Sam lost to Cary Middlecoff by a stroke. In 1953 he entered the final round of the Open at Oakmont just one stroke behind Ben Hogan. Perhaps reflecting on his many past frus-

trations, he went on to shoot 76 and lost by six. When reporters asked afterward if he'd been tight, Sam gave them a look of pure countrified disgust
and remarked: "Tight? I was so tight you couldn't-a drove flaxseed up my
ass with a knot maul." Vintage Sam Snead, even in the bitterest of defeats.

In all, the pride of Hot Springs played in twenty-six national Opens,
seriously contending in more than half of them, amassing one of the finest
Open records in history. "Would I give half of what I did win just to have
one of those Open titles?" he mused rhetorically the afternoon we played
the Old White in West Virginia. Looking over at a patch of clover just off
the fourteenth tee, he smiled and hopped out of the cart where we were
riding with his beloved golden retriever. He walked over to the clover patch,
stooped, and ran his long fingers over the grass. A few moments later he
came back to the cart delicately holding a perfect four-leaf clover, still grin-
ning beneath his brightly banded straw-hatted hat—another Snead trademark. "Lookee here. Nobody in this game could ever find four-leaf clovers
the way I could," he said, presenting it to me, the sly old smile fading just
a bit. "But I reckon I'd give up that talent and half of what I won just to
have just one of those damn Opens."

Snead's tough luck in national Opens haunted golf's Grand Old Man
to the grave, and bothers the kind of historian who feels that particular
shortfall is a black mark against his greatness, but it certainly won't dimin-
ish the fact that nobody who ever picked up a golf club swung it any finer
or more naturally than the Peckerwood Kid.

As he related in his engaging memoir *Education of a Golfer* (1962), written with Al Stump, a must-have for any serious book collector on golf and
still one of the most instructive books of its kind on the game, Snead's first
golf club wasn't even a golf club. It was a "swamp maple limb with a knot
on the end with bark left on for a grip" he hacked off a tree and whittled
into the rough approximation of a club like the one his idolized older
brother Homer used to hit golf balls in the family pasture.

The Homestead resort was located a few miles down the road from the
Snead place, and that's where Snead, the youngest of five athletic dirt-poor
kids, eventually wound up caddying, cleaning clubs, running errands, and
teaching himself to play the game on the side with a cast-off set of cheap
wooden-shafted irons he had picked up from his meager earnings. "Nobody
would give me lessons, so I basically experimented until I got it down
right," he said, recalling how he eventually graduated to apprentice teach-

ing pro and picked up a few bucks showing hotel guests how to swing a golf club. "After about a year of not many pupils, but with plenty of time to practice on a real course, I was thin as a razorback hog and had sharpened into a long hitter with a fair amount of ability at chipping and putting, while not having a prospect in sight for getting up in the world."

His big "break" came when he was invited to play in a foursome "over the mountain" at the famed Greenbrier in White Sulphur Springs, West Virginia, that included Lawson Little, the former British and U.S. amateur champion, and two past U.S. Open winners, John Goodman and Billy Burke. Snead beat them all and was hired as teaching pro at the Greenbrier—a job he nearly promptly lost by driving the 335-yard fifth green and striking a prominent hotel guest on the rear end while the guest was bending over to fetch his ball. That guest was powerful Alva Bradley, president of the Cleveland Indians baseball club and director of the Chesapeake & Ohio Railroad, the company that owned the Greenbrier. Outraged, Bradley attempted to have the young pro summarily fired and refused to believe the offender had driven the green from the tee until he saw him repeat the performance and appointed Sam his personal teacher for the rest of his days.

It was the stuff of legend—Horatio Alger meets Bobby Jones. Or so Fred Corcoran later packaged and peddled it.

When twenty-four-year-old Snead ventured west with $300 in his pocket staked to him by several Greenbrier members who believed the long-hitting phenom might be able to hold his own on the winter touring circuit, Snead himself figured "I'd just do it until I could find me a real job and the money ran out."

It never did. He made $600 his first week and three weeks after that collected $1,200 first-prize money at the Oakland Open. He went on to win four more times and finished second in his first Open Championship that year—one of the most sensational and unlikely debut years in the history of the professional game.

What's not widely conveyed in the popular mythology that sprang up around the laconic wisecracking cracker from the hills of Ole Virginny is the fact that driving the golf ball—probably the factor behind Snead's meteoric rise to fame—was initially the aspect of his game that troubled him most. His favorite and most effective club, in fact, was his pitching wedge, followed by his putter and his long irons. Driving the ball, he figured, was what he did about "fifth best . . . and at times I spray-hooked balls all over the field."

Slammin' Sam Snead wasn't nearly the natural the sportswriters always have made him out to be, he confided in *Education of a Golfer*. "My long-artillery game needed plenty of fixing in the beginning" and bedeviled him so woefully during the early days of his pro career that he considered giving up and going home. One day on the practice range at the L.A. Open, though, tour journeyman Henry Picard watched him duck-hook several balls and deduced that Sam's driver was too light and whippy, then offered to let him try out a heavy stiff-shafted driver made by Philadelphia club-maker George Izett. A week later, his hook miraculously cured, Sam won the Oakland tournament with his new Izett driver and went on to capture the Crosby Invitational days after that. That club—which he paid Picard $5.50 for—became Sam's favorite club, the driver he used to win the hearts of fans and win most of his major championships with, "the single greatest discovery I ever made in golf and [that] put me on the road to happy time."

If Slammin' Sam was a uniquely American phenomenon, as natural as rabbit tobacco or heat lightning on a southern summer evening, his was an image and down-home appeal that failed spectacularly to translate across the ocean to the game's birthplace. Peering from the window as his train approached St. Andrews for the 1946 British Open, Snead commented to a passenger across the aisle, "Say, that looks like an old abandoned golf course." It was, of course, the Old Course at St. Andrews and the man, according to Sam's account, or at least Corcoran's, which wound up in several prominent London broadsheets, was a local lord who took severe umbrage at the Slammer's remarks.

Never one to spend his folding money unless it was absolutely unavoidable, Sam claims he had no interest whatsoever in contending for the Claret Jug but showed up only to appease his manager and his sponsors at Wilson Sporting Goods. The British Open paid $600 first-place prize money, which Sam calculated would scarcely cover his travel expenses. But Wilson and Corcoran leaned on him to go, so off he went—and seemed to be jinxed from the very beginning.

Leaving New York for England, his airplane blew an engine and failed to get off the ground. Arriving in London, still ravaged by the recent world war, he couldn't find a hotel and actually napped on a depot bench before catching a train to Scotland. He hated the rationed food and later claimed to be dizzy from just "beans and porridge." Then came the encounter with the lord on the train to St. Andrews and his insult to the royal and ancient game. "Snead," the *Times* of London fired back, "a rural American type, undoubtedly would think the leaning tower of Pisa is a structure about to totter and crash at his feet."

Things didn't go much better in the tournament itself. He went through three or four caddies in four days, the first of whom whistled through his teeth every time the Slammer started to line up putts, the second of whom could not tell distances "worth a lick." His third caddie, guaranteed to be St. Andrews's best, went to jail for public drunkenness the night before the Open started and barely got out in time for Sam's starting time.

For all of that, using a heavy-bladed putter, deprived of sleep, and disgruntled by the chilly weather, Snead somehow mastered the Old Course's huge double greens and claimed he was almost dumbfounded to find himself tied for the lead by the end of the third round. In the final round a St. Andrews gale "made every putt a guess," but Sam lagged his way brilliantly around the course to capture the venerable Claret Jug and meager prize money. He gave the winning ball to his caddie, who broke down and, according to Sam, wept gratefully, saying he would cherish it forever—then promptly went and sold the ball for fifty quid.

The Slammer didn't exactly endear himself to his Scottish hosts by later commenting that he had no intention of trying to defend his British crown because "my traveling expenses alone were $1,000, and nobody but me picked up the tab. On top of that, all my hitting muscles 'froze' in the icy wind at St. Andrews. For days I ached in every joint." Soundly criticized by both American and British sportswriters for passing up golf's oldest tournament, the unflappable Sam Snead rejoined that anytime you left the U.S.A., "you're basically just camping out." It was yet another example where, if he'd only had "Wee Ice Mon" Ben Hogan's brain, he might have left well enough alone and simply said nothing—and done his reputation a world of good in the process.

Pigeons, hawks, and vultures—those were Slammin' Sam's nicknames for the various golf hustlers and player wannabes that drifted their way across his long and colorfully illustrious career. Most came with "juicy fat bankrolls," looking to gun down the longest driver in the game of golf, a feat only a few ever accomplished.

That's because early in his life, weaned on the fine art of wagering, with a week's groceries often hanging in the balance, Snead developed firm rules about whom to play for money—and whom to avoid at all costs. Pigeons were usually well-to-do gentlemen golfers who didn't mind the prospect of losing a bundle for a little fun with the greatest name in golf, whereas Hawks were smooth talkers who shot well above their average abilities until the game was set, at which point "they cleaned out your pockets." Vultures were professional gamblers, golf "hustlers," and cheaters who preyed on the vanity of pros and amateurs alike. Knowing one from the other, Snead maintained, and recognizing the various dodges and wrinkles that came with their propositions, was the key to successful betting in golf. "Early in life I developed one basic rule, and I lived by it," he told me the afternoon we breezed around the Old White Course together: "Never play for money with a stranger and don't believe what a man says his handicap is until you've seen him play at least a dozen times. That's the rule I lived by most, and I'm happy to say it's why I rarely lost my money."

He said this as we approached the White Course last hole, a wee par three over a small pond. Both of us were playing pretty well that afternoon, but especially Sam, who was beating his age by a country mile. Jokingly at the first tee, I'd suggested we play a quarter Nassau, and—ever the tight-wad with the tomato can buried in his backyard—he'd steadfastly refused. Now, as we arrived at the tee, a couple of elderly men were waiting for us in a cart—Snead cronies, looking for a little action.

"What are you boys doin' out here in the sun?" the Slammer drawled affectionately, scratching his dog's head. "Y'all ought to be home havin' your naps."

"We thought you might want to put a little something on the last hole," one of his buddies replied, winking at his partner in crime.

Sam smiled lazily, looked at me, then took the bait.

"All right, tell you what. We'll all shoot at the green. One shot for ten bucks. Closest to the pin takes the dough."

The two old birds in the cart grinned and hopped out, ready to play.

I asked Snead—one of my childhood heroes—if he minded if I played, too. He fixed me with a stern expression.

"I've seen you play only seventeen holes," he began. "That's not nearly enough. You play pretty well, I'll grant you, and figure you're probably fairly honest. But lookee, you're not related to ole Leonard Dodson, are you? That sumbitch couldn't play a lick until there was money ridin' on it, and at that point you couldn't beat him!"

I assured Snead that I wasn't related in any way to Leonard Dodson, a South Carolina pro who never amounted to much except on the club hustlers circuit. I used the moment to explain that I'd grown up in Greensboro, North Carolina, a block from Sam Snead Boulevard and the golf club where he had won several of his record eight Greensboro Opens.

"Well I'll be damned," he said, smiling hugely.

"Tell you what," he whispered and winked. "I'll take the money off these old bird dogs and just play you for a bowl of chocolate ice cream and maybe a little whiskey."

I replied that, under the circumstances, that was fine by me.

Snead's buddies teed up and fired highly respectable tee shots to the middle of the green, cackling like teenagers. I teed my ball and put it ten feet to the right of the flag, causing one of the old boys to whistle and needle Sam about having met a "true ringer." Sam shook his head and said, "Maybe so. But at least I'm gonna send you boys back home to your naps. Watch this."

With that, he deposited his golf ball maybe eight inches from the cup. Both bird dogs howled as if stung by a swarm of yellow jackets, and Sam Snead slid me a coy little smile that said he'd played this little scene a thousand times in his life.

Before I could reach my ball, the Slammer pocketed his friends' folding money and picked up my ball, which he playfully underhanded to me across the putting surface where I was totaling up his amazing score.

"C'mon," drawled the Peckerwood Kid who'd just shot 73 but was fast approaching his mid-80s. "I'm buyin' the ice cream *and* the whiskey."

I reminded him that I'd lost the wager. So it was my job to buy.

"Not today," he said graciously and winked again. "Tell you what, though. You come back in ten years and we'll have us another little match. Maybe I'll let you buy then."

SAM SNEAD

	Total New Money	Wins	Top10s	Top25s
Majors	$ 21,055,884	7	48	76
Other Official Tournaments (and International Wins)	102,306,809	77	296	381
TOTALS	$123,362,693	84	344	457

MAJOR CHAMPIONSHIPS

	New Money	Wins
Masters	$7,689,127	3
U.S. Open	4,450,252	0
British Open	1,418,229	1
PGA	7,498,276	3

BEST OTHER EVENTS

	New Money	Wins
Greensboro	$8,894,673	8
Miami Open	5,534,820	6
Palm Beach Round Robin	4,761,875	5
Western Open	4,060,067	2

Year	New Money	Total Wins	Top10s	Top25s	Majors	Other Events
1936	$ 1,007,200	1	4	5	$ 0	$ 1,007,200
1937	6,962,340	5	20	25	898,726	6,063,614
1938	8,647,202	7	20	22	594,000	8,053,202
1939	4,098,018	3	15	16	865,577	3,232,441
1940	4,576,810	3	14	17	852,964	3,723,846
1941	6,433,987	6	20	21	490,295	5,943,692
1942	3,737,608	3	10	12	1,164,533	2,573,075
1943	0	0	0	0	0	0
1944	1,672,000	2	4	4	0	1,672,000
1945	6,870,247	6	22	27	0	6,870,247
1946	8,271,339	6	20	27	1,404,849	6,866,490
1947	2,374,413	0	8	14	709,897	1,664,516
1948	2,626,157	1	9	14	502,341	2,123,816
1949	8,202,172	6	19	22	2,477,583	5,724,589
1950	10,818,810	10	26	29	535,874	10,282,936
1951	3,815,681	2	10	12	1,272,015	2,543,666
1952	5,787,254	5	12	13	1,131,293	4,655,961
1953	3,903,287	2	9	15	737,897	3,165,390
1954	2,510,128	2	5	8	1,328,542	1,181,586
1955	5,204,168	4	11	18	753,168	4,451,000
1956	1,715,360	1	6	8	579,222	1,136,138
1957	4,222,462	2	11	13	866,066	3,356,396
1958	3,500,000	2	10	11	514,000	2,986,000
1959	859,003	0	4	6	395,253	463,750
1960	2,908,479	2	7	11	533,146	2,375,333
1961	2,536,304	2	8	12	202,594	2,333,710
1962	896,679	0	3	7	381,779	514,900
1963	1,481,500	0	6	6	324,800	1,156,700
1964	582,023	0	2	4	0	582,023
1965	1,925,318	1	6	12	246,934	1,678,384
1966	369,256	0	2	4	172,150	197,106

Year	New Money	Total Wins	Top10s	Top25s	Majors	Other Events
1967	$252,570	0	2	3	$128,800	$123,770
1968	767,409	0	4	4	120,539	646,870
1969	729,088	0	2	5	0	729,088
1970	334,722	0	0	5	161,215	173,507
1971	295,963	0	2	3	0	295,963
1972	767,186	0	4	6	227,333	539,853
1973	630,911	0	3	7	148,500	482,411
1974	949,643	0	3	7	334,000	615,643
1975	120,000	0	1	2	0	120,000

Gary Player

Ben Wright

Gary Player has made a monumental contribution to the history of golf, but perhaps the most significant aspect may be overlooked in the passage of time, as the traditions of a great game have been swept away on a sea of green and professional golf has become big business.

Let no one ever forget that Player, the diminutive South African who has never stood above five feet seven inches tall or weighed more than 145 pounds, in a career lasting with distinction well into its sixth decade, almost single-handedly persuaded his fellow professionals that they had also to be athletes to realize their full potential and, more important, to endure in the white heat of world competition.

In my early days as a cub reporter, Ben Hogan and a host of his rivals smoked cigarettes almost continually, and Arnold Palmer was little better when he burst on the scene with such an enormous impact as the "blue collar" champion.

Jack Nicklaus earned the sobriquet "Fat Boy" despite the fact that he, too, smoked. Player's guide, mentor, and early partner for South Africa in the Canada (now World) Cup, Bobby Locke, was similarly derisively named "The Bishop" for his bloodhound jowls and fulsome potbelly.

Pleasantly plump professionals of the Locke build, who enjoyed the camaraderie of their colleagues over a daily postround tipple, were legion.

Not today, thanks to the persistent preaching of Player, a winner of 163 championships and tournaments worldwide in five decades and still convinced that, heading into his upper sixties, he can win during his sixth.

I hope Player does so, because I remember his emergence in Great Britain as a raw nineteen-year-old with a magnificent work ethic and overflowing determination but minimal talent or knowledge of the golf swing. Thankfully, Gary was a quick study. I remember vividly one afternoon in the middle of that, the 1955 season, after Player had missed yet another cut, this time at the Royal Liverpool "Hoylake" Club in Cheshire, England. I was walking to the railway station with Player and Hugh Lewis, the professional at a nearby municipal club, an occasional tournament aspirant who had also been ousted at the halfway stage of the event. The rain was beating on our umbrellas as it came at us horizontally on a serious gale. We had nary a raincoat among us.

Player turned his big brown eyes up at the burly Lewis, who stood well over six feet in height, and asked him urgently: "How can I possibly improve myself, Hughie, quickly, before I'm totally broke and have to go home?"

Lewis, in typically dour North Country tones, replied in a booming voice: "Gary, lad, why don't you use whatever money you have left to buy yourself a one-way ticket on a banana boat sailing for Johannesburg, forget about golf, and find yourself an honest job? You've no business being out here."

Tears coursed down Gary's cheeks as we walked on in silence. Many others in the game had castigated Player for his golf swing, his grip, his hairstyle, and his sloppy clothes. Later Gary was to write in his book *Grand Slam Golf*: "When I went home in the autumn, having more or less come out even and covered my costs financially, I was very bitter and shaken by this first experience of British golf. But it did a great service to my drive and determination."

Player returned to Britain in 1956 as the South African Open champion and recorded a famous first victory, battling and beating the great Arthur Lees, a tough-as-nails Ryder Cup player and the home professional, over both courses at the Sunningdale Club in the five-round Dunlop tournament with a record-winning aggregate of 338.

Gary was on his way, improving his technique all the time—and never too proud to learn from any Tom, Dick, or Harry who would offer him advice—absorbing golf technique like a veritable sponge. In *Grand Slam Golf* he recalled: "It led me quickly to the certainty that the crease in my pants was not going to win championships for me. Having a beautiful swing is no guarantee of success."

Player has never had to worry about the latter! But by sheer hard work and abundant courage, not to speak of self-reliance, he has made his rather unsightly "walk through" swing work repetitively for decades. And not for nothing has he been acknowledged widely as the best bunker player of all time.

When Player decided that he would move on to America in 1957, I was frankly amazed at his temerity. He had no sooner scratched the surface in the minor league than he felt himself ready to tilt at windmills in a huge country wholly unknown to him, when he could not even yet afford to buy a car. Full marks for guts—or was it foolhardiness? I remember very vividly, some years later, when Gary said to me in all seriousness that "Jack Nicklaus could become a really great player if he ever chose to play regularly outside America."

I asked him what the hell he was talking about, since Nicklaus was palpably the most successful competitor the game had ever known. With typical Player logic, Gary replied, "Do you know how tough it has been for me to travel from my native land to take on the Americans—and beat them—in their own backyard? Just remember that when I have flown some fifteen to twenty hours from South Africa to London I have to turn left and start all over again. Jack has no idea how hard it is to travel like that." Point taken.

And it is a tribute to Player's outstanding physical condition that he has survived, despite flying as much as fifteen million miles during his incredible career.

On the subject of Player's fitness, I recall arriving at Portmarnock Golf Club, Dublin, Ireland, from my hotel in the city on the first day of the 1960 Canada Cup, eventually won by Arnold Palmer and Sam Snead. I was quickly fetched to the snooker room in the clubhouse, where Player was laid out on one of the leather benches against the wall, suffering a severe asthma attack. Because I had been a childhood asthmatic myself, I always traveled with medication. I was whisked back into Dublin to fetch the stuff, fed it to Gary, and, in the company of Locke the little fellow shot 65, then a course record, that very afternoon.

That same evening my first wife, Pat, and I were invited to dinner in Players' suite, to find him demonstrating his complete recovery, by walking round the room on his hands talking nineteen to the dozen!

But I'm getting ahead of myself. Player hitchhiked his way around America in 1957 and returned to South Africa with a very small profit financially but with an enormous legacy, a golf education. In 1958 he finished second to Tommy Bolt in the U.S. Open at Southern Hills, which earned him the then princely sum of $5,000. In *Grand Slam Golf* he summed up that win: "I could afford to have my pants pressed now!"

Player's increasing fame cut little ice with the secretary at Muirfield Golf Club, Scotland, Colonel Evans-Lombe, when he arrived there ten days in advance to practice for the 1959 British Open, hell-bent on becoming the event's youngest champion of the twentieth century. Evans-Lombe coldly informed the South African "interloper" that he could use the practice area and chip and putt but that he could not play the course. When Player explained that he had traveled many thousands of miles to play in the Open and that he could see many people out on the course, Evans-Lombe countered with an immortal reply: "Oh yes, but they are members." Enough said. Thankfully Muirfield has improved since then, albeit mighty slowly.

After considerable to-ing and fro-ing, Lord Brabazon, then president of the British PGA, was called to intervene. Player was finally allowed to practice. But Evans-Lombe had the last words: "Only one round per day!" Gary used the time to good effect but was so keen to learn the intricacies of Muirfield that one day he sneaked in an extra nine holes. His caddie was promptly banned for some days. This time the club captain stepped in and smoothed out what by then had become an increasingly ridiculous situation, allowing Player to complete his preparation for the championship in peace.

After thirty-six holes Player was eight shots behind the leader, Fred Bullock, an English-born teaching professional employed at nearby Prestwick St. Nicholas. In those days two rounds were played on the final day, Friday, to allow such brethren to return to their clubs for weekend duty. Moreover the leaders were situated wherever they were drawn, and not yet bringing home the field, so Gary Player was due to finish at least two hours before Bullock and a more likely rival, the elegant Belgian Flory Van Donck, who was six shots ahead of Gary in second place.

On Thursday evening Pat Mathews, who represented the Slazenger Company, told me that Player had just said to him: "Pat, tomorrow you're going to see a small miracle; in fact you're going to see a large miracle. I'm going to win the Open." I roared with almost hysterical laughter. The South African has plainly developed his body at the expense of his mind, I replied. And the rest is history.

Player scored 70 and 68 on that historic Friday and beat Bullock and Van Donck by two shots. Not without high drama, however. In the final round Player was phenomenal for seventeen holes as he cruised past the nine players still ahead of him at lunchtime. He stood on the eighteenth hole needing a par four for 66, the score for which he had aimed.

Alas, the hook that had dogged Player throughout his career intervened, and his final drive found one of the deep left-hand fairway bunkers. He hacked out his ball a hundred yards from the green with a six iron, then used the same club to punch a low third under the wind. Perhaps he'd needed one more club, for the ball came up very short, on the lower tier of the deep green from where he three-putted for six.

He was inconsolable, and one of my photographic treasures is a shot of Gary, head in hands, quite unable to sign his card at the scorers' hut, his wife Vivienne's arms around him. Player's wonderful sponsor, South African George Blumberg, whisked him back to the Marine Hotel in North Berwick for a cold bath and a strong drink to await his fate. Player was absolutely convinced that he had thrown away the championship.

Harold Henning, Player's friend and later World Cup–winning partner in Madrid in 1965, had backed Gary to win some eight hundred pounds sterling. He telephoned continually from the clubhouse as the scores came in and potential rivals fell by the wayside. When victory finally was confirmed, Player was so elated he went out and sat alone at the podium for fully half an hour before the presentation began—basking in his moment—to the delight of the Scottish crowd.

I was only fortunate enough to witness one of Player's thirteen South African Open victories, at Royal Johannesburg Golf Club in 1972. Then it was that Bobby Cole, South African pretender to Player's throne, was having troubles with *his* swing and phoned Player for advice on the eve of the championship. "I'll see you and talk next week," said Player. And the South African press—to a man—unloaded on him.

Yet perhaps the most apocryphal Player story concerned Ben Hogan, who was Gary's idol when Gary was a young man. On one of the many occasions, in even such a distinguished career, Player was having trouble with his swing, he phoned Hogan for advice. "Whose clubs do you play, Mr. Player?" asked Hogan tersely. "I play Dunlop at the moment," replied Player. "Then go ask Mr. Dunlop for advice," Hogan is said to have hissed as he put down the phone.

In 1960, when Player was defending his British Open title at St. Andrews in the centenary event, I was called from the dinner table at the Association of Golf Writers Annual Dinner in Rusacks Hotel. I was working for the *Daily Mirror*, London, and Hugh Cudlipp, then the managing editor, whom I had yet to meet, came on the line to tell me to go and ask Player if there was any racial significance in the slacks that he had worn on the Old Course that day—with one black and one white leg! A suddenly ashen-faced Player told me at the top table that he would never wear that pair of slacks again—nor did he.

In more recent times Gary Player, the self-styled Black Knight, has become the darling of the media by usually saying absolutely the right thing. For example, when asked for his thoughts about a particularly obnoxious and unworthy golf course, he will say, quite deadpan, "It is probably the best of its type I have ever seen." But when the great man wags his index finger in your face and says "I've got to tell you one thing," you can be on the receiving end of a lengthy but never, ever boring monologue.

Player has no illusions about himself, however, or about how seriously people take some of his public and private utterances. In *Grand Slam Golf* he described himself as "Small, dark, deliberate, painstaking, the feeling of the man without talent who has done it all by sheer hard work and nothing else, a highly-strung faddist who bores the ears off you with weight-lifting and diets and nuts and raisins and talk of God, dark clothes, somber under the big peaked cap, and above all, a little fellow, a little man." And the name Gary Player? A plain, honest Anglo-Saxon pairing, good enough for a golf player but without any identifiable flavor to it. Non-vintage. But there is a little more to Master Gary Player than that.

For a start he was recognized as one of the "Big Three" with Palmer and Nicklaus for his stature as a golfer. And he more than held his own. He became one of only five players to win all four major championships and accomplished the feat at the age of twenty-nine in his lone U.S. Open victory in a thirty-six-hole play-off against Australia's Kel Nagle at Bellerive CC, St. Louis, in 1965. At the time only Gene Sarazen and Ben Hogan preceded Player. Jack Nicklaus and Tiger Woods joined this exalted group in 1966 and 2000.

His nine majors include three Masters titles (1961, 1974, 1978), three British Opens (1959, 1968, 1974), two PGA championships (1962 and 1972)—a record by far and away the best ever of any non-American—while his career record around the world is vastly superior to any compiled in the entire history of the game, regardless of nationality. And, oh! that travel!

Player won five World Matchplay titles at Wentworth, England, in the days when his manager, Mark McCormack, who conceived the event, rarely allowed into the field anyone but his own stable of clients. But a match is a match is a match. And Player's semifinal victory over the late Tony Lema in 1965 was without doubt the best match I ever had the privilege to witness. In a nutshell Player was one up after nine holes, six down after eighteen, seven down after nineteen—with seventeen holes to play—five down with nine to play, and all square after thirty-six holes. Player won at the thirty-seventh. Lema scored 67 in the morning, Player 68 in the afternoon on the completely tree-lined course measuring over seven thousand yards, known as the "Burma Road."

Over his career three Player strokes stand out in my mind, having watched them from close range, each possibly representing the best of his extraordinarily complete repertoire. Each ensured a major championship victory and in sum are perfect examples of the little South African's indomitable courage under the fiercest pressure.

In 1968, at Carnoustie in the British Open, Player was battling Nicklaus, Billy Casper, and Bob Charles down the stretch in the final round. With Nicklaus miraculously close to the green at the fourteenth hole after an amazing three-wood second from the copse to the right, Player, with the ovation for Jack's shot still ringing in his ears, launched his own three-wood shot between the "Spectacles" bunkers in the middle of the fairway at this great par-five hole. His ball pulled up no more than two feet from the cup, having never left the flagstick. Nicklaus chipped and putted for his birdie, but Player's marvelous eagle allowed him to prevail over the most arduous finishing stretch of holes ever faced in the British Open.

Rather than trusting my fading memory, I quote from Mark McCor-mack's *World of Professional Golf* for the 1972 season, describing the clos-ing stages of the PGA Championship at Oakland Hills that year, played in miserably insistent, weeping rain over another of the most daunting fin-ishing stretches in championship golf. With three holes to play, Player shared the lead with Jim Jamieson, up ahead on the eighteenth hole. I quote: "Gary's dilemma magnified when he sliced his tee shot behind and close to weeping willow trees well off in the rough at the sixteenth. Rodgers—Phil, that is—Player's playing partner, told British golf writer Ben Wright later that Gary was so discouraged over that tee shot that he was talking like he had already blown the tournament."

Now I will take up the story, since I was standing alongside. Player had 150 yards to the flagstick, with the insidious pond between him and the green. He required a nine-iron loft to get the ball up quickly enough to clear the drenched trees. That was just not enough club, but Player simply added "heart." The lie was a good one on long grass flattened down by the gallery. The South African simply launched himself at the ball, then imme-diately ran away to his left toward the fairway, in time to see his ball land four feet from the hole for the decisive and astonishing birdie.

The third masterstroke is the most celebrated, since it enabled Player to win his second Masters title in his most magical year, when he also won the British Open and a veritable host of other titles around the world.

On that Sunday afternoon in 1974 a gaggle of the world's best were vying for the lead down the stretch. When Nicklaus birdied the fifteenth with an unbelievable pitch from the mud—he took off his right shoe and sock to stand in the water—he tied Player and Tom Weiskopf for the lead. But less than a minute later Player birdied the seventeenth to reclaim the leadership.

I have long ago lost count of the times I have watched the diminutive South African nail that nine-iron second shot to the undulating seventeenth green, that glorious strike that finished six inches from the hole—but it never gets old. The goosebumps get me every time. It is a constant source of wonderment that the little man was able to dig so deep and so often.

My favorite of all my Player memories happened that same year, because it lasted two weeks! I hasten to explain that I was commentating on Aus-tralian television at the 1974 Australian Open at Lake Karrinyup Golf

Club, Perth, Western Australia. Gary spread-eagled the field with a third round—a course record 63—in wind and rain that enabled him to coast to victory with a 73 the following day. Qantas Airlines, the event's sponsor, held its Boeing 747 at the Perth airport—it was en route from Sydney to London—to accommodate Player and me. Imagine my embarrassment when Player insisted on going to the practice tee after the presentation. At last he had found the secret to straight driving, he dared to tell me when he eventually condescended to join us in the first-class cabin.

All the way to London, Player either slept like a baby or read me passages from one of Sir Winston Churchill's literary tomes, of which he was, and probably still is, an ardent student. We were met at Heathrow Airport and whisked to my home in Epsom, Surrey, for breakfast. Then off again this time to visit the late Brian Swift, a racehorse trainer friend, on the Epsom Downs. After a tour of Swift's pristine stables Player bought a four-year-old mare called—appropriately enough—Look Lively. The horse later became a stalwart broodmare at the Gary Player Stud in South Africa.

Then it was back to Heathrow Airport for the flight to Murcia in southern Spain, via Madrid, where we were seemingly inevitably delayed for some hours. When we eventually reached La Manga Campo de Golf on the Costa Blanca, I adjourned for some strong drink and bed, while Gary, believe it or not, made for the practice tee. I shall never forget drawing the drapes in my room, having watched the little man hitting balls in the twilight, obviously the last man out there. But imagine my surprise on drawing those drapes very early in the morning to see Player hitting practice balls. Was this really real, or some frightening dream, I asked myself? It was real.

Greg Peters, an American of Russian extraction who owned the La Manga complex at the time, had devised a most interesting format for his seventy-two-hole pro-am by which the professionals took the team score of their amateur partners only, not their own. He had received some scornful treatment from professionals in pro-ams because his game was perhaps sketchy in the extreme. He aimed to force the professionals in this field to look after their amateur partners—and, my goodness, did Player look after my team? He coached us on every shot in the second round to a phenomenal 54 that allowed him to win the professional event at the first hole of sudden death against Briton Clive Clark. And our team won the Amateur

Division by no fewer than six shots! Practice, practice with dividends for all!

While we celebrated, Player dashed off to Madrid to win the Ibergolf tournament there over the next two days, beating another Briton, Peter Townsend, at the second hole in extra time. And then it was home to South Africa to win the General Motors International Classic the following week at Wedgwood Park Golf Club, Port Elizabeth. Hard as it may be to believe, Player then flew on to Brazil to win the Brazilian Open at Gavea, par 69, and there cracked the 60 barrier—the first time ever accomplished in any national championship—with a 59 in the third round. Player had halves of 29 and 30 against par of 34 and 35, recording nine birdies, an eagle, plus a bogey at the par-three second hole. He required but twenty-four putts and to keep the crowd on their toes holed a bunker shot for a two at the sixteenth hole, then dropped a fifteen-footer at the last. Phew!

In recent years Player has performed with similar distinction as a senior and super senior, has and will assimilate most of his six children and thirteen grandchildren into his businesses, and is able to spend more time with his wife, Vivienne, his childhood sweetheart.

Pound for pound Gary Player has to be the best golfer-athlete of all time.

GARY PLAYER

	Total New Money	Wins	Top10s	Top25s
Majors	$20,373,985	9	44	70
Other Official Tournaments (and International Wins)	55,110,137	115	262	350
TOTALS	$75,484,122	124	306	420

MAJOR CHAMPIONSHIPS

	New Money	Wins
Masters	$6,621,272	3
U.S. Open	3,799,923	1
British Open	5,660,590	3
PGA	4,292,200	2

BEST OTHER EVENTS

	New Money	Wins
World Series of Golf	$3,356,237	3
Tournament of Champions	3,094,133	2
Memphis	2,287,663	1
Colonial Invitational	2,238,764	0

Year	New Money	Total Wins	Top10s	Top25s	Majors	Other Events
1955	$ 9,000	1	1	1	$ 0	$ 9,000
1956	839,346	4	5	5	316,040	523,306
1957	662,587	3	4	10	109,782	552,805
1958	3,337,091	5	15	17	774,624	2,562,467
1959	1,987,179	7	9	13	1,368,849	618,330
1960	2,278,286	7	13	21	488,574	1,789,712
1961	5,963,872	5	22	27	1,151,189	4,812,683
1962	3,575,230	4	13	18	1,772,487	1,802,743
1963	5,141,280	8	26	29	675,774	4,465,506
1964	3,477,476	3	11	16	497,852	2,979,624
1965	4,478,790	6	12	15	1,492,800	2,985,990
1966	1,842,210	4	9	12	633,451	1,208,759
1967	2,459,936	2	11	15	666,803	1,793,133
1968	4,822,942	8	20	22	1,349,024	3,473,918
1969	3,874,828	5	14	18	646,147	3,228,682
1970	2,721,532	3	10	14	492,175	2,229,357
1971	3,565,184	6	15	15	603,422	2,961,762
1972	4,687,199	9	16	21	1,448,426	3,238,773
1973	1,722,041	3	5	10	193,785	1,528,256
1974	4,320,935	9	14	19	2,447,442	1,873,493
1975	1,813,243	3	9	13	0	1,813,243
1976	1,766,717	4	11	17	167,533	1,599,184
1977	2,294,553	3	12	17	233,314	2,061,239
1978	3,417,393	3	9	12	1,159,364	2,258,029
1979	1,907,300	3	9	13	670,141	1,237,159
1980	678,822	2	5	7	169,400	509,422
1981	346,380	2	2	5	92,400	253,980
1982	258,200	1	1	4	92,400	165,800
1983	108,413	0	0	2	67,028	41,385
1984	915,539	1	2	6	544,480	371,059
1985	96,299	0	1	3	0	96,299
1989	65,042	0	0	2	0	65,042
1990	49,280	0	0	1	49,280	0

Billy Casper

Al Barkow

Asked once at the far end of his tournament career what he might have done differently, Billy Casper said he wished he hadn't taken Ben Hogan as his model of deportment on the golf course. He speculated that if he had not gone about his business in the stone-cold, robot style of the "Wee Ice Mon," the golfing public might have had a warmer response to him. Not that Casper was given the cold shoulder, but his record as an outstanding champion might have been better recognized. And it is a very good record indeed.

The gallery must assume from a distance the character and nature of its champion players, or get it in dribs and drabs from journalists, who may miss the essence of their subjects. Thus the gallery did not catch on to Casper as the San Diego pool shark/hustler he'd been in his younger days or the quick-witted needler hidden beneath the automated golf shot machine.

Instead the world in general picked up mostly on Casper's rather bizarre diet. Because of a lifelong genetic problem with weight—his paternal grandfather was a 300-pounder, his father weighed in at 350—Casper included in his bill of fare such supplements as desiccated ox blood and buffalo meat. The latter, joined with his given name, produced the all-too-obvious Big Bill sobriquet.

Would Casper have won more tournaments, more major championships if he had displayed the looser and more open Billy his close friends knew him to be? His response is that he probably wouldn't have done as well.

Casper's deportment decision was not only Hogan-inspired. After winning his first U.S. Open, at Winged Foot in 1959, Casper began his journey into the Mormon Church, which had at least as much of an impact as Ben Hogan on his demeanor both on and off the course.

Immediately following the victory at Winged Foot, he was invited to play in the Utah Open. "It was the first time I had ever met Mormon people as a group," Casper noted in the introduction to *The Good Sense of Golf*, his 1980 instruction book.

"Both my wife, Shirley, and myself were raised as Protestants. We had no experience at all with Mormonism, and no other real religious background except a belief in the Bible. In Utah the Mormons impressed us with their close family-unit structure. This was especially important, because both my wife and I had come from broken homes and we now had two children and a third on the way. And, I was almost completely tied up in my golf game. My life consisted of playing golf, fishing, watching television, and playing cards."

Realizing that his lifestyle not only had the potential for an unsatisfactory marriage but also would stand in the way of his optimizing his talent for golf, Bill (and Shirley) adopted the Mormon religion. The circumspect conduct this church demands of its followers was a significant factor in his private and public deportment, while in adopting it Casper also went against his grandfather's advice to live up to the German meaning of his last name—*Casper* means "clown."

Golf is a game best played by those with more than a little self-control. Billy Casper understood that, acted on it, and became one of the best golfers the game has ever had. Yet because of his totally understated public persona, the public at large is frequently surprised that Casper is currently sixth on the PGA Tour's all-time winner's list. (He also won five foreign titles—two Brazilian Opens, the Italian and Mexican Opens, and the Havana Invitational, in the days when Cuba was a golfing mecca.) Among these victories are two U.S. Opens and a Masters, not to mention victories in such prestigious nonmajors played on highly challenging layouts as the Western Open (four), the Colonial Invitational (two), the Doral Open (two), and the Los Angeles Open. Casper also played on eight U.S.

Ryder Cup teams, captained another, and was a five-time winner of the Vardon Trophy, awarded by the Tour for low stroke average of the year. Yes, Bill Casper had a lot of game.

Casper's personality was shaped by a need or desire to live a balanced life, but the more exuberant spirit of his youth was evident in the way he played the game. His swing featured a laterally sliding right foot as he got to and past impact, and his basic shot was a beautifully controlled fade. Then there was his short game, in particular his putting. He was, and will always remain, one of the best putters the game has ever had.

He stood at the ball with the putter held in close to his body in such a way that his left hand more or less bumped into his left thigh in the follow-through. It was a conscious thing, Casper's way of not letting his left hand break down in the forward stroke and cause pulled putts. As a result, Casper was the archetypal "pop" putter. He kept the club face so square in the take-away it appeared shut. The stroke itself was fairly short and firm. It is a stroke seldom seen in postmodern golf, what with the incredibly smooth greens the professional golfers now play over day after day, week after week, on the tournament circuit. Casper's stroke was a response to the slower, more uneven public-course greens on which he grew up around San Diego. It was exceptionally effective because the stroke was so sound in its simplicity. To this Casper added the cool nerves of the pool shark he had been as a kid.

Bill Casper was the total package when it came to high-quality golf. He could drive it in play with adequate length, hit shapely approach shots, and when a green was missed he had all the stuff to get it up and down in two—or fewer. The best example of Casper's complete game was when he won his second U.S. Open, in 1966, at the Olympic Club in San Francisco.

It was a kind of sweet-and-sour victory because he defeated golf's most beloved icon, Arnold Palmer. As a result, it's a U.S. Open that has gone down in history as the one Palmer lost, not the one Casper won. Which he most certainly did.

Going into the final nine holes of regulation play in the '66 U.S. Open, Palmer had a seven-shot lead over Casper. The conventional read of what happened next was that Palmer was so sure of the victory that he began taking chances to beat Ben Hogan's record-winning score of 276 in the national championship.

Playing too boldly, even for him, Palmer came back in four-over-par 39. But here is where Billy Casper gets short shrift. He completed the championship with a very fine 32 to get the tie. A 39 isn't great golf for a guy out to win the U.S. Open, but with a seven-shot lead it would probably pass muster under most circumstances. This wasn't most circumstances. Billy Casper was in it, and the ex–pool shark had the spunk and talent of a masterful predator when he saw a good meal on the hoof.

In the play-off, Palmer again took a nice lead into the final nine—two strokes. But he came back in 40 to Casper's solid one-under-par 34. Palmer wasn't going for any record in the play-off. He just didn't have the stuff that day to close the deal against a player who was not at all intimidated by his presence and had all the tools to emerge the victor. Alas, it is still thought of as the Open Arnie lost. "*C'est la charisma.*" Here was an Open Billy won, fair and square.

It is a further mark of Casper's pride of achievement that he made a major change in his swing action when he became a senior Tour player, to continue as a viable competitor. The basic left-to-right shot that had brought him to the pinnacle of his profession takes more energy and flexibility than the swing for a right-to-left trajectory, and by the late 1970s Casper was no longer up to it.

The wear and tear of more than twenty years playing the PGA Tour (he began in 1954 and played a few years beyond his last victory, in 1975) and his ongoing overweight problem found Casper having considerable difficulty playing par golf—incredible, given his record. Bad timing, too, for the Senior PGA Tour was beginning to take shape in the late seventies. It presented a fine chance for him to continue making a good living playing his game.

Casper sought out fellow San Diegan Phil Rodgers for help. Rodgers was seven years Casper's junior and had been a fine tour player (winner of five events, loser to Bob Charles in a play-off for the British Open) and was turning himself into one of the best teachers in the game.

"With Phil I changed my grip," Casper recalled, "strengthened it, and he got me to take the club back to the inside on a flatter plane. He also eliminated the big lateral slide that had been a central aspect of my swing since I was a youngster. The idea was to go for the ball in the downswing more from the inside, instead of down the line."

The goal was to turn Billy into a right-to-left player, which would give him more distance, to make it easier on his body, and to repeat. The attempt came within a few shots of foundering on the shoals of exasperation.

Casper just couldn't get the knack of it and was on the verge of giving up the idea. But on the very last day of the effort Casper got it. He began to hit a nice draw and with it went on to win nine times on the official senior circuit, three times otherwise, and just over $2 million. Most significant of all his victories as a senior was the 1983 U.S. Senior Open, his fourth career major and once again in a play-off, on this occasion outgunning Rod Funseth at Hazeltine CC.

In recounting the highlights of his career for this profile of a great champion, Casper said there were five moments that counted most. The first, not surprisingly, was his first PGA Tour victory, the 1956 Labatt's Open. First victories, even if it's a much smaller event than those that come after, have a way of etching themselves most deeply on the competitive psyche.

But Casper's achievement at the Labatt's had even more significance than a maiden breakthrough into the winner's circle. He also got from it a piece of advice that helped write the rest of his superb competitive career. "I was going to the twelfth hole with the lead in the last round at the Labatt's and was paired with a seasoned veteran named Ted Kroll. As we walked off the eleventh green Ted told me that from then on to the end of the round to put a club in my hand off the tee that would get me in the fairway. I did for a couple of holes—went with the two-iron—but on the fifteenth hole I took the driver and put the ball in the rough. I got a look from Ted that said everything needed to be said. On the sixteenth and seventeenth holes I went back to a two-iron off the tee and kept my lead to the end. I've always been grateful to Ted for that counsel and made it a for-all-time part of my game plan."

The second significant moment in Casper's career was when he won the 1959 U.S. Open at Winged Foot, doing so with a miserly 114 putts over the seventy-two holes, an average of 28.5 putts per round. He had three-putted just one green, the tenth, a surface even more severely sloped then than today.

"I was always a good chipper and putter," Casper said, "simply because I was too lazy to practice the long game. I just hung around the green chipping and putting."

Then there was the momentous incident when Casper suffered a serious hand injury after hitting a nine-iron out of a divot during the 1963 Greensboro Open. "A bone in my left had was moved out of place, and it affected the little finger of the hand. I played the following week, in Las Vegas, and was close to the lead but had to pick up. I was worried about my career being over. But a young man who had come to live with our family knew of a retired osteopath who manipulated the hand and effectively fixed it." Indeed. The first time out after the rehabilitation, Casper won the Hartford Open. "That answered all my doubts about my future."

We have already reviewed Casper's victory over Arnold Palmer in the 1966 U.S. Open, but Billy here adds a most interesting comment. He saw with his own eyes, and to his everlasting surprise, Arnold Palmer panic. "I had seen other guys tense up, panic under pressure, but not Arnie. But once it looked like I might get into his lead, his swing got shorter and faster, and even with a two-iron he was pull-hooking into the rough, which was very deep at Olympic that year.

"It began on the sixteenth hole. I drive in the fairway, he pull-hooks into deep grass beyond where the gallery trampled it down. I get three shots back right there. On the next hole he pull-hooks another one and makes a bogey six with a great putt. I pick up another shot, and we're tied.

"On the eighteenth he pull-hooks again into deep grass; that's three in a row. I drive it up the right side in light rough. Arnie hits his second to the back of the green and putts down to four feet. He asks me if he should mark his ball, and I tell him to knock it in. He does, I two-putt, and into the play-off we go next day."

The fifth great moment came in 1970, at age thirty-nine, when he captured the Masters in a play-off with Gene Littler, a contemporary who had emerged from the same outstanding San Diego junior golf program as Casper. That Augusta National victory also produced the most unforgettable single shot in Casper's career.

"I played in my first Masters in 1957, and once I had the experience I wanted to go back forever. But in 1959 I missed the cut and worried that I wouldn't get back to Augusta next year. But I won the U.S. Open that same year, and I always remember that when I next came into the Augusta clubhouse Cliff Roberts didn't congratulate me so much as he thanked me. He liked my being there, and that made me feel pretty good.

"Anyway, I get into a play-off with Gene [Littler] for the '70 Masters, and on the second hole I hooked my tee shot badly to the left, deep into the trees. I was on some tamped-down grass, but a small branch half-covered my ball. I couldn't move it for fear of moving the ball.

"All I wanted to do was put a nine-iron back into the fairway, from where I could get back into play on the par-five. I had to hit it very high, though, and with that branch on my ball I wasn't sure I could do that. I managed to get the club head between the branch and the ball and got it out. I had a five-iron third shot I put on the back of the green. Litt was in front of the green in two, but he chili-dipped it and made a bogey.

"I two-putted for a par and was off and running. It seems odd, somehow, but the one shot I remember most was a nine-iron I played back to the fairway. That's golf, I guess."

In good part because of his mien on the course, Casper was often said to play too conservative a game. Since he was also playing during the heyday of the ever-aggressive superhero, Arnold Palmer, that tag may have gotten more currency than it deserved. Casper puts that aspect of his reputation into historical perspective. "There is definitely room in golf for a more conservative approach to the game. Certainly there was in my day, when the purses weren't quite as generous as they've become.

"Take that fellow Goosen, in Tulsa [the 2001 U.S. Open]. He needed two putts from twelve feet to win the U.S. Open, and he charges it. Not smart. But they can do that now, because the money is so great.

"Nowadays, you can catch lightning three times a year and make a million, which is all you need. In my first year on the Tour, 1955, I won $4,000 and was fifty-fifth on the money list. Next year I won a tournament and a total of $18,000 and was twelfth on the money list. We pulled a Spartan trailer with a Buick Roadmaster the first year and a half on tour. I got $650 a month from my backers for three years and more as I won more money. Finally I paid them off. I owned a car and a little house and had four or five thousand in the bank. Things were good, and a little different, moneywise, in those days."

What does someone who has devoted his life to playing a terrifically demanding game learn about himself and, if you please, life in general? For Billy Casper it has been patience, with himself and his game and in his private life. In the end, it is what it takes to be a winner.

"You must have the ability to control your mind and your heart," says Casper. "The golf swing is really a small part of it. It comes from all the practice and routine. But you need a strong will and the ability to think yourself around the course when not playing well.

"That is what heart is, when you're not hitting the ball well and still staying with it. That is something I learned. It didn't come with the territory."

BILLY CASPER

	Total New Money	Wins	Top10s	Top25s
Majors	$10,590,000	3	24	47
Other Official Tournaments (and International Wins)	78,224,588	53	252	384
TOTALS	$88,814,588	56	276	431

MAJOR CHAMPIONSHIPS

	New Money	Wins
Masters	$3,496,780	1
U.S. Open	3,403,900	2
British Open	603,636	0
PGA	3,085,684	0

BEST OTHER EVENTS

	New Money	Wins
Western Open	$3,929,657	4
Hartford Open	3,819,500	4
Los Angeles Open	3,248,737	2
Pebble Beach	3,138,452	2

Year	New Money	Total Wins	Top10s	Top25s	Majors	Other Events
1954	$ 34,560	0	0	1	$ 0	$ 34,560
1955	494,597	0	2	7	0	494,597
1956	3,115,022	1	9	27	108,757	3,006,265
1957	4,157,751	2	14	25	95,200	4,062,551
1958	6,549,544	4	19	26	780,751	5,768,793
1959	5,137,540	5	16	22	1,069,575	4,067,965
1960	4,578,641	4	15	23	437,743	4,140,898
1961	3,942,115	1	19	25	367,544	3,574,571
1962	5,873,583	4	15	20	101,920	5,771,663
1963	3,102,648	2	10	19	123,200	2,979,448
1964	6,438,177	4	24	26	600,477	5,837,700
1965	5,968,513	4	17	23	568,430	5,400,083
1966	6,467,583	4	16	24	1,426,000	5,041,583
1967	4,568,368	2	16	20	389,297	4,179,071
1968	6,522,224	6	16	22	717,304	5,804,920
1969	4,441,995	3	12	17	465,539	3,976,456
1970	4,252,892	4	10	15	1,286,822	2,966,070
1971	2,910,734	1	7	16	869,742	2,040,992
1972	1,535,070	0	4	12	426,513	1,108,557
1973	2,538,494	2	7	11	75,787	2,462,707
1974	1,233,190	0	6	11	0	1,233,190
1975	2,579,987	2	10	13	410,600	2,169,387
1976	1,031,206	0	8	11	173,600	857,606
1977	934,952	1	3	7	95,200	839,752
1978	189,994	0	0	4	0	189,994
1979	190,335	0	1	3	0	190,335
1984	24,874	0	0	1	0	24,874

Nick Faldo

John Hopkins

In 1957, England still bore the signs of the war that had ended only a dozen years earlier. There was no obvious prosperity. Colors were drab and unimaginative. Food rationing for meager portions of milk, meat, and eggs had only recently ended.

The wireless, as it was called then, was the primary medium for home entertainment, and the cinema—known as "the flicks" for the flickering images that were projected on the screen—the preeminent nonsporting public entertainment. Even the Mini, the car of which more than five million would eventually be sold, was still only a pencil drawing on the board of Alex Issigonis, its brilliant engineer, at his Birmingham office.

It was into this country, a Britain that had not yet fully struggled clear of the final embers of World War II, that Nick Faldo was born at 57 Knella Road, Welwyn Garden City, on July 18, 1957. Faldo was one of a quintet of golfing prodigies who would go on to win major championships that were all born in Europe in a ten-month span between April 1957 (Severiano Ballesteros) and March 1958 (Ian Woosnam). Bernhard Langer (August 1957) and Sandy Lyle (February 1958) rounded out the five-ball that would contribute so much to the success of professional golf in Europe in the years to come.

George and Joyce Faldo were a typical family who, if not struggling to make ends meet when their son was born, had not yet established any last degree of financial security. George Faldo worked in the financial planning department of ICI Plastics. Joyce Faldo was a cutter and pattern drafter for a firm that sold silk. They lived for Nicholas Alexander, their son and only child.

We are all children of parental influence, the way we are because of the way they are, or were, by example—genetically shaped by them, influenced by them, taught by them, and frequently one parent more than the other has a dominant influence during the formative years. On the other hand, some children seem motivated to outstanding feats as a direct consequence of their failure to gain a parent's approval.

Harry Vardon, for example, never received the appreciation he expected from his father, and its lack may have been one of the most powerful influences that drove him to win six Open championships, the first in 1896, the sixth some eighteen years later in 1914. "Harry is the golfer, but 'tis Tom who plays the golf," Vardon's father once wrote of his two sons. There was a similar *froideur* between Greg Norman and his father, and it wasn't until Norman was well into his thirties that he and his father were able to sit down and talk it over. Charlie Nicklaus, a genial pharmacist, was the dominant parent in the eyes of young Jack, and Arnold Palmer always knew that if Deacon Palmer, his father, was angry with him he could expect Deacon's heavy hand or worse. Deacon was a disciplinarian. Earl Woods certainly implanted powerful genes into his son.

If George Faldo, a quiet, somewhat shy man, provided his son with a considerable physique—long legs and broad shoulders—most of the rest of Nicholas Alexander Faldo has come from his mother, a tall, vivacious woman with his high cheekbones. Nor was the early driving force in young Faldo's life ever in doubt. Ask if Nick is the son of his mother or father and the answer is always his mother.

They doted on their son as the parents of only children often do. Joyce Faldo once recalled the extent of her ambition for him. "We wanted Nick to be an actor," she said. "We thought he'd be another Olivier. We took him to dancing lessons. We tried to interest him in music; we knew he would win the Tchaikovsky piano prize. He has smashing legs, and I wanted him to be a model, so we used to go with him to Harrods fashion shows. And then I realized he lived for sport and wanted nothing else. So that was the end of those dreams."

Joyce Faldo would take young Nicholas anywhere he wanted to go in the small family car and take his friends too, fitting these journeys in around her work as best she could. Later neighbors and colleagues told her they thought she was doing too much for her son. "We thought you were mad the way you did everything for Nick," Joyce Faldo remembers being told years later by a neighbor. "We thought you were spoiling him."

Such criticism was of no concern to Joyce Faldo. She was demonstrating such confidence in her son that not only did he never dream he would fail but she instilled her own belief in him. He is living proof of Freud's theory that "a man who has been the undisputed favorite of his mother keeps for life the feeling of being a conqueror, that confidence of success that often induces real success."

"We didn't think for a moment that what we were doing was wrong," she said years later. "It seemed to us to be the most natural thing in the world to do everything in our power to help Nick. It did not enter our heads that he might fail. He was so sure of his ambitions to be a professional golfer and win titles that we knew he had what it takes. Besides, people kept coming up to me and saying, 'You know Nick is very good, don't you?' All we had to do was to sit back and wait."

The time between 1987 and 1992, and particularly between 1987 and 1990, must have been a joyous time for the senior Faldos. They saw their son play to a level of consistency that was unmatched.

In July 1987 he won the Open at Muirfield, parring every hole in his fourth round, an achievement that down the years became rather devalued by criticism that it was boring golf. A year later he was edged into second place in the U.S. Open—but only after an eighteen-hole play-off in which Curtis Strange outlasted him. He won the U.S. Masters in 1989 and again in 1990, and in the Open at St. Andrews in 1990 he won by five strokes. In the thirteen major championships in this period Faldo won four, came in second once, and five times finished in the top 11.

This was a dominance that was rare in those days. It took one back to Jack Nicklaus at his peak, and it was not until Tiger Woods came along at the end of the century and won the four successive major championships that Faldo's record was overshadowed.

It can be instructive and revealing to learn how champion golfers take up the game. Severiano Ballesteros came to it because his brothers played, and he started when he was no more than a mite by hitting a ball around on the beach at Santander, his home in northern Spain. It was something similar with Sandy Lyle, who, at the age of three, was to immediately prove extraordinarily accomplished when a golf club was placed in his tiny hands. Likewise, perhaps more so, the case of Tiger Woods, who started swinging a cut-down golf club around the same time as he started to walk.

Faldo, however, knew nothing of golf until the Easter of 1972, about the time of his fourteenth birthday. He was watching television at home when Jack Nicklaus appeared on the screen competing in the Masters at Augusta National. At that time Faldo was an outstanding swimmer, a good runner and cyclist. Even then he preferred individual sports, those in which there was no one else with whom to share the credit, no one to blame when things did not work out as planned. Seeing this burly man with blond hair moving among the stately pines at Augusta National was a life-changing experience for the young Englishman sitting in his parents' house in Hertfordshire. Entranced, he moved nearer the edge of his seat, and soon his mother was arranging for the lanky teenager to have a series of golf lessons.

Such was the beginning of golf for the man who would become the best English golfer (Sandy Lyle's a Scot, Ian Woosnam Welsh) since Henry Cotton in the 1930s and 1940s or Harry Vardon several decades earlier.

The best in Britain? The best in the world for a while, the most consistent, the most respected, the most admired. At this time, he talked of how he wanted to know that in years to come people would say to one another: "I saw Nick Faldo play golf. He wasn't bad." That laconic British understatement appealed to Faldo's humor, a humor as frequently misunderstood as the man himself.

Where Faldo was so good was in the fact that all aspects of his game were strong. His driving was straight, if not as long as one would expect from such a big and powerful-looking man, his irons were crisp, his short game clinical, and his putting was lethal, a result of years spent putting on differing surfaces in his parents' home, from slippery linoleum on the bathroom floor to carpet in the sitting room.

As a champion Faldo had none of the thunderous power of Nicklaus, nor the velvet touch and imagination of Ballesteros. Yet he was straighter and steadier than Tom Watson and, at their respective best, certainly as good a putter. Sandy Lyle probably had more God-given talent, but possibly less application. There is one famous story concerning the rivalry between Lyle and Faldo, a rivalry that drove Faldo on and on because it seemed that Lyle always got better more quickly. Lyle was British-boy and youths international, was selected to play for his country, won professional tournaments, and then won his first major championship, all ahead of Faldo. One day in Boston in 1988 Faldo revealed the depths of his feelings on this subject. He had just come in from a practice round before that year's U.S. Open. He was getting ready for a session on an exercise bike followed by an hour in the gym. Across the other side of the pool was Lyle, sitting with a group of friends. "Look at Sandy's swing," Faldo said with feeling. "It goes over, up, down, around, through, in, and out. By rights it should not work at all, but it does." He sighed and consigned himself to a longer session than usual on the bike and in the gym to make up for what was clearly a differential in talent between him and Lyle.

Faldo's talent may have been slower in arriving, but it lasted longer. Lyle's victories in major championships came in the Open at Sandwich in 1985 and the Masters in 1988 compared with Faldo's six victories—the Masters of 1989, 1990, and 1996 and the Open of 1987, 1990, and 1992.

In his array of talents Faldo could not claim to be the best in the world at any individual skill in the way that Ben Hogan was so coolly precise and that flexible Sam Snead was such a remarkable athlete. Nicklaus's mind was stronger than any since Hogan, a category that now includes Woods. Ballesteros was more thrilling. Norman was longer. Bernhard Langer's long irons were more deadly, Faldo's equal in physical fitness.

Nor would Faldo win a contest for the game's all-time individual categories. Driving accuracy and driving distance would belong to Nicklaus, greens-in-regulation to Hogan, putting to Watson, while Gary Player owned the sand section outright. But in such an analysis Faldo would certainly be very close to the top of the all-around statistics. And remember that such a measure does not include one of Faldo's greatest strengths, his analytical mind, one that was always open to advice, and his visceral instinct that more often than not he was the one who knew best for himself. Again and again in the first four decades of his life Faldo did things that appeared to fly in the face of conventional wisdom, and almost without exception he was proved right. Over his career Faldo demonstrated the strength of his mind again and again, starting with his decision to quit a university place in the United States after a mere couple of months and return to Britain. Many questioned this decision, suggesting he was a quitter. Faldo, however, maintained he was falling back in the Unites States, not moving forward. He did not like the endless medal rounds and wanted instead to hit balls on a practice ground as he had done at home.

No less important was his decision in the early 1980s to change his swing under the tutelage of David Leadbetter. Faldo won the Order of Merit in Europe in 1983 for the first time. This was not enough to convince him that his swing was strong enough to withstand the pressure of the final rounds of tournament golf, and so he sought out Leadbetter, a leading teacher of the era. It was close to four years before Faldo began to play really good golf again, and during that time there were many who felt he had made a grave mistake. "If it ain't broke, don't fix it" was the view of his swing. Once again, over the next five years Faldo would prove his decision to have been the right one for him.

In the Open championship at Muirfield in 1992 Faldo led midway through the last round, then fell behind. Having led and then lost the initiative, few thought he could regain it. One who did was Faldo himself, the other was Leadbetter—and on that breezy Sunday they might have been the only two!

Faldo recaptured the lead and won, as much by willpower as by skill. Legend recalls that on the fifteenth tee Faldo turned to his caddie and said, "I am now going to have to play the best four holes of my life," and promptly did so—for his fifth major championship.

In the 1995 Ryder Cup at Oak Hill, Faldo walked onto the sixteenth tee two down in his singles match against Curtis Strange. An hour later he had won, the manner of his winning of the last hole the stuff of fairy tales. A drive that tailed off into the rough was followed by a recovery shot hit to precisely ninety-five yards from the flagstick, a distance with which Faldo felt most comfortable. There followed a wedge to four feet from where Faldo rapped home the putt for the one-hole victory that in the final analysis assured Europe of an historic Ryder Cup triumph on U.S. soil. Indeed over his entire career, the greater the pressure, the more cerebral Faldo seemed to become at the critical moments. Still, the greatest triumph of mind over matter might have been the following April when Norman and

Faldo, who had so often been cast together as the central figures in a crucial round of golf, played out the last round of the Masters.

Norman, who had begun leading by six strokes, was behind by the eleventh hole and would eventually lose by five, a swing over the eighteen holes of eleven strokes. As well as the sheer scale of the achievement, in time that meeting of the two great players of the day would take on even greater significance. It would be Faldo's last victory in a major championship and virtually Norman's last high finish in any future major. It was as if the enormity of what they had gone through had worn them both out.

For much of the time that he was at the top of his career, Faldo had a female caddie, Fanny Sunesson, who came from Karlshamm, a town two hours' drive from Malmo. At this time female caddies were far from usual on the golfing scene, and choosing Fanny was yet another mark of Faldo's unwavering individualism. Sunesson was and is a hardworking, genial bag carrier who kept to herself. Faldo had noted her incessantly cheerful attitude, her attention to detail, her vast appetite for work. For the best part of a decade they were together before late in 1999 Sunesson, by now tiring of Faldo's lack of success and seeking the sort of challenge that had originally drawn her to Faldo, ended their partnership. Faldo, asked what he would miss most about Fanny, replied: "Well, it will be hard getting used to not hearing her say things like: "Did you know there are seventeen different types of hummingbird in this town?" Yet time would heal whatever dissent may have occurred, maybe none, and their longtime partnership was revived in obvious good humor in April 2001.

The recurring pattern throughout Faldo's career was that women played an extraordinarily important part in the shaping of his life. By the age of forty-two, he had been married and divorced twice, had one highly publicized fling with a girl barely more than half his age, which was ended, the tabloid newspapers in Britain took some pleasure in reporting, when she took a nine-iron and set about the bonnet of his Porsche. He was proposing to marry a Swiss in her twenties who had walked out of her relationship upon meeting Faldo in Switzerland.

The truth is that Faldo is like Coriolanus. He was molded by women, first his mother, then Melanie, his first wife, then Gill, his second, then Brenna Cepelak, and currently Valerie Bercher, whom he married in July

2001, with Fanny Sunesson and her relentlessly cheerful presence on his golf bag for most of the winning streak.

The ultimate test for any sportsman in Britain is the opinion of "the man in the street," and there were plenty of times when Faldo was shopping or getting out of his car when someone, unprompted, would shout out: "Good on you, Nick" or "Well done, Nick. Good luck."

Nonetheless he remained a figure with a checkered history in the eyes of the British public, and it was not until the 1995 Ryder Cup, just one week before news of his leaving his second wife became public knowledge, that this slight snootiness toward Faldo began to disappear, and it did so then because of his astonishing fight back to defeat Strange. After this, Faldo grew in popularity as fast as he had fallen in the past, despite the fact that by now he was spending most of his time playing the U.S. circuit.

If the case against Faldo is that he became the great champion he surely was because he was totally preoccupied by golf, then he would probably plead guilty. An example of that dedication is that the births of all three of his children were induced to fit with their father's golf schedule.

Remember, however, how few truly world-class and lasting sportsman Britain has produced down the years. Nick Faldo is certainly one of those.

NICK FALDO

	Total New Money	Wins	Top10s	Top25s
Majors	$13,206,043	6	25	44
Other Official Tournaments (and International Wins)	37,200,504	32	189	298
TOTALS	$50,406,547	38	214	342

MAJOR CHAMPIONSHIPS

	New Money	Wins
Masters	$3,576,133	3
U.S. Open	1,737,425	0
British Open	6,234,853	3
PGA	1,657,632	0

BEST OTHER EVENTS

	New Money	Wins
Volvo PGA	$4,531,949	4
French Open	1,839,154	3
European Open	1,810,359	1
Cisco World Match Play	1,773,666	2

Year	New Money	Total Wins	Top10s	Top25s	Majors	Other Events
1976	$ 107,573	0	1	3	$ 0	$ 107,573
1977	802,224	1	6	6	0	802,224
1978	1,457,540	1	6	12	154,069	1,303,471
1979	497,411	1	6	11	63,208	434,203
1980	1,395,241	1	8	13	90,861	1,304,379
1981	2,023,852	1	8	16	102,713	1,921,139
1982	2,377,153	1	13	23	346,681	2,030,472
1983	3,503,319	5	14	20	192,717	3,310,602
1984	2,249,162	2	8	14	362,446	1,886,716
1985	607,050	0	3	11	45,360	561,690
1986	1,224,227	0	6	13	252,832	971,395
1987	2,581,931	2	12	16	1,106,140	1,475,791
1988	3,956,230	2	16	18	1,237,852	2,718,378
1989	3,857,105	5	8	18	1,340,566	2,516,539
1990	3,829,950	3	11	16	2,493,683	1,336,267
1991	1,892,222	1	9	15	333,926	1,558,296
1992	5,120,945	6	18	23	1,804,038	3,316,907
1993	2,527,989	2	12	14	1,006,080	1,521,909
1994	1,531,761	1	10	14	369,551	1,162,210
1995	2,611,087	1	7	14	46,480	2,564,607
1996	2,637,133	1	8	13	1,401,844	1,235,289
1997	1,429,520	1	6	9	0	1,429,520
1998	208,639	0	2	4	0	208,639
1999	321,765	0	3	4	0	321,765
2000	417,312	0	3	6	168,153	249,159
2001	478,008	0	4	5	0	478,008
2002	760,199	0	6	11	286,843	473,356

Walter Hagen

Dr. Stephen R. Lowe

Bow ties, bathtub gin, jazz, and the Charleston. Wall Street, Fords, and flappers. The Roaring Twenties. It was the most colorful decade in American history, as well as an era of intense, rapid change. Long-held traditions and standards were challenged repeatedly. A booming economy produced millionaires in every walk of life and helped fuel a Golden Age of Sports.

Golf thrived and changed with the new prosperity. Mounds of sand became factory-made tees, hickory shafts hardened into steel. A new international rivalry, the Ryder Cup competition, was born. The game's stars, like the decade in which they played, were some of the brightest ever, but none of them outshone Walter C. Hagen, the charming, well-built son of a poor, immigrant family from Rochester, New York.

A true original, "Sir Walter" perfectly suited his times. Hagen was the first "unattached" touring pro, as well as the first player to dress flashily during competition, to endorse a matched set of irons, to employ gamesmanship, to hire a full-time agent—and to make a million dollars in golf. In competition Hagen was the first American-born player to win the British Open, the first U.S. Ryder Cup captain (and competitor), and the first player to win the same major championship four years in a row. Grantland Rice, the Golden Age's top sportswriter, considered Hagen "the irresponsible playboy of golf, and at the same time a keen and determined competitor." To some, Sir Walter was an arrogant rebel; others saw him as their personal champion, leading the way to golf's future. On one point all were agreed: Walter Hagen embodied change.

There was nothing in Hagen's humble background that suggested future wealth and fame. He entered the world on December 21, 1892, in a small, two-story home built by his father, William Hagen, on the outskirts of Rochester, New York. Before Walter came along, all of the Hagen men made a living as manual laborers—and none of them had the wherewithal to play golf. Walter's dad worked as a blacksmith in the railroad yards of East Rochester, and his mother, Louise Balko Hagen, was a German immigrant who raised five children while keeping up the house and garden on the quaint two-acre Hagen homestead.

Young Walter developed a lifelong passion for the outdoors, especially hunting and fishing. He passed the long winters of upstate New York by sledding and skating with his four sisters. When the snow melted, he loved to play baseball, and although his pitching prowess has been exaggerated over the years, Hagen was good enough as a teenager to excel in tough local semipro leagues. School was one of the things Walter didn't enjoy, and like so many from his social class, he dropped out early, barely finishing the sixth grade. In all, Hagen's childhood was rather ordinary.

There was one crucial difference, though, between Hagen's background and that of most other working-class kids. The Hagen house happened to be located near property that was purchased by Rochester's wealthy sportsmen for the purpose of constructing the city's first golf course. If not for that coincidence, the persona of "Sir Walter" would probably never have been born. But in 1895 the Country Club of Rochester (CCR) was formed, and soon after, golf was played within a mile of the Hagen land. By his seventh birthday little Walter was caddying at the CCR, toting and cleaning clubs for the city's elite.

Hagen quickly became a favorite with club members, and the feeling was mutual. He remembered admiring "the ease with which they spoke of huge money deals—and I certainly eyed wishfully their fancy golfing outfits." Rochester's professional, Andrew Christy, noticed Hagen and took the young caddie under his wing. When Hagen turned fourteen, Christy offered him the assistant professional's job. Christy taught Hagen the fine art of club making and repair, management of the pro shop, and the basics of greenkeeping. Hagen also learned how to swing the club; actually, the most valuable aspect of Hagen's job promotion was the chance to play more rounds at the country club, many under the instructional eye of Christy.

By 1912 Hagen was ready for his first competition. Never one to think small, he made plans to enter the U.S. Open, but Christy encouraged him to wait another year and instead play in the Canadian Open. Hagen reluctantly agreed, traveled to Toronto, and finished a respectable twelfth place. Weeks later Christy resigned his post at the CCR, and at nineteen years old Hagen became one of the first American-born club professionals.

Hagen spent most of 1913 settling into his new job, but by September he was ready for more competition and took the train to Brookline, Massachusetts, to play in his first U.S. Open. Hagen fought hard at the country club and ended in a tie for fourth place, behind leaders Harry Vardon, "Big Ted" Ray, and Francis Ouimet, a young local amateur who put American golf on the map the next day by defeating the British professionals in a play-off. The valuable experience Hagen gained at Brookline helped him break through the following year at Chicago's Midlothian Golf Club, where he edged out rising amateur star Charles "Chick" Evans by one stroke to capture his first national Open in only his second attempt.

The Midlothian victory launched Hagen's competitive career. He would eventually win another U.S. Open (1919), four British Opens (1922, '24, '28, and '29), five PGA Championships (1922, '24–'27), and five Western Opens (1916, '21, '26, '27, '32). During the early 1920s, before Bobby Jones ascended to the emperor's throne, Sir Walter was widely regarded as the number-one player in the world. In the summer of 1924, after Hagen won his second British Open, the *New York Times* declared him the "greatest golfer who ever lived—bar none."

As for the number of "majors" Hagen won, it depends on how one counts them. He collected eleven of the currently designated "major" events, although only three of them were contested in the 1920s. In that decade the Masters was but a dream in the young mind of Bobby Jones. Golf writers, but more important the players themselves, generally considered the Western Open to be a fourth major, and including those victories, Hagen had sixteen contemporary majors. However one classifies them, Hagen compiled a record that easily ranks him among the best.

But Hagen's significance to golf runs deeper than his outstanding competitive career. Hagen changed golf fundamentally by pioneering the professional tour and thereby taking the sport from the private country club to the public. There were no professional golfers before Hagen, only golf club professionals, men who served wealthy members by performing the tasks that Christy had taught Hagen at Rochester.

Club professionals came from the lower classes and early in the century were almost always British immigrants. Their identity was defined entirely by their club; they played competitively for small amounts of money only a few times each year, and they were always listed in newspapers and tournament programs according to home club, such as "Walter C. Hagen, Country Club of Rochester." Members generally looked down on their pros, perceiving them as rough, uncouth, and subservient.

Hagen suffered such prejudice at Rochester and at Detroit's Oakland Hills Country Club, where he migrated for the 1918–19 season, because for a man of his social background second-class treatment at a country club was more comfortable than first-class treatment in the railroad yard. But after he won a second U.S. Open in 1919, Hagen had had enough. Displaying an old-fashioned German-bred pride, he decided to break free from the constrictions and condescension of the private club and become a full-time touring professional golfer. Never again would Hagen be contracted to a club. Beginning in 1920, he was identified in tournament summaries as "Walter C. Hagen, unattached." Hagen was the first to carry that label, which denoted economic free agency. Most observers either scoffed, believing that Hagen couldn't make a living through exhibitions and tournament play, or criticized him for "unduly commercializing" a gentleman's sport. The great British professional J. H. Taylor, for example, castigated Hagen for playing "unattached," saying that "real pros" worked for the "honor, prestige, and dignity of the clubs" they served. Hagen simply went his way, proving some wrong and cordially disagreeing with the rest.

Hagen carried his challenge further by pushing boundaries at some of the most famous clubs around the world. In 1920 he traveled to Deal, England, for his first try at the British Open. Europeans were much more tradition-bound than Americans, and at Deal the professionals were not even allowed to enter the clubhouse but rather were asked to use a nearby shed for their locker room. Upon arrival, Sir Walter alighted from his chauffeured Austin-Daimler motorcar wearing a Savile Row overcoat, looked over the accommodations, and concluded that they were no place for his fine wardrobe. In protest, Hagen used his limousine as a locker room that week, parking it each day in front of the clubhouse's main entrance.

Three years later at Troon, Hagen refused to take part in the trophy presentation ceremony, despite the fact that he was the runner-up, because professionals had not been admitted into the clubhouse during the previous week. If club members deemed him unworthy to enter their sanctuary during the tournament, Hagen reasoned, then why should he enter it for their trophy presentation? Instead, Hagen marched up the steps to the front door, turned to the crowd, and said, "I'd like to invite all of you to come over to the pub where we've been so welcome. If the [tournament] committee likes, they can present the trophy to the new champion over there." Democratizing golf and developing respect for its professionals became a crusade for Hagen.

It was just that cause that led sportswriters to christen Hagen with his primary nickname, "Sir Walter." The name conjured up images of honor, chivalry, and egalitarianism; to his supporters Hagen was like a medieval knight, slaying unjust prejudices. The crusade required pluck, hard work, charisma, flair, and a lot of moxie. Sir Walter had them all—in spades. In fact there was not another golfer in 1920 who could have carried it off.

To help wage his campaign, Hagen recruited Robert "Bob" Harlow to be his personal manager and agent. Harlow created and then sold "Sir Walter." He scheduled exhibitions, convinced civic leaders to organize open events, and negotiated Hagen's endorsement contracts for products ranging from equipment to knickers to long-playing instructional albums. Smooth talking, well groomed, and disciplined, Harlow was the perfect promoter for Sir Walter's show. With Harlow at his side, Hagen not only survived as an "unattached" professional but did better for himself than any other golfer ever had. During the 1920s his annual income was somewhere between $50,000 and $75,000; H. B. Martin once estimated that Hagen made $1.5 million throughout his career.

The most lucrative seasons were those immediately after Hagen won a major tournament, such as the summer of 1922, following his first British Open victory. Harlow usually invited a headliner, like the entertaining and skilled "Australian trick-shot artist" Joe Kirkwood, to play in foursome exhibitions with Hagen, and the troop would cover the country in trains, boats, automobiles, and even an occasional airplane. The barnstorming tour quickly became a Hagen-Harlow specialty.

While Harlow made tough-minded business decisions behind the scenes, Hagen performed grandly on the stage. Herbert Warren Wind wrote that Sir Walter was a "born showman," who "loved the big gesture." Hagen attracted thousands of customers to exhibitions and open events with his knack for the spectacular in dress, mannerisms, and style of play.

In 1924 the *Detroit News* dubbed Hagen "Golf's Fashion Plate," revealing a wardrobe that included two dozen pairs of custom-designed golf shoes. In the spring of 1925, O. B. Keeler described Hagen as "the leading showman of sport" and compared him to the great prizefighter of the late nineteenth century, John L. Sullivan. Sportswriter Al Laney recalled that Hagen's "mere arrival on the scene did something, caused something to happen. His every appearance seemed to be accompanied by the figurative blaring of trumpets and a metaphorical waving of banners, and Walter was perfectly conscious at all times of his role as a performer."

Hagen's biggest gesture may have come at the 1926 British Open, when he strode down the final fairway, trailing Bobby Jones by two strokes. Hagen needed to sink a 150-yard approach shot for an improbable eagle and the tie. With Jones sitting on the clubhouse balcony and a tension-filled throng gathered around the home green, Hagen paced off the distance to the hole and then sent his caddie to tend the flag! Sir Walter had every intention of making the shot. He failed, but only narrowly, running his ball within inches of the cup and offering the spectators one of the greatest golf shows of their lives.

Of course, one man's showmanship is another's gamesmanship, and Hagen became just as famous for the latter. One of his favorite match-play tricks was to select the wrong club when hitting first in an effort to confuse his opponent. Hagen might, for example, hit an easy mashie into a well-guarded par three and then watch his opponent hit a full mashie into a hazard behind the green. If competing against a player with a shaky putting stroke, Hagen would purposely concede two- and three-footers early in the match but look the other way during the late holes. Hagen would even use his mouth to throw an opponent off balance.

One of his brassiest lines came at the 1925 PGA Championship, when he walked into the locker room and casually asked Leo Diegel and Al Watrous, "Which one of you is going to finish second?" As it happened, they both did that week—Watrous succumbed to Hagen's match-play wizardry in the first round over thirty-nine holes, while Diegel fell to Hagen in the third round on the fortieth green. In a piece entitled "What Makes Hagen a Great Player?" the *New York Times*' William Richardson argued that Hagen's greatest assets were his "head" and "confidence." "Others, his mechanical equals, maybe superiors, have to give way to him when it comes to headwork on the links."

Hagen specialized in the psychology of the game because he needed to; his swing was not a pretty sight to behold. The word most commonly used by writers to describe it was *lurching*. Hagen had a wide stance, strong grip, and flat swing plane—a remnant from the baseball diamond. His weight shift was dramatic as he moved to the right on the backswing and then practically lunged at the ball on the downswing. His ideal ball flight was a low draw, but in reality it was unpredictable, especially from the tee. Hagen's forte, however, was the short game; he was the master scrambler.

From a hundred yards inward to the hole, Hagen was deadly accurate, and once on the green, he putted with a deft touch and steely nerves. British golf writer Arthur Croome once observed that Hagen "makes more bad shots in a single season than Harry Vardon did during the whole period 1890–1914. But he beats more immaculate golfers because three of 'those' and one of 'them' count four, and he knows it." H. B. Martin thought that Sir Walter was "superbly unorthodox, self-taught, and not in the slightest measure a copyist or a patternist" in his golf swing. Hagen was pragmatic about his style; he cared far less about what old-timers thought of his swing than about whether or not it won him tournaments, and he always played to win. Harlow believed that "if Walter got into a game of tiddlywinks with a couple of kids on the nursery room floor, he would try as hard to beat them as he did to win the British Open."

Hagen was unconventional and controversial away from the course as well. His other nickname was "The Haig," most likely an effort to connect Hagen to "The Babe," another hedonistic, charismatic athlete from the 1920s. As with Babe Ruth, the stories about Hagen's carefree lifestyle are legion. Wind recorded that Hagen drank "what would have been for other people excessive quantities of liquor. He broke eleven of the Ten Commandments and kept on going."

Anecdotes about Hagen's spending all night at a party, then showing up at the first tee of a tournament in a tuxedo and patent leather shoes became widespread. On that score, though, the image rarely reflected reality. In fact the evidence indicates that Hagen took good care of himself during his prime, sleeping more and imbibing less than has been commonly assumed. Later in life Hagen attempted to correct some of the myth, writing, "I could make one highball last longer in my own glass than any Scotchman ever born." Hagen became skilled at holding a drink for long periods, appearing to consume it, while actually using it as a sort of prop as he held court.

But if Hagen's drinking has been exaggerated over the years, then the tales about his womanizing are most likely all true. The largest segment of his gallery was often comprised of women, and Hagen usually found his evening's companionship among them. Handsome and debonair, the Haig was as bold with a woman on his arm as he was with a putter in his hand. Early in his career Hagen was introduced to Ernestine Shumann-Heink, famous contralto of the Metropolitan Opera. He had never seen her before and, after noticing her "ample bosom," supposedly commented, "My dear, did you ever stop to think what a lovely bunker you would make?" Such behavior did not make for a happy marriage, and during a decade in which divorce was relatively rare, Hagen was married and divorced twice. A family friend recalled the popular explanation for the breakup of Hagen's second marriage: "The story is that the dissolution began one night in a Florida hotel, when Walter, returning at a very unseemly hour, was discovered by Mrs. Hagen, as he hastily prepared for bed, to be without underwear." Hagen's only defense was that he'd been "robbed."

Yet Hagen had other, more admirable qualities. In spite of his gamesmanship and self-promotion, he was remarkably popular among his peers, who understood that whatever was good for him would probably benefit them in the long run, too. Moreover, Hagen was just likable; he never forgot his roots, consistently impressing people with a sincere common touch forged by his own modest upbringing. He became famous for giving large sums of money to caddies and friends, and he played dozens of exhibitions for charity. Finally, according to H. B. Martin, Hagen's two most outstanding traits were his refusal to court sympathy or self-pity and his utter disregard for making alibis—whatever the breaks. Those attitudes endeared him to competitors and took the edge off his otherwise cocky behavior. "I love to play with Walter," declared Bobby Jones. "He goes along chin up, smiling away; never grousing about his luck, playing the ball as he finds it. He can come nearer beating the luck itself than anybody I know."

In his rise to wealth and fame in golf, Hagen had beaten the odds. But no one can defeat Father Time, and as the Golden Twenties gave way to the Gray Thirties, Hagen slipped past his prime. The transition was made easier, though, by the realization that his crusade had been a huge success; professional tour golf was growing strong, and more people than ever were caught up in the sport. Bob Harlow became the PGA Tour's first tournament manager in 1930, drawing on the experience and success of his barnstorming days with Hagen. Inspired by the example of Sir Walter, other club professionals acquired more freedom—some followed Hagen, touring the world "unattached," while others simply demanded and received more respect, as well as time for competitive play. "All the professionals who have a chance to go after the big money should say a silent thanks to Walter each time they stretch a check between their fingers," Gene Sarazen concluded. "It was Walter who made professional golf what it is."

Hagen won his last event in 1935 and by 1940 was through with competitive golf for good. Always something of a vagabond, he finally purchased some property of his own in 1953, about twenty acres of wooded land on Long Lake, near Traverse City, Michigan. With the help of Margaret Seaton Heck, he penned *The Walter Hagen Story*, an entertaining autobiography filled with favorite anecdotes. Hagen spent his remaining years in northern Michigan, where, with a few exceptions, he lived in surprising obscurity. One of his last moments in the spotlight occurred in 1968, when Hagen became only the fourth American, alongside President Dwight D. Eisenhower, Francis Ouimet, and Bobby Jones, to be made an honorary member of the Royal and Ancient Golf Club of St. Andrews, Scotland. The following year, on October 6, 1969, while resting peacefully in his cottage, Walter Hagen died at the age of seventy-six.

For weeks thereafter sportswriters around the country stammered to explain Sir Walter's significance. Unfortunately for Hagen, his image as a Roaring Twenties rebel somewhat overwhelmed his competitive record. Al Laney astutely reflected, "All of us who wrote golf in Hagen's day made too much of his flamboyant showmanship [and] not nearly enough of his golf." The result has been that for the uninitiated, Hagen is often confused with Hogan—a terrible injustice to both men.

And for all too many informed fans, Hagen is remembered as a wonderfully colorful figure and just a good—not great—golfer. Fortunately, his record and contributions speak for themselves, and history has a way of putting things in perspective. The *Times* of London was one of the few that got it right in 1969, reminding its readers that even if Sir Walter "had dressed for the fairways in sackcloth, he would stand in comparison with the best in the world."

WALTER HAGEN

	Total New Money	Wins	Top10s	Top25s
Majors	$18,986,325	11	33	44
Other Official Tournaments (and International Wins)	43,362,895	34	119	151
TOTALS	**$62,349,220**	**45**	**152**	**195**

MAJOR CHAMPIONSHIPS

	New Money	Wins
Masters	$ 361,200	0
U.S. Open	6,043,434	2
British Open	5,918,750	4
PGA	6,662,941	5

BEST OTHER EVENTS

	New Money	Wins
Western Open	$7,534,950	5
North & South Open	4,862,225	3
Florida West Coast Open	3,393,400	4
Metropolitan Open	2,593,500	3

Year	New Money	Total Wins	Top10s	Top25s	Majors	Other Events
1913	$ 258,330	0	1	1	$ 258,330	$ 0
1914	1,000,000	1	1	1	1,000,000	0
1915	391,106	1	3	3	113,906	277,200
1916	3,131,521	3	7	7	506,221	2,625,300
1917	949,100	0	2	3	0	949,100
1918	774,000	1	1	1	0	774,000
1919	2,173,850	2	5	5	1,000,000	1,173,850
1920	3,022,422	4	5	6	142,253	2,880,169
1921	3,590,848	2	8	9	1,641,148	1,949,700
1922	4,236,117	4	9	10	1,366,917	2,869,200
1923	5,874,589	5	11	12	1,320,089	4,554,500
1924	4,515,640	5	8	8	2,378,172	2,137,468
1925	2,486,272	1	6	6	1,307,472	1,178,800
1926	4,726,039	4	9	9	1,809,301	2,916,738
1927	3,679,721	2	8	10	1,177,221	2,502,500
1928	2,636,260	1	6	7	1,673,493	962,767
1929	3,699,382	3	9	12	1,509,519	2,189,863
1930	1,187,503	0	5	7	89,763	1,097,740
1931	3,165,366	2	10	11	216,899	2,948,467
1932	3,501,380	2	11	16	186,358	3,315,022
1933	2,067,139	1	7	8	375,939	1,691,200
1934	1,277,499	0	5	11	166,897	1,110,602
1935	2,602,778	1	7	17	477,766	2,125,012
1936	858,888	0	5	9	145,600	713,288
1937	0	0	0	0	0	0
1938	163,212	0	1	2	0	163,212
1939	214,200	0	1	2	0	214,200
1940	166,063	0	1	2	123,063	43,000

Raymond Floyd

Ron Green, Sr.

On the Sunday that he would win the 1976 Masters championship, Raymond Floyd walked into the locker room, sorted through some telegrams from well-wishers, told some reporters that he had slept peacefully the night before, then went to his locker.

He set a cup of Coke on the floor. Going through his belongings in the locker, he accidentally knocked a box of golf balls off a shelf. The box landed on the Coke, crushing the top of the cup, but the drink didn't turn over. Floyd, smiling, said, "I drop a dozen balls on my Coke and don't even spill a drop. See how good I'm doing this week?"

How good he was doing was leading by eight strokes with one round to play, a lead he would protect through the long afternoon. When he slipped into the green jacket awarded the champion, he had tied Jack Nicklaus's record 271 for seventy-two holes, the record that had moved Bobby Jones to say Nicklaus "plays a game with which I am not familiar."

Floyd made a career of dropping golf balls on Cokes without spilling a drop, so to speak, defying the odds. He defied golf's calendar, winning at an age thought to be too young and winning at an age thought to be too old. He went from being one of the PGA Tour's playboys to being the father of *Golfweek*'s "Family of the Year" in 1994.

He graduated from hothead to leading citizen in the golf community. Thanks to his wife, he conquered an attitude problem that threatened to drive him off the Tour, and he became one of the great players of the century.

None of this was easy.

Floyd won the 1969 and 1982 PGA Championships, the 1976 Masters, and the 1986 U.S. Open, as well as eighteen other events on the PGA Tour. He had twenty-one top-ten finishes in majors, including a second in the PGA Championship and a second and third in the British Open.

He won fourteen times on the Senior PGA Tour, four of the victories coming in senior majors—two Senior Tour Championships, the Tradition, and the Senior Players Championship. He played on eight Ryder Cup teams and captained another.

If there was one moment, one event, that defined Raymond Loran Floyd, it was his selection to play on the Ryder Cup team in 1993 at the age of fifty. Floyd was already into his second season on the Senior PGA Tour. No man had ever competed in the Ryder Cup competition at that age, but Tom Watson, captain of the team, chose Floyd. Watson said he was looking for "heart and guts" when he made the selection.

He was also choosing a man who in 1992 had become the first to win on the PGA Tour (Doral Ryder Open) and the Senior PGA Tour in the same year (three times) and with his Doral Ryder Open win joined Sam Snead as the only players to win on the PGA Tour in four decades. Floyd justified Watson's confidence, winning three points for the United States in the Ryder Cup matches and helping to secure a victory over the European team.

Floyd's father, L.B., was a career army man. Raymond was born at Ft. Bragg in North Carolina. He started whacking golf balls around at age four or five at the driving range his dad owned, and by the age of seven, his dad said, little Ray was hurting business because so many customers would stop hitting balls to watch the kid.

Raymond's first love was baseball. It wasn't until he won the National Jaycee Junior Championship in 1960 that he got serious about golf. After high school, he gave college a brief try at the University of North Carolina, fulfilled his military obligations, and then set out to play professional golf.

On March 17, 1963, Floyd went into the final round of the St. Petersburg Open in second place, three shots behind Dave Marr. Floyd had been on the Tour for four months and hadn't won a dime. On that sunny Sunday afternoon, though, he shot 69 and won $3,500, the first deposit in what would become more than $17 million in prize money.

The champion was twenty years, six months, and thirteen days old. Only Johnny McDermott, Gene Sarazen, Charles Evans, Jr., Francis Ouimet, and Horton Smith had won at a younger age. After his win at St. Petersburg, Floyd said, "A lot of people told me I played well enough to win a lot of money. I guess I finally believed it. I came here with the hope of winning, not just making the cut."

He won despite having to scramble much of the day, but history would show that asking Raymond Floyd to scramble was like throwing a rabbit into a briar patch. Over the years, though his swing was not classic in style, he had all of the skills necessary to win, but he excelled in two things: the short game and the ability to concentrate. He could play all of the little shots around the greens, and he was an artist with the putter.

During the 1982 PGA Championship, which he won in Tulsa, he said, "I love it when somebody comes up and says, 'All I saw was rear ends and elbows, you down there pullin' the ball out of the cup all day.' I tell him that's where I was aiming. I want that reputation, because putting can make up for a lot of bad swings." As a senior, Floyd reflected: "Throughout my career I've always had a fabulous short game, and I've always been a good putter. I tend to putt well under pressure. I think I focus better." The concentration revealed itself in what fellow competitors called "the Stare." When Floyd was in the hunt, and especially when he was leading, he would get a fixed look in his eyes, as if he were seeing nothing but the next shot. It was obvious from their comments that the look chilled his competitors.

After the win in Pensacola, Floyd won only once over the next six years. In 1969 he won three times. He blew away Ken Venturi's seventy-two-hole record in the American Golf Classic at the tough Firestone Country Club course by seven strokes. Floyd also won the PGA Championship that year on the testing National Cash Register Course in Dayton, with police escorting his group after threats of a civil rights demonstration. "I've had a couple of police escorts before," he cracked, "but never on a golf course."

After the big 1969 season Floyd went another six years without a victory. Winning so young had made him think it was easy, he said, and it took him several years to understand that it wasn't. He later admitted, "Winning tournaments meant nothing to me. I thought the Tour was just one big ball, traveling from Miami to Los Angeles to New York and all those other exciting places."

It was during those early years that he developed a reputation for partying heartily. One writer even credited him, or charged him, with bringing back the bacchanalian days of Walter Hagen. In later years Floyd would agree that he hadn't left much undone, that there was nothing in the back of his mind that he wished he had done. "I'm not proud of it," he said, "but that's the way it was."

It wasn't as wild as advertised, though, said Floyd. He became friends with Doug Sanders and Al Besselink, colorful tour stars who knew their way around the hot spots, and with Super Bowl quarterback Joe Namath, who had a reputation as America's most eligible bachelor, and Floyd's reputation for night life grew.

Then, in 1973, he met a pretty brunette named Maria Primoli. They married after a whirlwind courtship. The marriage would produce two sons and a daughter and a new Raymond Floyd. In 1974, Floyd was playing so poorly in Jacksonville that he decided to pull out midway into the second round. Maria told him no, that he couldn't go through life pulling out of tournaments. He withdrew anyway, and they spent the next two days thrashing out their clash of wills. "Maria jumped on me like a tiger," said Floyd. "It helped put my life in proper focus. From that moment on, I was a more mature, patient, and responsible man."

The next year he broke his winless streak, and in 1976 he blitzed the Masters, opening with a 65, following with a 66, then putting together a pair of 70s on the weekend. He was fourteen under par on the sixteen par fives, using a five-wood and his outstanding fairway woods game to great benefit. He beat Ben Crenshaw by eight strokes and left the rest of the field in his dust. Tom Weiskopf, a fellow competitor, labeled it "one of the greatest feats this game has seen."

"That's a great feeling walking up that amphitheater on the eighteenth at Augusta with everybody applauding you," said Floyd. "After you've won a tournament, you have sort of a warm glow. When I was a bachelor, I used to celebrate some after I'd won. Now I usually have my family with me, and we don't do much different than what we would normally do, but you enjoy everything you do more. When you win, you're kinda king for a week. If a man doesn't cherish winning, doesn't appreciate the thoughts of winning, he won't be a winner."

Floyd won his third major championship in 1982, another PGA Championship. The venue was Southern Hills Country Club in Tulsa. The weather was brutally hot. He opened with a 63, which he said was "a marvelous round of golf, probably the best round of golf I've ever played, anywhere. With it coming in a major, and on a golf course like this, it's something I'll remember forever."

One particularly memorable aspect of it was the stretch of holes from the seventh through the fifteenth, when he had nine straight threes. The 63 matched the best round in tournament history. He shot 69 on Friday, and his 132 total set a new record for the halfway mark in the PGA. On Saturday he shot 68, his 200 total setting another record and his five-stroke lead tying one. Confident, he said, "I'm a good player from in front. I don't think I've ever lost a tournament when I've had a big lead. By big lead, I mean three or four shots." He began shakily on Sunday but finally regained control of his game and won.

For all the records he had broken over the years, though, and all the titles he had won, nothing was quite as remarkable as his victory in the 1986 U.S. Open over the rugged Shinnecock Hills course in Southampton, New York. For one thing, his best finish ever in a U.S. Open had been a sixth, and in twenty-two starts he had managed only two top-ten finishes, a shortcoming that he had analyzed at great length without coming up with a satisfactory answer. He had won tournaments on courses where Opens had been played but never the one he had dreamed of winning since childhood. Another thing, he was three months shy of his forty-fourth birthday. No one that old had won the national championship.

There was also an uncharacteristic collapse still fresh in his mind. The previous Sunday, he had led the Westchester Classic with nine holes to play but had bogeyed seven of the last nine. On the drive from Westchester to Southampton that night, he and Maria talked at length about it and concluded he should make it work for him as a learning experience. "We took a bad experience and turned it into a good one," he said.

It was especially helpful on the first day of the Open, when cold, windy, rainy weather was blowing scores out of sight. Floyd was determined to keep control of himself, and he got around in 75, a good score in those conditions.

That day, and in the three days to follow, he focused on keeping things in sync, never letting anything bother him. He even walked with the same rhythm he had in his swing.

He followed the 75 with a 68 and a 70, and on Sunday, with ten players leading or sharing the lead at one time or another, he closed with a 66, under extreme pressure, on a golf course so tough it will make your clubs bleed, to win by two strokes. He never smiled, not when he was making birdies, not when he was quick-stepping up the eighteenth fairway to a standing ovation from the gallery, not until he dropped the last putt.

"Raymond had that look in his eyes," said his old friend and competitor Lanny Wadkins. "When he gets that look, he's hard to handle. There's probably none better than him in that situation. We've been partners in Ryder Cup matches and played a lot of money matches as a team, and we haven't lost a lot. We're a lot alike. When I think of him, I think of playing with Ben Hogan one time in Fort Worth. We were joking around and having a good time, and Hogan said, 'I don't like to play jolly golf.'

"I've never forgotten that, and I think Raymond and I are the same way. When we're playing golf, we aren't very jolly. Raymond's a good door slammer. It's great to see him win."

Maria saw "the Stare" too. She said he passed her between the tenth green and eleventh tee, made eye contact, but never acknowledged her presence. "That was the first time this week his eyes were glazed, the way they get when he's mentally in gear," she said. "He didn't even see me. I knew then they were going to have to beat him; he wouldn't falter."

She was holding a telegram. It read: "Dear Raymond, I knew it was in the making. It was just a matter of time. Congratulations. Arnold Palmer."

On Saturday, someone had asked Floyd if this might be his last good chance to win an Open, given his age. "Believe me," he said after Sunday's round, "the conversation I had with myself last night after those questions was pretty stern. I said, 'I'd better get on with it.'"

It would be his last U.S. Open title, but he won another PGA Tour event that year, and then six years later, in 1992, at the age of forty-nine, he was second in the Masters and won the Doral Ryder Open. At age fifty he tied for seventh in the U.S. Open and at fifty-one tied for tenth in the Masters.

In 1989 he was inducted into the World Golf Hall of Fame. He left the PGA Tour and joined the Senior PGA Tour without the thing he wanted most by that time, a British Open title. With wins in the three U.S. majors, a British title would have moved him into the company of Jack Nicklaus, Gary Player, Ben Hogan, and Gene Sarazen as the only golfers to have won the four major championships (a rare feat since accomplished only by Tiger Woods). He had made a serious assault on that championship in the five-year span from 1976 through 1981, with a second, third, fourth, and eighth, but never challenged again and eventually gave up trying as the years mounted up.

On the Senior PGA Tour, Floyd was a terror. Sixteen days after turning fifty, he won the GTE North Classic and donated the winner's check of $67,500 to the Hurricane Andrew Relief Fund, which benefited families whose homes had been destroyed by the Florida storm. He played only seven seniors' events that year but won three of them. He played fourteen the next year, splitting time with the regular tour, and won two more. After he won his thirteenth Senior PGA Tour title in 1996, which was the Ford Senior Players Championship, his third senior major, hip and back problems curtailed practice, and a reluctance to get up and go to the next town took their toll. Floyd went three years without a win. He had those problems corrected, then tweaked his game. In 2000 he saw some good things start to happen, including a fourth place in the U.S. Senior Open. And then the man who never let the calendar tell him when he could and could not win won again. At age fifty-seven he came from six strokes back with eighteen holes to play to win the Ford Senior Players Championship in Dearborn, Michigan. That made him the oldest man ever to win a senior major. Floyd shot a closing 66, holing a twenty-footer for birdie on the last green to win by a shot. Whether "the Stare" was there could not be detected. He was wearing dark glasses. But the result suggested that it was.

It was his fourth senior major, but he dismissed the notion that it was as significant as those he had won on the PGA Tour. "It's not even in the same ballpark," he said. "The other tour is what it's all about, winning majors. This is nice, and it's a mulligan, if you would, or life after, but it's not like winning a major on the other tour."

The British Open would be played the next week, but Floyd wasn't going. Time, which had meant so little to him, had finally subdued him. "I can't compete on that Tour," he said. "That's like some sprinter running against Michael Johnson. Those kids are longer, stronger. I'm not that hungry."

Anymore.

RAY FLOYD

	Total New Money	Wins	Top10s	Top25s
Majors	$13,065,117	4	28	65
Other Official Tournaments (and International Wins)	46,061,860	21	149	307
TOTALS	**$59,126,977**	**25**	**177**	**372**

MAJOR CHAMPIONSHIPS

	New Money	Wins
Masters	$4,791,467	1
U.S. Open	2,603,528	1
British Open	1,660,474	0
PGA	4,009,648	2

BEST OTHER EVENTS

	New Money	Wins
Doral	$3,702,470	3
Byron Nelson	3,242,337	1
World Series of Golf	2,017,881	0
Tournament of Champions	1,959,133	0

Year	New Money	Total Wins	Top10s	Top25s	Majors	Other Events
1963	$1,173,150	1	3	5	$ 0	$1,173,150
1964	1,314,394	0	4	11	89,444	1,224,950
1965	1,454,825	1	3	9	262,937	1,191,888
1966	1,510,590	0	6	12	242,250	1,268,340
1967	693,705	0	3	9	61,820	631,885
1968	1,972,755	0	7	16	162,960	1,809,795
1969	3,156,285	3	6	10	1,077,452	2,078,833
1970	931,956	0	3	10	222,664	709,292
1971	1,707,154	0	6	12	270,073	1,437,081
1972	780,688	0	4	7	227,333	553,355
1973	756,667	0	2	7	91,597	665,070
1974	2,243,225	0	8	14	260,348	1,982,877
1975	1,879,194	1	5	14	279,035	1,600,159
1976	4,118,746	2	10	17	1,916,621	2,202,125
1977	2,914,788	2	9	16	303,620	2,611,168
1978	1,968,761	1	7	17	603,824	1,364,937
1979	1,743,665	2	8	12	78,400	1,665,265
1980	2,506,137	1	9	15	169,300	2,336,837
1981	5,361,065	4	17	21	585,658	4,775,407
1982	4,669,162	3	9	17	1,238,803	3,430,359
1983	2,239,535	0	8	20	481,742	1,757,793
1984	744,859	0	2	8	210,700	534,159
1985	2,803,053	1	9	15	467,396	2,335,657
1986	2,926,090	2	5	16	1,072,689	1,853,401
1987	825,505	0	3	11	152,378	673,127
1988	793,001	0	3	8	340,546	452,455
1989	169,683	0	1	3	0	169,683
1990	1,033,658	0	3	6	604,800	428,858
1991	1,072,220	0	5	10	376,047	696,173
1992	2,565,654	1	5	12	690,131	1,875,523
1993	446,630	0	2	4	264,230	182,400
1994	279,347	0	1	3	140,000	139,347
1995	128,740	0	0	2	73,280	55,460
1996	169,240	0	1	2	47,040	122,200
1998	72,850	0	0	1	0	72,850

Emperor of the Game

Robert Tyre Jones, Jr.

Sidney L. Matthew

When the eighteen knights of golf's eternal roundtable have taken their chairs on history's ultimate green, it is inevitable that one of their number be universally acclaimed as "the Greatest." He is, of course, the greatest Hero of Heroes, sometimes called Emperor.

One might ask whether such a resolution is really necessary. After all, there are eighteen able heroes all seated at the roundtable, which features no head, no foot, no corners, and no sides. Can't we just say that every able man who made it to the table is equally worthy and nobody should be acknowledged as Emperor? If the history of mankind is any teacher, the answer is "probably not."

Hero worship has been studied by deep thinkers and observers of the human condition for centuries. Plato postulated that the amateur sportsman should be held up before the republic and regarded as the model citizen. In his lectures titled "Hero Worship," nineteenth-century Scottish philosopher and historian Thomas Carlyle theorized that "it is the business, well or ill accomplished of all social procedure whatsoever in this world . . . to raise the able-man to the supreme place and loyally reverence him" in creating the perfect state or the ideal government. The ablest man, said Carlyle, is the truest-hearted, most just, noblest man who tells of the wisest, fittest, and most valiant thing that will always behoove us. The

Emperor of Heroes is the summation for us of all these qualities that command our respect and willing subordination.

How then do we identify this ablest of men and heroes? Over the ages, Carlyle notes, we seem to have settled on particular qualifications and identifying characteristics. The ablest of the great men illuminates all those who surround him. He emanates a sincerity that genuinely utters forth the inspired soul of his original genius. Conscious of his faults, the greatest hero never boasts. His voice ably speaks for all others. There is something that attracts other great men to be in the Emperor's presence: the absence of anything false or selfish. And a perceptible quality of balance about his life that indicates he is worthy of the appellation. All things considered, the chorus of heroes' voices in golfdom does resound the name of Robert Tyre (Bobby) Jones, Jr., as the Emperor of Golf.

What They Said Back Then

The marshaling of evidence to support the Emperor's selection is a tap-in. As the only amateur in the elite eighteen, Jones's fourteen-year total playing career was perhaps the shortest. The historians who were privileged to see him play spared little ink praising not only Jones's technical skills but also his artistry. Is there a golf writer today who claims to be the equal of Bernard Darwin? With "faltering pen," Darwin wrote his tribute to Bob Jones in 1944 as part of *Golf Between Two Wars*. Titled appropriately "The Greatest of Them All," it spared few accolades addressing why Darwin positioned Jones at the head of the class:

It was in 1921 that we here first met Bobby. . . . His fame had preceded him. . . . Now he was a battle worn warrior of nineteen with, as all the best judges united in thinking, the makings of the greatest golfer in the world. No reasonable expectations were disappointed for the greatness was there to see for anyone with eyes. I can remember the precise spot at Hoylake where I first saw the swing soon to be familiar in the imagination of the whole golfing world; so swift in that it occupied so little time, with no suspicion of waggle, and yet so leisurely in its almost drowsy grace, so lithe and so smooth.

Darwin's appraisal was hardly a lone voice in the wilderness. The great Peter Doberiner pronounced Jones "the finest golfer of all times":

To say that Jones was the greatest golfer there ever was, or ever will be, is to do him an injustice, for his golf was never much more than a diversion.

The *London Observer*'s Geoffrey Cousins wrote: "Every generation of golfers has provided its great men and it is often reasonable to hail some outstanding player as the finest of his time. That distinction, of course, belonged to Jones, but in his case one could go further and suggest that he was the greatest golfer the world has ever seen."

In the London *Sunday Times* Henry Longhurst wrote about Jones in equally reverent tones, announcing, "My but yer a wonder, sir." His obituary tribute to Jones went as far as one needs to support the Emperor's coronation as the greatest ever: "Let me close this brief tribute by quoting a friend of mine who was once partnered with Jones in the Open: 'If I had sons,' he said, 'I should have sent them out to see him—as much for his behavior as for his play.' Jones was probably the greatest and certainly the best-loved golfer of them all."

Pat Ward-Thomas of the *Manchester Guardian* echoed these sentiments: "Down the years people have wondered whether Jones was the greatest of all golfers. Comparison is invidious for no man can do more than win and Jones won more often within a given period than anyone else has ever done. To the majority of golfers the name of Robert Tyre Jones can only be a legend and a legend unchallenged and undying it will remain for as long as golf is played. Jones was the champion of champions. No golfer has achieved or is ever likely to achieve a supremacy over all the players in the world for as long as he did. No golfer will command more lasting affection and respect for his qualities as a person."

American golf writers who knew Jones well and share the literary mantle of respect were no less extravagant in their views that Jones rates the top shelf. Grantland Rice watched Babe Ruth and Ty Cobb, Red Grange, Knute Rockne and the Four Horsemen, Jack Dempsey, Gene Tunney, and a host of other spectacular sports superstars. But Rice reserved his top spot for Jones, stating: "There has been no champion like him that sport has yet given to the game."

Charles Price minced few words: "Bob Jones was the greatest championship golfer in the history of the game, amateur or pro, and I mean championship golfer, not a tournament player. This is a statement you could make unequivocally only if, as I have, you have also been friendly with almost every golfer of historical consequence in this century, save Harry

Vardon. Bob would be mad at me for making such a statement, but I doubt any of the others would. He was the most un-falsely modest person I ever knew."

One of Price's contemporaries who shared the breadth of his experience with the legends of golf is Herbert Warren Wind. In his *Story of American Golf*, Wind wrote the following in the chapter titled "The One and Only": "Only Harry Vardon, Ben Hogan, and Jack Nicklaus merit comparison with Jones as major championship golfers."

Mr. Wind eloquently states the case for each player and can only conclude "they belong in a class by themselves. . . . In some ways each is incomparable. Bobby Jones certainly was."

Eustace Storey was the 1924 runner-up to Cyril Tolley in the British Amateur Championship and thrice on the British Walker Cup Team. On June 25, 1972, Storey wrote the following appraisal in the Sunday *New York Times*:

> To the Editor: I do not know whether it would be of interest to your golfing correspondent, but on the occasion of the Open being played at Pebble Beach, I would like to recall the occasion when the first Amateur championship was played there in 1929. Four Englishmen went out for the tournament: Cyril Tolley, myself, T. A. Bourn and Lord Charles Hope (now dead). On the Sunday before play began, Bobby Jones, Tolley, myself and Harrison Johnston, who subsequently won, had a four-ball match. We were all playing reasonably well and went around in 74 or so, but Jones did 66. I don't believe this has ever been beaten. He did the 9th, 10th, 11th, 12th and 13th in 3 each and at the 14th, the long dogleg up the hill, he carried the green with his second shot, chipped back and got his 4. I might tell you that Johnston and I had to play a 7 iron for our thirds and Tolley, who was considered at that time the longest man in the world, put his second into the cross bunker in front of the green. During my life I have seen all the great players of their time playing fairly well: Vardon, John Ball, Travers, Chick Evans, the lot. No one was comparable to Jones, not even Jack Nicklaus. Jones never hit a ball off the course and he was an absolutely first-class putter in that if he didn't hole a long putt it was stone dead and no worry at all.

How right he was! Jones won. Nicklaus might take a hint from this too.

The Desperate Business of Superlatives

Dealing in superlatives is a desperate business for all writers whether they traffic in golf or tiddledywinks. That is precisely why the string of pearls set forth above about Emperor Jones must be ultimately substantiated. You are wondering whether Jones really was that good, whether Nicklaus or Woods eclipsed Jones, and whether Jones deserves to be Emperor. A close look at Jones's record, his life, and the way he lived it justify what these people have said all along. Jones is truly *sui generis*.

From his earliest days as a six-year-young lad following Carnoustie native Stewart Maiden around the links at Atlanta's East Lake CC, Jones knew not only how to strike a golf ball but also why a ball could be golfed. Jones had a genius for the theory of the game.

He had more than a knack for the sport. Young Jones understood the mechanics intimately. He later translated this knowledge into theorems of mechanical engineering that he could articulate as a college student at Georgia Tech, where he received his first degree in 1922. But Jones knew the physics of golfing the ball long before college. Simply by perfectly imitating Maiden's technique, Jones shot 80 on East Lake at age eleven. At twelve little Bob was pounding out two-hundred-yard drives. He won both the East Lake and the Druid Hills CC men's club championships at age thirteen. And he was the "medallist" as the youngest-ever competitor in the 1916 Amateur Championship at Merion CC at age fourteen.

That started a fourteen-year career that ended with the Impregnable Quadrilateral—the Grand Slam in 1930. Jones then retired from the championship scene at the ripe old age of twenty-eight. Unlike Muhammad Ali or Babe Ruth or Mike Tyson or Michael Jordan, however, Jones never was tempted to make a "comeback" from retirement. He never felt that his record was insecure enough that it needed propping up.

A quick look at the record shows why he was entitled to be confident. Jones played in fifty-two championships and won twenty-three of them. He finished first or second in eleven of thirteen U.S. and British Open Championships in which he played. Bob won "The Double" (U.S. and British Opens) twice, in 1926 and 1930. He won a total of thirteen major championships during a thirteen-year span. And, of course, the pièce de résistance is the capturing of all four recognized major championships in the Grand Slam of 1930.

The Grand Slam is the longest streak of sustained excellence in virtually any respected sport, eclipsing Babe Ruth's sixty home runs (which lasted thirty-four years after he set it in 1927), Joe Dimaggio's 1941 hitting streak of fifty-six games, Wilt Chamberlain's average 50.4 points per game set in 1961–62, and Byron Nelson's PGA Tour streak of eleven straight victories set in 1945.

It is little wonder that in 1997 the World Golf Hall of Fame international voting body elected the Grand Slam "The Greatest Moment in Golf History"—also selected by the Associated Press as the "Supreme Athletic Achievement of this Century" in 1944. Jones himself was voted the Greatest Golfer of the Century by all sportscasters and sportswriters in 1950. They knew what they were talking about.

It is not intellectually honest to explain away Jones's record by claiming that he played with hickory shafts on hardpan unwatered fairways against weak fields. And that today's professionals would destroy Jones with their newfangled technology and buffed-up physiques.

Today's professionals and amateurs alike are perhaps better trained than most in Jones's era. But Jones was no wimp. He could tear a pack of playing cards in half with his powerful grip. Seldom did he use his strength to full advantage. Instead Jones had a "fifth gear." Half a dozen years after retirement Jones showed this to Sam Snead, who was renowned as a long hitter. "Bob just cruised his drives short of mine until we reached the parfives. Then he somehow crushed them twenty and thirty yards past mine. Nobody had ever told me he was that long. I was flabbergasted."

When Jones first played the Olympic Club in San Francisco, he was the first man to hit the par-five 604-yard sixteenth hole in two strokes. Sportswriter O. B. Keeler witnessed Jones's drive over the green into a greenside bunker on Merion's 350-yard eighth hole in 1916 when Jones was fourteen years old. Ten years later, in 1926, at Scioto, Keeler saw Jones drive his ball 310 yards from the seventy-second tee. These were not Titleist Pro V-1 golf balls. You don't even want to know their compression!

But Jones could post some incredible scores with these mush balls and without the sand wedge (invented by Sarazen in 1931) that carries with it a two-stroke-per-round advantage over the old niblick. Jones was frequently returning scores in the 60s long before others caught up with him. He was the first player to return a score in the 60s in the British Open, in 1927 (a "most obscene" 68). Bob set the East Lake CC course record in 1922, posting a 62. He set the record low score of 67 in the 1927 Amateur. Jones shot the "perfect round" of 66 at Sunningdale in 1926, coupled with a 68 to win the club's Gold Vase. He also shot 66 in winning the 1927 Southern Open at East Lake CC.

How would Jones compare with today's Robin Hood–type ball and trampoline-faced metal woods? We got a good glimpse of the answer when Jones designed clubs for Spalding as a director, beginning in 1932 with his registered matched sets featuring the sweet spot in the center of gravity throughout the set. Jones returned scores in the 65, 66, 67 range with regularity. He was not dubbed the "Mechanical Man of Golf" for nothing.

Jones thought Nicklaus played a game with which he was not familiar, but Jones would have handled Jack and Tiger the same way he handled Cyril Tolley in the 1926 Walker Cup matches at St. Andrews. Jess Sweetser asked Bob on the evening before their storied match, "Bob, how are you going to handle Tolley? He is the longest hitter in Great Britain." Bob softly replied, "Jess, don't worry about Tolley." The next day Tolley drove from the first tee about 240 yards, which was good in those days. Jones powered past him 20 yards. On the second tee Tolley stretched out to about 250 yards on his drive. Jones passed him again by 20 yards—yes, 270 with that old mush ball. After that Jones didn't have to worry anymore about Tolley because Cyril was pressing his luck trying to outdrive Jones. Bob won by the lopsided score of 12 and 11.

Ben Hogan recognized that the true secret of Jones's success was not his considerable physical skills but rather the strength of his mind. In this dimension Jones knew no peers, and it is why Jones should be acknowledged as Emperor.

The Slam

The hallmark of Bob Jones's accomplishments on the golf course will always be that he played as a gentleman. The Grand Slam came second. It is "that granite fortress that Jones alone could scale by escalade but others may attack in vain forever." A forgotten aspect of the Grand Slam is that Jones actually conceived of the notion in 1926, fully four years before he went out and realized his dream. Bob Jones thought that whoever won the Open Championship on both sides of the Atlantic in the same year had achieved the right to be recognized as the champion golfer of the world. When Jones did just that in 1926, it was hailed as "The Double Open." It ain't that easy to do. In fact, other than Jones, the Double Open has been achieved only by Gene Sarazen (1932), Ben Hogan (1953) and Lee Trevino (1971). But Jones did it not once but twice (1926 and 1930), just for punctuation that the initial occasion was not a fluke.

Yet another feat of perhaps comparable wonder is the "Double Amateur," comprising the American and British Amateur Championships won in the same year. Again an accomplishment by an elite few. Chick Evans started that parade in 1916 when he showed that both Amateur titles could be annexed in the same year. Jones did it in 1930. And Lawson Little won both titles in 1934 and 1935. Still another incredible "Double" is the couplet comprising the British Open and the British Amateur Championships. John Ball captured both in 1890 followed by you-know-who-Jones in 1930. You will remember that quite a number of other champions have won a combination of the major titles in their careers, but only Jones has won the Double Open, the Double Amateur, the Double British, and the Double American in the same years.

All this points up the chief difficulty of the Grand Slam won by Jones. Not only did he buck up against "Old Man Par," his adversaries and the golf courses, but also Jones won against a more auspicious adversary—himself. The self is certainly a worthy opponent, especially in a cerebral contest like golf. There are more hobgoblins and demons in the six-inch course between the ears than ever were confronted on the links. Make no mistake, Jones wrestled each one before the last trophy was presented.

Thirty years after the original Grand Slam, the media struggled to fill the void left by Jones's absence coupled with the stark realization that the Grand Slam was indeed out of reach. Sportswriter Bob Drum and Arnold Palmer then stirred the imagination of the Fourth Estate by concocting the modern Grand Slam. Palmer wondered what were the chances of a player like himself winning all the professional major championships on both sides of the Atlantic. "Can't be done," said Drum. And the race was on.

Palmer came close in 1960. He won the Masters and U.S. Open and could have won the British Open except for the St. Andrews Road Hole. There's always something getting in the way. Hogan strung together three pearls in 1953—the Masters, U.S. Open, and British Open. But neither his legs nor his schedule could sustain him for the fourth title, the week-long match-play PGA.

Until Eldrich Woods came along, everyone began to settle for a cheap imitation of the modern Grand Slam known as the "career" Grand Slam. That list is growing, but to date there are no names at all listed in the "modern professional Calendar Year Grand Slam" category. So far, not even the best professionals can put the puzzle together, which again goes to show you that the "genuine Grand Slam" is a unique element of Jones's genius and the prime reason why he truly is the Emperor.

Since Woods's emergence on the golfing scene in 1996, considerable attention has been paid to his purported full-scale assault on Jack Nicklaus's assembly of twenty major titles in a single career. The sportsman's hobby of winning lots of major titles and stacking them up in a mathematical race to the highest total is as old as Young Tom Morris's four consecutive British Open titles and Harry Vardon's six Open titles.

Watson won a remarkable five championships and showed everyone just how redoubtable Vardon's record really was. This major business was certainly not lost on Jones, who collected thirteen major titles in the space of seven years. Walter Hagen won eleven. Tiger has so far won eleven. Hogan and Player each have nine, Palmer eight. Vardon, Sarazen, Snead, and Watson each won seven total majors. By the time Jack Nicklaus was twenty-eight years old, he had won nine majors, whereas at the same age Jones had won thirteen. Jack clearly has the upper hand in total majors, twenty in twenty-five years. But Charles Price extrapolated that "Jones would have been working on his forty-sixth national title at the age Jack Nicklaus won his twentieth." But total majors does not an Emperor make. There must be more facets to the diamond than that.

Those handy with the record archive could possibly weave a more particularly revealing comparison of these champions' records. A study of the records of the top champions leaves Jones in an Emperor's role.

Perhaps one relevant toe-to-toe comparison might focus on the efficiency of a champion in winning his major championships. For example, Bobby Jones won thirteen major championships in thirty-one attempts, which means Jones won 42 percent of those major championships he entered. Using the same perspective, Ben Hogan won 17 percent of those major championships he entered (9 of 53) and Jack Nicklaus won 12 percent of his major attempts (20 of 162). Tiger has won 33 percent of the majors he has attempted (11 of 33). Ben Hogan won 17 percent of contested majors (9 of 54 entered). Walter Hagen won 24 percent (11 of 46 majors entered). *Jones is the most efficient champion in the majors.*

If one looks at the periods of time when a player was "hottest," it may cover the span between a player's first major championship and last major championship won. Here Jones leads the pack again. Jones won thirteen of twenty-one majors contested between 1923 and 1930. That is 62 percent. Ben Hogan won nine of sixteen majors entered between 1946 and 1953. That is 56 percent. Walter Hagen won eleven of thirty majors from 1914 to 1929 for 38 percent. Again Tiger is at 33 percent (eleven of thirty-three majors between 1994 and 2002). *Jones was the hottest champion in the majors.*

Some have commented on the "youth" at which players such as Tiger have won major titles.

Young Tom Morris was the youngest British Open champion (seventeen years, five months, eight days in 1868). Gene Sarazen was the youngest PGA champion (twenty years, five months, twenty days in 1932). John McDermott was the youngest U.S. Open champion (nineteen years, ten months, fourteen days in 1911). Tiger Woods was the youngest Masters champion (twenty-one years in 1997). Jones won his first major in 1923 at age twenty-one. (He should have won the 1919 Amateur against Davey Herron, but that's another story.) Jones was *not* the youngest major champion. But he was the youngest U.S. Amateur competitor in 1916, at age fourteen. And who is remembered as the "Boy Wonder from Dixie"? Of course, R. T. Jones.

Still another comparison focuses on the pace at which various champions achieved the highest total of majors earned. For example, Bob Jones achieved his thirteenth major at age twenty-eight. Nicklaus was thirty-two when he achieved his thirteenth major in 1972. In the 2003 season Tiger Woods must win two of his next four majors to tie Jones's record of thirteen majors at age twenty-eight—50 percent! As Tiger has won 33 percent of the majors he has played thus far, the odds are slightly less than even money that he may do it, all other things being equal. Again, subject of course to the 2003 season, *Jones matured as major champion the fastest.*

The record books aside, what really makes Jones the Emperor over all others was his gentlemanly demeanor and incredible strength of character.

Jones played golf for fun and never for money. When it became akin to a job, he quit, since Bob already had a profession as a lawyer. He had his life's priorities right early on: God, family, the law, and last was golf, but never a life unto itself. Jones had more ambition than to play professional golf—not because it was a dishonorable pursuit but rather because he had greater ambition.

Bob's nongolf pursuits were extraordinary and swallowed up his short golf career. He invested in an extravagant education with degrees from Georgia Tech and Harvard. And he short-circuited the need for a law degree by passing the bar exam halfway through the law curriculum. Some critics have claimed Jones was not a part-time golfer after all. If not, he surely squeezed more out of a single day in life than most wring out of a week.

Jones attended school followed by real estate sales for a short stint in Sarasota and then dived into his law practice. When he retired at age twenty-eight after achieving the Grand Slam, Jones made the Warner Brothers movies, designed the Spalding golf clubs that bore his name, wrote five books, designed and built Augusta National, started the Masters Tournament, and served as a national and international ambassador of golf.

Jack Nicklaus and Gary Player were conferred well-deserved honorary doctorates by St. Andrews University. Only Jones was bestowed the singular honor of citizenship in the Freedom of the Royal Burgh of St. Andrews. In receiving this honor, Jones stands alone with Benjamin Franklin, who was similarly honored in 1759.

Whereas other champions seemed to struggle in reaching the pinnacle of general public adoration, Jones was almost immediately accepted. Hogan was the "Wee Ice Mon," Jack the "Golden Bear," Palmer "the King," and Tiger the "Phenom." Only Jones was acknowledged as the Emperor of Golf.

But Jones was not a one-trick pony. Like his golf swing, he was a remarkably balanced person in equal measure of humanity, humor, courtesy, and consideration to all those about him. As the consummate "southern gentleman" Jones was instantly likable because he was genuinely modest and self-deprecating. When presented with the enormity of his accomplishments in a written tribute, Jones simply looked down and said, "I only wish I were that good."

He was always ready to attribute his success to others about him. He once said that his biographer, O. B. Keeler, wrote so many good things about him that he felt obligated to live up to them or else "he might let old Keeler down." Jones's puckish sense of humor was infectious. He once crumpled up a twenty-dollar bill and asked his caddy to drop it in the bunker by Walter Hagen's ball. Hagen reflexively picked up the twenty and put it in his pocket. He then splashed his ball onto the green.

Jones calmly asked, "What did you get on that hole?"

Hagen answered, "I got a four. I was up and down out of the bunker."

"No, Walter, you got a five. You removed a loose impediment in the bunker."

Who doesn't know that Jones called not just two but four single-stroke penalties on himself in competition, saying, "There is only one way to play this game and that is by the Rules. You might as well praise a man for not robbing a bank"?

To be sure, other players have done the same thing, but Jones set the standard. Instead of fiercely competing against his playing partners, Jones played against "Old Man Par." For that reason he was, in Gene Sarazen's words, "like a friend, when you played with or against him."

Jones had the respect of his peers and all others not because he was the best sportsman. Rather, Jones was the most able man anyone has ever seen. He was the truest-hearted, most just, and noblest of all the golfers who ever lived. He represents the summation of all the qualities that command our willing subordination. Which is why Robert Tyre Jones, Jr., is and will forever remain . . . the Emperor.

BOBBY JONES

	Total New Money	Wins	Top 10s	Top 25s
Majors	$10,306,008	7	13	17

MAJOR CHAMPIONSHIPS

	New Money	Wins
Masters*	$ 258,907	0
U.S. Open	6,728,682	4
British Open	3,318,419	3

Year	New Money	Total Wins	Top10s	Top25s	Majors
1920	$ 162,003	0	1	1	$ 162,003
1921	219,717	0	1	1	219,717
1922	479,583	0	1	1	479,583
1923	1,000,000	1	1	1	1,000,000
1924	585,000	0	1	1	585,000
1925	585,000	0	1	1	585,000
1926	2,106,140	2	2	2	2,106,140
1927	1,218,519	1	1	2	1,218,519
1928	585,000	0	1	1	585,000
1929	1,000,000	1	1	1	1,000,000
1930	2,106,140	2	2	2	2,106,140
1934	108,267	0	0	1	108,267
1935	58,240	0	0	1	58,240
1938	92,400	0	0	1	92,400

*Jones's appearances in the Masters are included "simply for the record." He retired from competitive golf after the Grand Slam in 1930.

PART TWO

Back Nine

Severiano Ballesteros

John Huggan

The bald facts are impressive enough. Between his first win, the 1976 Dutch Open, and his last, the 1995 Spanish Open, Seve Ballesteros won forty-eight European tour titles. During the same period he was World Match Play champion five times, won thirty-three other titles around the world, played in eight Ryder Cups (winning three), played in four World Cups (two wins), and picked up five major championships—three British Opens and two Masters.

But those are mere numbers. It isn't so much what Ballesteros achieved during his colorful career; it was how he achieved it. For the great Seve, hero to a continent's youngsters reared on generations of American golfing triumphs, the journey was always much more important than the arrival. So it is that, while his great rival Nick Faldo may have won more majors—six to five—and in the minds of many may even have been the better player, there is no doubt that it is Seve who is the most significant in historical terms.

Although he and Faldo were part of Europe's so-called "big five"—Ian Woosnam, Sandy Lyle, and Bernhard Langer the others—Ballesteros showed the way. He was always the leader. First of the five to win a major— the 1979 British Open at Royal Lytham. First to win in America—the 1978

Greater Greensboro Open (his debut on the PGA Tour). And first to win an American major title, the 1980 Masters. Seve broke the mold when it came to golf at the highest level.

In retrospect, the eleven months between April 1957 and March 1958 represented a special time in European golf. Not only were the Americans defeated in the Ryder Cup match at Lindrick, but five seemingly unconnected births would, some two decades later, change the face of the professional game across the globe. Remarkably, the five Europeans who would push the mighty Americans off the top of the golfing tree and who all would win at least one major championship first saw the light of day within one year of each other.

Appropriately, as it would turn out, the first born was Ballesteros. Christened Severiano Ballesteros Sota in Pedrena, a small fishing village in the north of Spain, he was the fifth son of Baldomero Ballesteros Presmanes and Carmen Sota Ocejo. Young Seve's father was a sometime farmer, sometime fisherman whose home, a modest two-story building, was, significantly, close to the Club de Golf de Pedrena.

Within a few short years, the game he could see across the stone wall at the back of his house would consume the youngster.

"The golf course was only a hundred yards from my house," he remembers. "Most of the people from the village worked there. The children were all caddies, making a few pesetas to help the family. My uncle, Ramon Sota, was a successful professional, good enough to finish sixth in the 1965 Masters. He was probably the best Spanish golfer before myself. And my brothers were all caddies and then professionals. So I was surrounded by a golfing atmosphere. Straightaway the game got into me. I would practice on the beach because I was not allowed on the golf course."

Which isn't to say that he never played. Long after his parents thought he was fast asleep in bed, young Seve would sneak onto the course and play by the light of the moon with his trusty three-iron. Through his obsession with golf his schoolwork suffered. "I would go to school in the morning," he says, that distinctive smile across his face, "go home for lunch, then I was supposed to go back to school. But I didn't. I would leave my books in a big pipe that was between my house and the school. I would take my club and go to the beach. Or, if no one was around, I would sneak onto the far end of the golf course where I couldn't be seen. I'd be there all afternoon."

As he owned only one club, Seve had to manufacture every kind of shot—high, low, short, and long—an informal education that would be just one of the factors setting him apart from his peers later in life. But it wasn't winning the local caddies' championship—his only competitive golf before turning pro—that persuaded him to play for pay. "The reason I turned pro in March 1974 was because I was banned from the golf club for a month in January that year," he says. "On the 31st of December I would always get together with my friends. That year there were a lot of pipes on the course; they were going to be put in for drainage. On the sixth hole, which is downhill, four or five of us were on the tee, and a couple of my friends pushed the pipes down the hill. They rolled maybe 250 yards. No one saw us, but word got out. I was suspended because I was there, although I didn't push any of the tubes.

"That was a crucial moment in my life. My nephew came to me then and offered me a job in a factory making boats. My mother was in favor. She thought I needed a future. But my father was against. He said I must start playing golf for a living because I was good."

A fact the world at large would soon discover. By August of 1974 Seve was the best player in Spain under the age of twenty-five. One year later he was the best in Spain, period. And two years after that he was the best in Europe. In the midst of that period came the first of many defining moments for the dashing young Spaniard who put so many in mind of Arnold Palmer.

In July of 1976, Ballesteros arrived, unknown and unheralded, in Southport for the Open Championship at Royal Birkdale. He left, seven days later, as golf's newest star. At the age of nineteen he tied for second with Jack Nicklaus behind Johnny Miller. The story of that week is a remarkable one. Seve came, almost literally, from nowhere. He spent two days carrying his brother's bag in the qualifying event. His own caddie was a policeman who did not play golf and knew next to nothing about the game. And at that time Seve did not speak English. "I shot 69 in the first round," he remembers. "Everyone was congratulating my brother, Manuel. He was helping me with the press. I was enjoying myself. I knew it was the Open, but I had no idea it was that important.

"In the second round I shot 73 or something; I don't remember. Then I was playing with Johnny Miller in the third round. The night before the last round—I was leading—I wasn't worried about the next day. I was only nineteen, remember. I thought I could win. I was convinced. Anyway, I went out to a disco with my brother. We were dancing there until maybe midnight. Then we went back to our bed-and-breakfast place. As we were walking back, I could see that my brother was a little worried. He was obviously thinking, My God, my brother could win the British Open—this is unbelievable. I just wasn't that aware of what was going on, which was maybe a good thing. I told my brother I thought I was going to win. He just looked shocked. I asked him how I should play. He told me just to keep playing the way I did in the first three rounds. And that's how I went out in the last round."

He didn't win, of course. But it wasn't long until he did. Indeed, as the 1980s dawned, Ballesteros became the youngest British Open champion of the twentieth century. At the tender age of twenty-two he was not only taking on the world; he was beating it.

Yet his significance goes far beyond mere statistics. Over the next ten years of his career, the man from Spain—Spain!—transcended the game and became, outside of the United States at least, a true sporting icon. Simply by playing the way he did and doing what he did—winning and losing tournaments in the most unpredictable manner since Arnie—the young Seve became Europe's Palmer both on and off the course. His influence was everywhere.

For example: Prize money in Europe grew more than sixfold during the 1980s, in no small part due to the golf Ballesteros played and the charismatic way in which he played it. His drawing power and marketability were enormously attractive to prospective sponsors. The key was Seve's British Open victory at Lytham in '79. In that win were the seeds of many things, not least the effect it had on those players around him and the fact that, in the United States, he was destined never to reach the same heights of popularity he enjoyed in the United Kingdom. That was the year America christened Seve the "car park champion." His drive off the sixteenth tee in the final round finished under a parked car, from where he received a free drop.

For Seve fans it was a typically eccentric and endearing moment; for others like the sour-faced loser Hale Irwin it was a moment of outrageous and undeserved fortune. As so often in Seve's controversial career, he polarized opinion.

Still, his peers watched and learned. Inspired by their contemporary's ability to meet and beat the Americans, five other Europeans—Langer, Lyle, Faldo, Woosnam, and Jose Maria Olazabal—would, over the next fifteen years, follow him to major championship victories. "Seve was really the leader; the others followed in his wake," says former European Tour professional Ken Brown. "Because of the way he played and how successful he was, the others could see that they could do it, too. It was like, 'If Seve can win major championships, so can I.'"

It was in golf's four biggest events and in the Ryder Cup where Ballesteros would enjoy his finest moments. Individually, Ballesteros made himself the best player on the planet. With his European amigos alongside him, the Americans were soon losing the biennial tussle with the Old World.

It was, however, at St. Andrews in 1984 that Ballesteros enjoyed the biggest and best triumph of his career. In a pulsating duel between the best two players on the planet, he edged out Tom Watson to lift his second Open title.

Two shots stand out. Watson's approach to the penultimate green—"the wrong shot with the wrong club at the wrong time"—and the putt Ballesteros holed on the Old Course's final green. It was only ten feet or so in length. It didn't even go in the middle. But it provoked the most memorable reaction of the decade. Seve punched the air over and over, turning to all sides of the green, his face a picture of ecstasy. For those who were there it remains the single most powerful Ballesteros memory. At that moment Seve was at the height of his powers.

He was the Tiger of his time.

And there the similarities do not end. Seventeen years before Woods would eclipse his competition at Augusta National, Seve did the same en route to his first green jacket. Well, almost. The record book says that Seve finished a mere four strokes ahead of runner-up Jack Newton in the 1980 Masters. But look again. After sixty-three holes Ballesteros was sixteen under par, and the gap between first and second was a yawning ten shots. Had it not been for a potentially disastrous back nine of thirty-nine—which could have been a lot more—Tiger may have had to work a little harder for his record-breaking margin of victory.

But that was Seve. He always was more Arnie than Jack, a fact that became even clearer six years later, again at Augusta. One month after the death of his father and three years after his second Masters win, Ballesteros was standing in the middle of Augusta National's fifteenth fairway during the final round. Nicklaus was going crazy up ahead, but Seve had it all under control. Or so everyone thought.

All he had to do was hit the green with a four-iron, and the tournament was as good as over. It wouldn't matter what Jack did. But Seve didn't hit the green. In truth his shot did well to reach the water in front, so poor was the contact between club and ball. It was, no question, the worst swing made by a genuinely world-class player during the 1980s.

Two years later, Ballesteros won his fifth and last major championship at Royal Lytham when a closing 65 saw him lift a third British Open. But he never really was the same after Augusta '86. Neither was golf.

With that shot at fifteen, in a forerunner of the game's saddest quality in the nineties, came some unseemly cheering from the galleries. Strangely for one so obviously charismatic, Seve never was a popular figure in the United States. And, it must be said, the feeling was reciprocated, especially when it came to the Ryder Cup.

The emergence of Ballesteros, then many other world-class players from Europe, had far-reaching consequences. Before Seve the matches were nothing more than a garden party for golfers. The Americans won. The Brits lost. And everyone had a jolly nice time. Losing, particularly to Americans and America, wasn't something Seve had a lot of time for. Ever since he received a less than warm welcome on the eighteenth green at Greensboro as he was about to win his first U.S. Tour title ("Let's have a big "Ole!" for the Spic" is how many golfers recall that greeting) Ballesteros's relationship with Uncle Sam's nieces and nephews had been more frosty than friendly.

"The American players—not all of them—would never accept someone coming from overseas and beating them at home," he explains. "I heard many comments in the locker room. I remember hearing them say that I was 'stealing' their money." Such experiences only served, of course, to drive him on, especially when it came to the Ryder Cup.

"Seve was unbelievable," says Sam Torrance, eight times a Ryder Cup player. "He was always there when you needed a boost, always there when you needed help with your game. He always seemed to put the team first, which was remarkable, as he was the world's number-one player. Of course, he didn't like the Americans very much at all. He really wanted to win."

Soon enough then, the European side started kicking some Yankee butts in the previously all-but-dormant Ryder Cup. In 1983, at PGA National in Florida, the Europeans lost by the slenderest of margins, serving notice that their first victory since 1957 wasn't going to take them much longer to achieve. Still, for all that, it was clear who was the real star of the show. Even in ultimate defeat for his side, Ballesteros managed to distinguish himself.

All square on the final tee against Fuzzy Zoeller, the Spaniard hit a rotten drive, then an even poorer second into a fairway bunker well over two hundred yards from the putting surface. All looked lost, but Seve wasn't done. Marching into the sand with a three-wood in his hand, he struck an outrageous slice to the fringe of the green. It was, according to the American captain, one Jack Nicklaus, "the best shot I ever saw."

Two years later Europe did win the Ryder Cup, and ever since it has been the most exciting thing in all of golf. A bit like Seve himself, in fact.

Sadly, the glory days for Ballesteros ended in the mid-1990s. By the 1995 Ryder Cup at Oak Hill he was but a shadow of his former self. The peerless short game was still intact, but his long game—always erratic—had deteriorated to the point where he had trouble finding the fairway with a five-iron. Still, for all that, his final-day singles match against Tom Lehman remains one of the most vivid Ballesteros memories. It is no exaggeration to say that no one else could have played the way Ballesteros did that day and lost by less than eight and seven. That the match continued as far as the sixteenth green is a tribute to the remarkable tenacity and shotmaking abilities of a proud man.

Indeed, it was perhaps only his pride that carried Ballesteros through the following, declining, years. Between 1976 and 1992 he was never out of the top twenty on the European Order of Merit. Between 1996 and 2001 he was never inside the top one hundred.

"It is hard to know you don't have the game to win and that making the cut is the best you can hope for," he concedes. "When you do that, you never get the chance to compete. And you never have rhythm. Then you lose confidence. You are what you believe you are."

For the man himself then—and his many fans—those were harrowing years. Yet through it all, Ballesteros retained his enormous charisma. In 1997 he was an inspiring and enthusiastic nonplaying captain when the

Ryder Cup paid its first visit to his homeland, at Valderrama. As he cajoled and encouraged his men to a famous victory, he was seemingly everywhere. He even found time to concede the final meaningless putt to Scott Hoch in the deciding match with Colin Montgomerie.

For Seve, it was always center stage or nothing.

God, he was great!

SEVE BALLESTEROS

	Total New Money	Wins	Top10s	Top25s
Majors	$10,796,321	5	20	37
Other Official Tournaments (and International Wins)	39,285,806	64	203	261
TOTALS	$50,082,127	69	223	298

MAJOR CHAMPIONSHIPS

	New Money	Wins
Masters	$4,452,867	2
U.S. Open	1,052,015	0
British Open	4,665,539	3
PGA	625,900	0

BEST OTHER EVENTS

	New Money	Wins
Cisco World Match Play	$2,478,381	5
Volvo PGA	2,338,452	2
Spanish Open	2,187,101	3
French Open	2,140,172	4

Year	New Money	Total Wins	Top10s	Top25s	Majors	Other Events
1974	$ 62,200	0	1	2	$ 0	$ 62,200
1975	230,574	0	4	7	0	230,574
1976	1,814,126	2	11	13	521,466	1,292,660
1977	1,987,218	6	12	14	69,529	1,917,689
1978	3,507,399	7	14	17	226,585	3,280,814
1979	2,231,389	2	9	14	1,215,900	1,015,489
1980	3,283,828	4	11	14	1,069,628	2,214,200
1981	1,980,657	5	8	10	0	1,980,657
1982	2,637,091	3	10	14	531,161	2,105,929
1983	4,289,792	5	15	18	1,449,391	2,840,401
1984	3,072,740	2	9	15	1,326,140	1,746,600
1985	3,835,628	6	14	15	606,976	3,228,652
1986	2,949,154	6	15	16	518,556	2,430,598
1987	3,247,445	1	16	20	998,966	2,248,479
1988	4,602,934	7	14	18	1,234,940	3,367,995
1989	1,926,433	3	9	14	331,800	1,594,633
1990	1,028,516	1	11	13	157,267	871,249
1991	2,870,343	4	14	18	230,776	2,639,567
1992	852,156	2	4	9	46,879	805,277
1993	511,370	0	4	9	114,800	396,570
1994	2,206,771	2	11	15	145,562	2,061,209
1995	497,797	1	3	4	0	497,797
1996	248,500	0	2	3	0	248,500
1997	30,180	0	0	1	0	30,180
1998	71,661	0	1	2	0	71,661
1999	27,044	0	0	2	0	27,044
2001	79,182	0	1	1	0	79,182

Hale Irwin

Dan Reardon

You hear the question raised on wintry nights on sports talk radio shows. You can find it being kicked around a corner tavern the week of a major championship. Are golfers athletes? Grouped with jockeys, bowlers, and race-car drivers, golfers seem to threaten, for some, the integrity of the term *athlete*. While that argument may be waged endlessly with no satisfactory resolution, there can be no doubt that in at least one instance one of golf's all-time great players was a certified athlete.

Three-time U.S. Open champion Hale Irwin authored Hall of Fame credentials on the PGA Tour and subsequently on the Senior PGA Tour, but before he took his golf game to the professional ranks Irwin carved a football reputation in the tough Big Eight Conference as a two-time All-Conference defensive back for the University of Colorado Buffaloes. The same "do whatever it takes to win" attitude that typified his golf career was imprinted on Irwin as an athlete in his youth.

Introduced to golf by his father on a sand green municipal golf course in Baxter Springs, Kansas, Irwin also followed the sports path of every youngster of his generation in Little League baseball. "Baseball was my best sport, but I also had to work, and I decided I had to give up something, so I gave up baseball."

By age fourteen, and now living in Boulder, Colorado, Irwin was good enough to qualify for a national junior tournament in August. It was an inauspicious national debut with rounds of 79 and 90. His last two years in high school saw Irwin win the state high school tournament while at Boulder High School, but it was football that was his ticket to college. "Football was a way to go to college," says Irwin. It was also a way to hone a competitive intensity that became Irwin's trademark on Tour. "When I was playing college football, I was undersized, under speed, under everything. I had to do something a bit better than everyone else. I either studied more film or read my keys better or anticipated better. I really couldn't outphysical anybody. I just positioned myself to play better than the next guy. I think that helped me. I had the determination to get it done. The intensity that I had to play at allowed me to compete with others with better skills."

Despite his success on the gridiron, Irwin knew the NFL was not the direction for him as an adult, but the competitor in him has never allowed him to dismiss his chance of taking that sport to the next level. "There were players that I played with at Colorado, and players elsewhere in the Big Eight, that went on to success in the NFL. I felt I competed side by side with them and against them and, I think, held my own. Could I have made it? Down inside my soul I can come up with an honest maybe."

It was golf that he had envisioned for his future since he wrote an eighth-grade essay charting a life for himself as a professional golfer, and winning the 1967 NCAA Golf Championship was the accomplishment he needed to make the turn to professional in 1968. While he left his pads and helmet behind him, he took the mind-set of the game to a sport very different from the gridiron. "It's hard to separate that emotional, intense, physical game of football versus the more sedate, cerebral, and less physical action of golf. It's more likely that a football mentality will transcend into golf than a golf mentality will transcend into football. In my case that intensity carried into my younger years. People saw that intensity that I played with, and to this day that's me, that intense competitor. I can look into the eyes of a Jack Nicklaus or an Arnold Palmer, and that same look is there. It just wasn't as glorified because they didn't play another sport."

His first two years on the Tour were years of making cuts and posting few top tens. "I never doubted I would succeed," he remembered. "I just didn't know when I was going to make it. I just had to say OK to the timetable." That schedule found him breaking through for the first time as a professional at the 1971 Heritage Classic with a one-shot win over Bob Lunn. Two years later he solved Harbour Town Golf links for a second win, this time by five over Jerry Heard and Grier Jones.

Twice a winner on Tour and now top ten on the money list would qualify as success on the PGA Tour, but for Irwin it fell short of what he had set his sights on. "I was sort of a winner. But I felt for me to be what I wanted to be, not what others thought I might be, was to be a major championship winner." He crossed that threshold a year later.

In the history of the U.S. Open the 1974 championship at Winged Foot has an infamous reputation. Tagged by one writer as the "Massacre at Winged Foot," the course was the toughest Open setup since 1955 at Olympic. Longtime Open observer Robert Sommers noted in his book *The U.S. Open: Golf's Ultimate Challenge*, "Vandals drove a car across the first green after the opening round, but they were so hard that no one noticed except the men who set the cups early Friday morning."

It was Winged Foot that elicited perhaps the most famous comment on U.S. Open setups when Sandy Tatum responded to the question "Is the USGA trying to embarrass the best players in the world?" by saying "No, we're just trying to identify them." For Irwin, Winged Foot was an ideal convergence of an attitude and an approach that matched the demands on the field. "I can remember coming into that tournament that I had just come off a finish for second in Philadelphia and went up to Winged Foot, and the practice rounds were brutal. This was the hardest golf course that I had ever played, not only before but since. It was everything that you would ever want to see in a golf course and then some.

"So I thought if I can just be steady, keep my emotions under control— because everyone is going to make bogeys this week; just don't make as many bogeys as the next guy. Then if you make a birdie that is a gift from heaven, because there are so few birdie holes. So just go out there and play your game."

Three bogeys coming home on his opening round left him trailing Gary Player by three, but a second-round 70 tied him with Arnold Palmer, Ray Floyd, and Player. A patient 71 in round three left Irwin one off the pace of Tom Watson and strangely comfortable with his position. "As the week went on, I just kept keeping that in mind and kept playing my game, playing my game," says Irwin. "So we started the last day, and Tom Watson was leading, and Arnold Palmer and I are behind. Tom Watson was a young Tom Watson, and this was the only time in my career I wasn't too worried about Watson. I just didn't think his game was going to be a good fit for the final day.

"Arnie's career hadn't necessarily peaked, but he was just on the other side of that. My concern was to play my game . . . and then would somebody out of the pack come up behind us? But I realized no one could come up from far back in the pack because this golf course was just too hard. So I kept playing my game, made a big birdie putt at the ninth hole to take the lead, and never surrendered it."

It wasn't that simple on the closing nine. After the go-ahead birdie at the ninth he parred just one hole over the next seven. That set the stage for his first pivotal career moment at the par-four 444-yard seventeenth. "What epitomized my efforts that week was on that hole. I did not know what kind of a lead I had. Leader boards were not as frequent as we now have them. I suspected I had the lead, but I didn't know if I had it by one or two or what.

"I drove it into the rough on the seventeenth hole, and I just had to hack it out of there. I was 103 yards from the pin. I hit it in there about twelve feet or so. I felt I had to make this putt to keep the lead or at least be tied. It was not any easy putt, but I made it, and that was just the symbol of how I played that week. I kept grinding it out. I just had to do this shot now. I couldn't worry about that I had driven it in the rough, and I couldn't worry about eighteen, even though it's a tough hole. I had to do something right then. I had to keep it simple and sweet and straight in the hole.

"Then, when I got to the eighteenth tee, someone told me I had a two-shot lead, but a two-shot lead on the last hole could go very quickly. I drove it right down the middle and hit one of the best two-irons of my life up onto the green. Then I two-putted for the win."

Or perhaps, more appropriately, he'd survived his first major duel with the fates of golf. Irwin's seven-over-par total was the second highest since World War II, and he and runner-up Forrest Fezler, at nine over, were the only totals less than double figures above level par. The ex–football player had taken on one of the biggest brutes of major tournament golf history and proved something, to himself. "It proved that I could compete at that level," reflects Irwin.

Over the next five years he settled into a routine, winning and cashing big paychecks. Multiple win years followed in 1975, '76, and '77. At Medinah in 1975 he missed repeating as Open champion, finishing a single stroke out of a play-off with John Mahaffey and Lou Graham. Over that time he recorded eighty-six consecutive Tour appearances without missing a cut, one of the longest streaks in golf history.

Open win number two, like most middle children, is the overlooked jewel in his three-gem crown. The Inverness Club in Toledo, Ohio, had a history of denying good scores in previous Open Championships. No player had ever broken even par for the event when played at Inverness, and even though he threatened that record, Irwin too failed to post a red number after seventy-two holes, finishing at even-par 284.

As had happened at Winged Foot, he struggled early at Inverness, opening with a three-over 74 to sit four off the pace. That all changed when Irwin seized control with brilliant play in the middle rounds. A three-under 68 and a four-under 67 left him minus four for the championship—three clear of the field. A three-hole stretch starting at the eleventh in round three provided Irwin with the margin even a faltering finish on Sunday could not erase. He followed up two birdies with an eagle at the 523-yard par-five thirteenth. Again it was a two-iron second shot at that hole that highlighted a stretch of four under in three holes.

Four under, and enjoying a six-shot lead with nine holes to play, Irwin played an untidy inward nine that featured three bogeys and a double bogey at the seventeenth, giving him a closing 75 and a two-shot margin. He admitted afterward, "I started choking on the first tee." But he was a two-time Open champion and again had validated for himself that he belonged on the major championship stage. "I had had some great years between '74 and '79, and the second Open sort of added emphasis to that fact. It was underlining what I thought was proof that I could still play."

Five wins in the next four years continued the Irwin pattern of steady grinding on the PGA Tour, but it was during that stretch that he experienced his biggest disappointment in the game. In 1984 the Open returned to Winged Foot, and Irwin set his sights on win number three. On this occasion he had a special incentive to win.

"My father was quite ill with prostate cancer. It was apparent he wasn't going to make it. The only thing I could do for him before he died was to win. I was trying to give him one last little bit of happiness."

Three consecutive rounds in the 60s left him poised to deliver for his dad. It was Irwin and Fuzzy Zoeller a stroke apart in the final pairing of the day, but that was as close as Irwin would get. "I failed there. I just played so poorly on Sunday. But I had put so much pressure on myself that there was just no way I could win. I had just heaped this mountain of stuff on top of me. I needed to whittle it down to something I could deal with, and I just couldn't do that."

Following a win at the Memorial in 1985 Irwin was adrift professionally for the remainder of the decade. In 1986 he finished 128th on the money list without a top ten. Over the next three seasons he remained winless and cracked the top ten only four times.

It was a slump he understood and had the patience to endure. Irwin had made the decision during that time to venture into the golf design business. He knew the distraction of starting up a new company would be a hindrance to his game, but it was a sacrifice he was prepared to make, perhaps knowing from his football days that even if the game would drop him for a few losses, he could get still get up and recover.

"During that time I wasn't focusing completely on my game and developed some bad habits. I was not paying attention to detail," he now says. Starting late in 1989, he decided to "try to concentrate."

Like most great players, Irwin returned to his fundamentals in the game and the teacher who had provided them. For Irwin that teacher could be found in a mirror. Remarkably Irwin never ventured outside his own self-monitoring to reverse negative trends in his game. "There wasn't a teacher available when I started golf years ago. I knew by virtue of playing what I could do. I knew how I would react when I got nervous, what I did. I knew what I could do when I felt strong. I don't say that is necessarily the best way to go, but for me that was probably the best thing."

Through the first half of 1990 Irwin could see improved play, but the winless stretch continued. Nothing suggested he would return to form as the U.S. Open returned to Medinah in Chicago that June—*nothing but a dream.*

Two weeks before the championship Irwin told his wife, Sally, of a dream he had that he had won the Open. It may have been a wish more than a premonition because Irwin was playing on a special exemption from the USGA. Through most of that week it seemed his vision was merely a pipe dream.

An opening three-under 69 got his name on the leader board but only as an afterthought to the brilliant scoring that was going on ahead of him. A 70 in the second round kept him in the hunt at five under par, but Tim Simpson, at minus nine, was bidding to become the first-ever player in U.S. Open history to reach double figures under par.

On Saturday, Irwin could find just one birdie. Offset by three bogeys, his two-over 74 put him tied for twentieth, now four behind journeyman leader Mike Donald as Tim Simpson eased back into the pack. On Sunday, Irwin played "U.S. Open" golf, and had a relentlessly consistent string of outward-nine pars.

But this day was rapidly becoming a "red-numbers" affair, and Hale's consistency, normally the cornerpost of an Open challenge, was in reality losing ground. In football parlance he was facing "third and long" as he headed to the back nine.

After a par at ten, Irwin made his first move, a birdie at the 402-yard par-four eleventh. A string of three more birdies followed, taking him to seven under for the championship, but with the third-round leaders playing two hours behind him, it seemed that Irwin was headed merely for a final-day notebook item.

Pars on the next four holes failed to alter that impression and brought him to the eighteenth green facing a nearly-fifty-foot snaking putt for birdie and serious contention for a play-off spot.

Had he been in the final group, the long bomb he holed might have ranked as the most dramatic moment in U.S. Open history. His birdie sent a roaring message to the leaders behind him on the course, and the normally reserved Irwin punctuated the moment with a victory lap, high-fiving his way around the green. It was the signature moment of his career, but he still had two hours to wait to see if it meant anything at all. "Most people remember the seventy-second hole, and that's where the euphoria happened. That putt that I made was just to get to what I hoped would be a play-off. There were still hours of play behind me, but I had just played the last eight holes of the U.S. Open in five under par. That in itself was pretty amazing. But to birdie that last hole to possibly get into a play-off was my goal." Donald helped him attain that goal, bogeying the sixteenth hole to slip back into a tie.

U.S. Open play-offs are usually dull affairs, characterized by past-the-moment golf, and Monday's round lived up to that tradition. A birdie by

Donald at the ninth to Irwin's bogey opened a one-shot lead, and when Irwin added a bogey at the eleventh, Donald had his opportunity to take charge with a downhill attempt for birdie. Instead he three-putted, matching Irwin's bogey, and remained just one ahead. "I looked at that as leaving the door wide open," remembers Irwin, "when he could have shut it right in my face." Irwin bogeyed the next to give Donald the two-shot margin he had squandered just moments earlier, and Irwin was again playing uphill for a win.

"It was getting difficult for me to believe it could still happen, but I told myself to keep going, keep going. The mind-set is 'keep playing'—you never know what can happen. That's what I kept telling myself, because a two-shot lead can be overtaken in one hole. 'Just keep hitting the shots. Think only of the next shot, because it's the most important one you can play.'"

With that fortitude he found himself yet again with that trusty two-iron in his hands in the fairway at the par-four 436-yard sixteenth. "I was 207 yards uphill into the wind, and I had to hook it around some trees. I tried to tune out the situation. I tried to tune out the gallery. I tried to tune out what he was going to do. I tried to really focus on what I needed to do to get myself back in contention. It was just my turn."

He put his approach six feet from the hole and made the vital birdie to climb to within one. On the eighteenth tee it was Donald who blinked, a grievous tactical error, abandoning the three-wood that he had used so tirelessly throughout the round, for his driver. The choice left him in the rough from where fate determined the bogey that resulted in the first sudden-death play-off in U.S. Open history.

You don't let a competitor such as Irwin off the ground once, much less twice, and not expect to pay the price. At the first extra hole Irwin played to within ten feet and converted the birdie to become, at age forty-five, the oldest champion in tournament history.

"I've always felt that tenacity was something I've had. That would apply to most things that I have tried to do. Scaling a brick wall may be impossible, but if you can find a few handholds, maybe you can still do it. You can call it guts. You can call it confidence. You can call it experience. I've never abandoned my beliefs. They may have been set aside or temporarily misplaced, but they've always been there. Some things are improbable, but I've never thought many things are impossible."

With three U.S. Open triumphs, exactly twenty PGA Tour wins (the last coming at age forty-eight back at Harbour Town), with a reputation for unrelenting competitiveness, Irwin could legitimately lay claim to a place among the game's greatest ever.

One has to wonder, however, if he would have earned serious consideration if he hadn't authored the finest appendix to a playing career in golf history with his dominant run on the PGA Senior Tour. Although Irwin would argue that the longevity of his game, demonstrated by his record-setting run as a senior, should be factored into any assessment of him as a player, there seems little argument that he forced a reexamination of his career with his over-fifty performance. He redefined that tour with his competitive performances. He wrote or rewrote nearly every single season or career record established on the Senior Tour.

In 1997 Irwin assembled an unprecedented level of excellence with nine wins and eight additional top tens in nineteen events. His "worst" showing for the year was a tie for nineteenth at the Ford Senior Players Championship, and his earnings of over $2.3 million may stand forever as an unmatchable accomplishment. His money title not only secured Player of the Year honors on his own Tour, but despite a huge disparity in purses between the Senior Tour and the PGA Tour, Irwin outearned Tiger Woods, the money titleholder on the PGA Tour, by more than $250,000.

The man who said he knew it was time to walk away from football every time he picked himself up off the ground spent a lifetime picking himself off the very tailored grounds of professional golf.

Hale Irwin brought an athlete's mentality to his sport and forced others to consider his place in golf history. He may have learned how to play on the sand green course in Baxter Springs, Kansas, but he learned how to win on the practice fields of college football. "The uniqueness to the game of golf is that you do it yourself. You cannot hide. Your dirty laundry is hanging out there for everybody to see. There's not a teammate to cover for you. Every decision, every action that you make is yours and yours alone.

"The game has its own humility. One time you think you are on top of the game, and the next day it's got you by the throat. But if you can get your body working in the same motion as your mind is working, whether in a hard game like football or something as simple as chess—that requires a great deal of mental preparation—you don't have to be the world's fastest human or jump high or to throw it far to be an athlete or to be an activist in a sport or in an activity.

"You have to perform with heart and soul. What makes a person grow is that dedication to achieving a goal that is reachable and attainable but difficult."

HALE IRWIN

	Total New Money	Wins	Top10s	Top25s
Majors	$ 8,444,571	3	20	43
Other Official Tournaments (and International Wins)	46,377,824	25	155	274
TOTALS	$54,822,395	28	175	317

MAJOR CHAMPIONSHIPS

	New Money	Wins
Masters	$1,847,000	0
U.S. Open	4,335,260	3
British Open	1,115,423	0
PGA	1,146,888	0

BEST OTHER EVENTS

	New Money	Wins
Heritage Classic	$3,941,360	3
Memorial Tournament	3,494,400	2
World Series of Golf	2,572,421	0
Western Open	2,334,100	1

Year	New Money	Total Wins	Top10s	Top25s	Majors	Other Events
1968	$ 97,603	0	0	3	$ 0	$ 97,603
1969	389,226	0	1	6	0	389,226
1970	1,270,662	0	4	13	0	1,270,662
1971	2,185,270	1	7	13	227,773	1,957,497
1972	2,550,956	0	10	16	132,000	2,418,956
1973	2,755,740	1	11	17	217,595	2,538,145
1974	3,487,832	2	8	16	1,279,663	2,208,169
1975	4,363,576	3	16	19	855,947	3,507,629
1976	4,306,817	2	12	17	204,400	4,102,417
1977	3,500,699	3	8	13	224,000	3,276,699
1978	3,398,679	1	15	21	568,346	2,830,333
1979	2,667,779	3	9	15	1,271,068	1,396,711
1980	1,668,840	0	10	15	138,203	1,530,637
1981	3,467,724	3	9	13	136,483	3,331,241
1982	1,786,687	2	5	12	0	1,786,687
1983	2,906,653	1	10	16	806,816	2,099,837
1984	1,712,054	1	6	12	359,621	1,352,433
1985	1,416,323	1	2	8	102,520	1,313,803
1986	851,700	1	2	4	0	851,700
1987	474,004	0	2	7	0	474,004
1988	777,241	0	2	7	79,746	697,495
1989	537,780	0	2	6	0	537,780
1990	3,161,752	2	7	13	1,121,000	2,040,752
1991	1,457,521	0	6	7	254,788	1,202,733
1992	238,335	0	1	3	63,208	175,128
1993	750,058	0	2	9	155,031	595,027
1994	2,157,839	1	6	11	145,562	2,012,277
1995	483,042	0	2	5	100,800	382,242

Arnold Palmer

Mike Purkey

The great sports columnist Jim Murray once wrote, "God whispered into Jack Nicklaus's ear, 'You'll be the greatest player who ever lived.' Then he whispered to Arnold Palmer, 'But they'll love you more.'"

No other person in golf has been so universally loved, admired, and adored as has Arnold Daniel Palmer. The depth of his popularity cannot be measured except by the millions of golfers who devoutly worship at his feet every time he appears between the ropes and who yearn for his return every time he leaves.

Palmer is affectionately called the "king" and with good reason: he is treated like royalty everywhere he goes. And he rules over golf as a benevolent monarch who treats his subjects with equal parts fairness and affection. More important, Palmer ushered in golf's modern era, and many say he is single-handedly responsible for the millions of dollars those who followed him play for today. He had good looks, was raised among the working class, and was eerily unafraid of any shot in any situation. In other words he was perfect for the new medium that was beginning to bring the game to fans' homes: television.

Palmer had the biceps and the forearms of a man twice his size and drove the ball prodigious distances with that funny finish to his swing, kind of like a man about to sling a cat by the tail but who decided at the last minute to hang on to it. However, Palmer didn't always drive the ball straight, and he was often left with problematic shots over, under, around—or through—trees. He never met a trouble shot he didn't like. In fact it's suspected that he took a twisted pleasure in such dilemmas, which is probably why he was able to pull them off with such frightening regularity. That's one of the reasons we believe we can reach out and touch him and he won't even mind. Certainly he must be one of us. He smokes, sweats, and has trouble keeping his shirttail in. (All right, he doesn't smoke anymore. Neither do most of the rest of us.) He swears, stomps, and beseeches the sky. He hooks, yips, and lips out. Palmer is Every Golfer—only he has won major championships, and we live vicariously through his exploits.

He signs every autograph that is humanly possible—and then he signs some more. He submits to almost every interview request that his schedule allows—and then he bends over backward to accommodate. He plays in nearly every tournament that wants him—and then enters still more.

It is his unbridled enthusiasm for golf that endears him to everyone from the greatest to the least skilled of us. He simply loves to play golf, and it shows, even when his game is not up to his standards. In an era when the game's best players stow their clubs in a corner when they are away from the Tour, Palmer arranges his schedule so that when he is at his second home at the Bay Hill Club in Orlando, he plays every day with a regular group of pros and amateurs in a game lovingly called "the Shootout." And he plays those rounds with just as many equal parts seriousness and laughter as he does when he plays on Tour.

In other words, Palmer plays the game just like we do. More than that, he looks people in the eye—and smiles. For every person in the gallery, any contact with Palmer means that he has made him feel as if he or she is the only fan on the golf course.

What attracts us to him most is that he is perhaps the most human of all our famous athletes. He loves his job and his family and is modest almost to a fault. Yet he walks with a swagger that says he is a man's man, while also having the twinkle in his eyes that more than suggests he is a favorite of the opposite sex.

When he found himself in some trouble with the press and the USGA over some comments he made about nonconforming equipment, the fans remained loyal. For them it would take a lot more than a silly flap over the coefficient of restitution to lose faith in their king.

At age seventy-two, when his playing career was coming to an end, he puzzled the golf community when he gave his tacit endorsement to amateurs who wanted to play drivers that didn't conform to the Rules of Golf. He was the target of criticism from those who thought he was encouraging the use of illegal equipment. For his part, he simply wanted as many people as possible to enjoy the game he so loves.

Perhaps the seminal event of Palmer's career came in 1960 at age thirty at the U.S. Open. He began the final round seven shots behind fifty-four-hole leader Mike Souchak at Cherry Hills Country Club outside Denver. All week, he had been trying to drive the green at the 345-yard first hole, and all week he had been unsuccessful. Prior to the final round a conversation took place, a chat that has gone down in the myth and legend of golf. Not even the participants agree on exactly what took place, but it went down something like this:

In the Cherry Hills locker room, Palmer was eating a hamburger and passing the time with Dan Jenkins of *Sports Illustrated* and hometown writer Bob Drum of the *Pittsburgh Post-Gazette*.

"If I drive the first green, I could shoot something good," Palmer said.

"You couldn't drive that green if you were George Bayer in a Cadillac," Drum shot back, making reference to the longest hitter of the day.

"If I shoot 65, what'll that bring me?" Palmer wondered.

"About seventh place," Jenkins replied. "You're too far back."

"But that gives me 280, and doesn't 280 always win the Open?" Palmer asked.

"Only when Hogan shoots it," Jenkins quipped.

Jenkins said Palmer laughed when he left the locker room. Drum said Arnold was a little miffed. However he reacted, he burned a low hook over the corner of the dogleg at the first hole, and the ball bounded through the high rough and onto the green. He birdied the first four holes on his way to an outward thirty. He shot his 65 and won his only U.S. Open, setting a record in the bargain for largest eighteen-hole comeback.

He had won five other events in 1960, including his second Masters title. He would win two more that year for his best year as a professional.

More than anything, the Open victory established Palmer as a hero. He won with his heart exposed to the elements, slashing, thrashing, and holing putts from impossible distances. He was daring and dashing, even otherworldly in his exploits. He was capable of immense heroics and just as enormous blunders. Yet there he stood, a cigarette dangling from his lips, hair devilishly tousled, shirttail out in back—all seemingly within arm's length, even if you were watching on television.

That's why we pulled for Arnie, because he was us—our next-door neighbor, the plant foreman, the usher at church. Yet he was who we couldn't be—the star, the legend, the idol of millions. All the while, he looked every one of us straight in the eyes and smiled that genuine, heart-felt, killer smile. We swooned, even the guys.

Arnold Daniel Palmer was born on September 10, 1929, in the steel mill town of Youngstown in western Pennsylvania. He was the son of Doris and Deacon Palmer, who was the greenkeeper and de facto pro at Latrobe Country Club. Young Arnold learned the rudiments of the game from his father, who was demanding and stern. He placed the lad's hands on the club and demanded that he "Get the right grip. Hit the ball hard, boy. Go find it and hit it hard again."

Not much changed in the nearly seventy years that followed. Palmer's trademark would become his massive, gnarled hands, described often as belonging to a blacksmith. Those hands whipped the club through the ball at amazing speed, lashing drives long, straight, and true. Palmer for years was one of the longest, straightest drivers of the ball who ever lived.

When he did miss a fairway, however, it was a gargantuan error, and he often found himself with trees between him and the flag. That dilemma did not prevent him from seeking the shortest distance to the hole. There was no pin that Palmer couldn't shoot at, whether from the middle of the fairway or in the deep darkness of the woods. No one knows for certain when Arnold learned this swashbuckling style, but it is suspected that the genesis was from his pap, who taught him to hit the ball hard and worry about finding it later.

While at what was then Wake Forest College, Palmer blossomed into one of the best collegiate players in the country. He won the Southern Conference title his freshman year, beating Harvie Ward and Art Wall. He would go on to win another conference title and make the semifinals of two straight North and South Amateur championships, thus forging his growing reputation.

But the event that shaped Palmer the most during his college years was a tragedy. Palmer's Wake Forest roommate was Buddy Worsham, brother of PGA Tour star Lew Worsham. Buddy was killed in a weekend automobile accident, an event that tore at Palmer for years. Some speculate that was one of the reasons he left Wake Forest to join the Coast Guard.

Palmer won sixty-one times on the PGA Tour, including seven major championships. But perhaps the one title for which he feels the most pride is the 1954 U.S. Amateur Championship. It is certainly the most hard-fought big tournament he has ever won. The Amateur requires that its champion play eight matches in a week's time, including thirty-six-hole semifinal and final matches.

In 1954 two of his first three matches went to the eighteenth hole, and his fourth-round opponent, Walter Andzel, fell five and three. In the fifth round Palmer faced an old friend and foe, Frank Stranahan, one of the country's finest amateurs. Stranahan had defeated Harvie Ward, perhaps the best amateur in the nation, one up the previous round, a match that had been the talk of the tournament. Stranahan also had some experience with young Palmer, dusting him off eleven and ten in a thirty-six-hole North and South Amateur semifinal match and four and three in the 1950 U.S. Amateur. This time, however, Palmer played flawlessly, dispatching Stranahan three and one.

Don Cherry was the quarterfinal opponent, and Palmer was again taken to the final hole before emerging victorious. Palmer and Ed Meister locked in a pitched battle in their thirty-six-hole semifinal match and would wind up making history. Palmer, for his part, provided his share of drama to extend the match.

On the thirty-sixth hole Palmer's drive found heavy rough, and his second landed in high grass behind the green. His pitch finished five feet above the hole on a slick green. He holed the putt, in what would become typical Palmer style, to move to sudden death, which he would win on the third extra hole, making it the longest semifinal match in amateur history.

Palmer met Bob Sweeny, a forty-three-year-old investment banker from New York, in the final. Sweeny was the 1937 British Amateur champion and was said to give Ben Hogan strokes when they met in winter matches at Seminole Golf Club in Florida. The pair was a study in contrasts.

Sweeny was wealthy, refined, and well dressed. His swing was silky and classic. Palmer, on the other hand, came from working-class roots. He was a twenty-four-year-old ex–Coast Guardsman who was working at the time as a paint salesman. His swing was anything but refined.

But pretty swings don't win golf tournaments, and Palmer's action was always effective. Palmer didn't take the lead for good against Sweeny until the thirty-second hole, and he was extended to the thirty-sixth hole before the outcome was secured.

A major title in hand, Palmer headed out the next year for the insecure world of the PGA Tour. Armed with $5,000 per year and a $2,000 signing bonus from Wilson Sporting Goods, Palmer won the 1955 Canadian Open on his first full year on Tour. Three years later he made his way onto golf's grand stage at the 1958 Masters.

In the days leading up to the event, Palmer and Dow Finsterwald played a practice-round match against Hogan and Jackie Burke, Jr. Palmer played so badly that Hogan wondered aloud in the locker room how Palmer had managed an invitation to the Masters.

Perhaps Hogan's doubts fueled Palmer's desire to win the tournament, but Hogan had a point. Who was Arnold Palmer, and what had he done to make anyone think he could win a major championship?

He won twice in 1956 and four times in 1957, more wins than anyone else that year. Prior to the Masters he won in St. Petersburg and lost the Azalea Open in a play-off. At Augusta he shot rounds of 70-73-68 and found himself at the twelfth hole on Sunday with a one-shot lead. His tee shot at the par three carried over the green and embedded into the turf wet with heavy rains that soaked the course. He informed the officials that he intended to lift, clean, and replace the embedded ball without penalty under the rules of the day. The official told Palmer he couldn't proceed in that manner, and a rather heated discussion ensued.

He then told the official that he would play two balls, one as it lay and the other replaced under the rules that he insisted were in effect. He made a double-bogey five with the embedded ball and a par with the replaced ball. At the next hole Bobby Jones and the tournament rules committee chairman came out to inform Palmer that the par three would stand and that he would retain the tournament lead. Palmer finished with a one-over 73 and the tournament victory.

The win moved Palmer up a notch in the eyes of his peers and in the esteem of the golf world. Hogan proved to be wrong; Palmer did, indeed, deserve an invitation, and the Masters would prove to be the one major that Palmer owned over the next six years.

In 1960 Palmer enjoyed his best year on Tour, winning eight times, including the Masters and the U.S. Open. He shot rounds of 70-66-69— 205, eleven under par and a two-shot lead going into the final round. But he quickly gave that advantage away with a front nine of three-over-par thirty-nine on Sunday and stood on the sixteenth tee two behind Gary Player and Dow Finsterwald. Palmer faced a treacherous forty-five-foot chip that announcer Jimmy Demaret said he'd be lucky to get down in two.

In signature Palmer style, he holed the chip at the par-three hole and then made a twenty-footer for birdie at the seventeenth to draw even. A par at the eighteenth put him into a play-off with Player and Finsterwald. Palmer's 69 the next day beat Player by two and Finsterwald by eight. Palmer had made it two straight majors by winning the 1960 Open at Cherry Hills with his own brand of Sunday drama.

Typically, Palmer is also quite as well known for his colossal failures as he is for his sensational victories. At the 1961 Masters he squandered an opportunity to be the first player in history to win back-to-back Masters. He overcame a four-shot lead by Player to stand on the final tee with a one-shot lead of his own. All he needed was a par to win his second straight Masters.

As he walked down the last fairway, his tee shot on the left side, all he had was a seven-iron second shot to the green. On his way to his ball Palmer was stopped by legendary putting guru, George Low, who said, "Nice going, boy. You won it." At that moment Palmer's brain shut down. He hit his second shot into the right greenside bunker. The bunker shot was sent flying across the green. He needed to get the ball up and down from a side slope just to get into a play-off with Player. Instead he left the pitch fifteen feet from the hole and missed the bogey putt. He double-bogeyed the final hole to lose the Masters by a shot, perhaps the most ignominious loss of his career.

That same summer, Palmer made his second trip to the British Open, this time at Royal Birkdale, where he found conditions to be quite brutal. He shot rounds of 70-73-69—212, a shot ahead of Welshman Dai Rees, who had come close to winning the Open Championship many times. Palmer turned the front nine of the final round in thirty-six and led by four shots as he and Rees made their way home. He heroically saved a par four at the fifteenth after his drive found deep rough. He slashed a six-iron from the heavy stuff to within fifteen feet of the hole, a shot that probably saved the tournament. (To commemorate this remarkable recovery, the Royal Birkdale Club marked the spot with a permanent plaque.) Rees made a last-minute charge to get within a shot, but in the end Palmer became the first American to hoist the Claret Jug since Ben Hogan won at Carnoustie in 1953.

More important, Palmer's victory put the British Open back on the international map and established it as part of a modern Grand Slam—the Masters, U.S. Open, British Open, and PGA Championship. Until Palmer's trek, many American pros were unwilling to make the trip overseas for such a championship, one in which they would likely lose money after paying the high price for overseas travel. In fact Palmer himself said that the £1,400 he won at Birkdale just about covered his expenses. Not only that, there were no exemptions in those days, and Palmer had to go through the qualifying process just like everyone else. As a result Palmer was able to convince the Royal & Ancient Golf Club of St. Andrews to extend some exemptions to top American pros in an effort to entice them into making the trip.

In 1962 Palmer traveled to Scotland's Royal Troon, just weeks removed from an emotional play-off loss to Nicklaus in front of Palmer's hometown fans at Oakmont Country Club near Pittsburgh, Pennsylvania. Troon is long, narrow, and a difficult Open test. And when the wind kicks up, as was the case in 1962, the examination becomes even more demanding. Palmer was in third place after a first-round 71, a day when Nicklaus turned in an 80. Palmer followed with a 69 that put him three clear of the field. A third-round 67 gave him a five-shot lead, and 69 on the final day put him six ahead of his closest competitor. He broke the British Open scoring record by two shots and was the first American since Walter Hagen to successfully defend the Open Championship. At age thirty-two Palmer demonstrated the best golf of his career and was indisputably the top player in the world. He continued his Masters domination in 1964, which served to further fuel the Palmer-Nicklaus rivalry after Jack had won his first Masters the previous year. Palmer came to Augusta determined to win, and win he did. He took the lead with rounds of 69-68—137, seven under par—and after fifty-four holes he led by five with a third-round 69. After winning three Masters green jackets with high drama, his ambition was to be able to walk up the final fairway knowing there was no way he could lose.

Palmer got his wish and became the first four-time winner of the Masters in history. Commemorating Palmer's singular achievement, Masters officials erected a plaque on a water fountain behind the sixteenth green, a lasting monument to a monumental feat.

Palmer's dominance of the game came in an eight-year span, from 1957 to 1964. In that time he amassed thirty-nine of his sixty-one wins and all of his major championships. Not only had he captured the hearts and minds of America's golfers in a way no one had before, Arnold Palmer had taken the game to the people and connected with them on a level that had previously been reserved for team-sports athletes.

When he turned 50, his star power helped create the early success of the Senior PGA Tour. He won a major, the 1980 PGA Seniors, in his first attempt as a senior. He had actually made his debut in the unofficial World Seniors Invitational, an event conducted by his management company that would shortly find its way onto the Senior Tour schedule. He finished second to Gene Littler in the inaugural match.

Palmer won his second senior major in 1981 at Oakland Hills Country Club near Detroit when he beat Billy Casper and Bob Stone in a playoff. That victory legitimized the Senior PGA Tour as a viable entity. If Arnold Palmer would play—and become a star—on this fledgling circuit, then it was more than just an annuity for washed up players. It was its own tour with its own stars. And Palmer was the showcase, at least for the next 10 years when a chap named Nicklaus would join their ranks.

In 1984, Palmer won two senior majors, winning his second PGA Seniors title by two over Don January. He also won the Senior Players Championship, outrunning Peter Thomson by three strokes. He came within a whisker of sweeping all three senior majors that year, finishing second at the U.S. Senior Open, two shots behind Miller Barber. The next year, he defended his Senior Players Championship title, winning by a record 11 shots.

Five majors in six years made Palmer one of the stars of the Senior Tour, as if his stature didn't already. They were the halcyon days for the Senior Tour, times when you just knew that Arnold Palmer was going to be in the hunt most every week he played. The Senior Tour was billed as a nostalgia tour and no one could make us long for the old days more than Palmer could. Although he wasn't competing against the world's best anymore, he was still playing head-to-head against the players of his era. And he was still Arnie and that was good enough.

He still had his trademark swivel follow-through. He still had his electricity both with fans and his fellow touring pros. He could find his way into trouble and back out with equal ease. He was still Arnie, who could go on a birdie run at any moment and climb his way back up the leaderboard. In other words, he could make the Senior Tour relevant. Everybody loved Palmer and everyone loved watching him play, no matter how well or how badly. That's why he still plays, even past the year 2000, some 20 years after he first became a senior.

He was a hero, an idol, a star. And age has not served to dull that luster one bit. He was welcomed as warmly and signed as many autographs at age seventy-two—perhaps more—as he did when he was thirty-two.

Indeed he is the one player toward whom the modern golfer pays the most respect—he is called "Mr. Palmer" by nearly all. In fact, more than one veteran maintains that the spoils they enjoy as touring pros are owed to Palmer's charisma and popularity.

His legend, now and forever, knows no bounds of age or time.

ARNOLD PALMER

	Total New Money	Wins	Top10s	Top25s
Majors	$18,790,477	7	38	62
Other Official Tournaments (and International Wins)	79,599,243	64	242	369
TOTALS	**$98,389,720**	**71**	**280**	**431**

MAJOR CHAMPIONSHIPS

	New Money	Wins
Masters	$7,068,600	4
U.S. Open	5,349,147	1
British Open	3,812,297	2
PGA	2,560,433	0

BEST OTHER EVENTS

	New Money	Wins
Bob Hope Classic	$5,210,060	5
Tournament of Champions	4,299,800	3
American Golf Classic	3,601,895	2
Western Open	3,191,900	2

Year	New Money	Total Wins	Top10s	Top25s	Majors	Other Events
1955	$2,112,731	3	10	17	$ 218,228	$1,894,503
1956	2,882,836	2	9	15	252,153	2,630,683
1957	4,585,505	4	14	21	187,600	4,397,905
1958	5,669,730	3	16	25	1,067,421	4,602,309
1959	5,020,459	3	16	25	668,643	4,351,816
1960	9,000,004	8	21	26	2,817,455	6,182,549
1961	8,568,765	6	21	25	1,999,822	6,568,943
1962	7,997,931	8	14	20	2,773,573	5,224,358
1963	7,054,161	8	15	17	741,800	6,312,361
1964	6,800,420	3	19	25	1,691,187	5,109,233
1965	3,374,556	1	8	16	568,650	2,805,906
1966	5,596,007	4	17	19	1,137,867	4,458,140
1967	6,787,973	6	19	22	947,300	5,840,673
1968	3,315,046	2	10	16	597,248	2,717,799
1969	3,051,910	2	11	17	170,409	2,881,501
1970	2,998,188	0	12	16	586,713	2,411,475
1971	4,479,020	4	12	23	222,184	4,256,836
1972	2,248,100	0	11	16	613,485	1,634,615
1973	1,964,536	1	7	16	346,072	1,618,464
1974	700,359	0	2	7	312,043	388,316
1975	2,111,588	2	7	15	317,010	1,794,578
1976	648,777	0	3	9	82,500	566,277
1977	610,759	0	2	10	372,783	237,976
1978	375,440	0	2	4	0	375,440
1979	30,217	0	0	1	0	30,217
1980	195,638	1	1	4	51,520	144,118
1981	46,813	0	0	1	46,813	0
1982	35,100	0	0	1	0	35,100
1983	96,200	0	1	1	0	96,200
1991	30,950	0	0	1	0	30,950

Greg Norman

Phil Tresidder

Greg Norman is the stuff of which legends are made. Sadly though, he may not be destined ever to wear the legendary status himself. Legends are by tradition assessed and revered by the collection and weight of their trophy cabinet contents. Winning a modest two British Opens, some seventy-four tournaments worldwide, and securing a place in golf's Hall of Fame, notable as it might sound, might not be quite enough.

Wasn't it Johnny Miller who tagged Norman "Godzilla" in awe at first sight of his thunderous driving? And wasn't it David Graham who said positively that Norman would be the next great player in the world after Nicklaus? And again, Jack Nicklaus himself, who predicted the Aussie champion would "win a green jacket or two before he was through"?

Oh yes, Augusta has left its scars with hopes and ambitions unfulfilled, more than two decades of fruitless and frustrating visits, and a locker-room door barred to all but the green-jacket wearers. His Masters appearances are seemingly dogged by injustices (witness Larry Mize's freakish extra-hole chip-in) and then other self-inflicted injustices while primed for glory against Nicklaus and Nick Faldo.

For a record length of time, Norman headed the world rankings. Yet he confessed throughout his reign at the top that he never aspired to be the world number one. He just wanted to be the best player he could be. And as he reflects, he reassures himself that Greg Norman is successful in the eyes of Greg Norman. Yes, he always has been ego driven, protective, and sensitive about his image. Winning has been the supreme incentive. "To me, every victory is special, regardless of prize money or bonuses. I love to win; winning is the whole idea," he says.

Now in his late forties, Norman has drastically curtailed his tournament campaigns yet still probes hopefully to rekindle some old magic on the fairways. But the odds are stacked heavily against him and for a good reason.

He has built a multimillion-dollar business empire from his Florida headquarters, and time becomes his most precious commodity. When asked to estimate his respective commitments, he reckons it's about 60 percent golf and 40 percent business. So he parries, "The jury is out on my golf game, and it's too soon to assess my success in the business world."

But surely the giveaway line reveals itself when asked after his election to the World Golf Hall of Fame what artifacts he would donate to commemorate his career. "I figure I'd put in a plane, a yacht, a helicopter," he quipped.

Estimates of his wealth vary, but he says he is "no tycoon." But $280 million?

Perhaps, and his company did register a record $100 million in revenue to start the new millennium. His business empire is widespread and seemingly ever-expansive with tentacles embracing golf course design and construction in numerous countries, a highly regarded grass supply division, and a hefty wine export business from Australian vineyards to the American market. During a recent visit to his homeland Norman took a trip to the port city of Fremantle, on the country's western seaboard, to inspect a massive 230-foot cruising yacht he was having built. It's complete with swimming pool and cinema, and he's called it *Aussie Rules* in honor of Australian football.

If Australia has built a reputation as a land of opportunity, Greg Norman is the supreme example of grasping his with both steely hands. He is a product of the state of Queensland, which stretches to the north of the mainland, famous for its rain forests, exotic barrier reef, matchless game fishing, and rugged citizens devoted to sports. Queensland is the nation's winter playground, drawing locals and visitors alike to its glorious beaches when winter comes to the southern half of Australia.

Those sun-drenched beaches proved a surefire lure for a freewheeling teenager, Greg John Norman, who had made a grateful exit from classroom confines. He surfed the beaches as a self-confessed "beach bum," chasing the white-tipped breakers, lean-framed, superbly athletic, and a conspicuous and charismatic figure with his sun-bleached platinum hair. He barely escaped with his life on one occasion when he tackled a monster wave and was tumbled about on the ocean floor as if trapped in a crazed washing machine.

His father had nicknamed him "Buster," graphically descriptive of a bony-kneed youngster who scampered like Deerfoot along the beachfront with his black Labrador dogs at his heels, rode horses bareback, hanging on to the bridle, speared fish, sniped duck, and camped out under the stars. He went fishing with his father and mates, got stung by the spine of a John Dory, and was carted off to the hospital in terrible pain. On another occasion he was thrown into the killing pit when the fishing boat lurched and had his front teeth snapped. He was utterly fearless.

A professional golfing career, it seemed, was never a thought, let alone a destiny that would propel him onto the world golfing stage with Jack Nicklaus and other luminaries. Yet, as he quipped, he was getting around golf courses before he was even born. True, his mother, Toini, of Finnish extraction, was an enthusiastic golfer in their hometown of Mount Isa, spectacular for its blood-red sunsets, a massive mining center in the harsh, arid Queensland outback. Toini was seven months pregnant when her doctor said "enough." So she walked the course, then narrowly avoided a miscarriage to deliver an eight-pound, eleven-ounce son.

Norman was to join a Who's Who list of Australian golf champions and perhaps exceed them all. Norman von Nida, a tiny flame of a man, had carried the early banner for Australian golfers after World War II, competing on the British tournament scene with great distinction before his protégé, Peter Thomson, took over and annexed five British Open Championships. Then Crampton, Devlin, Graham, Marsh, Nagle, Grady . . . a momentum.

The golfing bug he had caught while caddying for his mother took full control through driving ambition and tireless practice. He celebrated his twenty-first birthday with his first tournament victory, the West Lakes Classic in Adelaide, which brought him to Sydney for the country's Open Championship in a blaze of glory and publicity.

Opportunist promoters promptly paired him with Nicklaus on opening day, only to see the new prodigy duff his drive from the first tee just
thirty yards. He was acutely embarrassed, but Nicklaus was full of encouragement. Years later it was Nicklaus again who walked across the restau-
rant at the Turnberry Hotel and quietly offered a few motivating words
that inspired the Shark to win his first major, the British Open.

Yes, he was the Great White Shark to an admiring golfing world. The
media had seized on the tag after hearing his exploits of shooting sharks
that had the audacity to steal fish snared by his speargun. The Shark took
his first sighting of the United States, later to become his golfing home and
headquarters, in the World Cup, partnering with Bob Shearer. He was to
become a familiar and much admired figure on the PGA Tour scene, certainly the most easily recognizable player on the course with his distinctive
Nordic features and boxerlike physique. The impact from his bold debut
in the Masters at Augusta produced some rousing praise and predictions
for his future, with his power hitting the key talking point.

The London *Sunday Times* writer John Hopkins enthused: "He hits the
ball as if his life depends on it. From the top of his backswing, when his
powerful shoulders are fully turned, he brings the club down at high speed,
often grunting with the effort and swinging so hard that his hands are swept
through, up and around his head until his body position resembles a reverse
'C.' When his dander is up, he creates such an impression of power that
you wince as he makes contact, and you half expect the ball to burst under
the onslaught."

The late Jim Murray, a legendary sports columnist with the *Los Angeles
Times*, asserted that the public enjoys watching go-for-broke golfers who
look like they're having a ball out there and not expecting a stock market
crash. Why was Gregory John Norman the pet of golf galleries all the way
from the temples of Malaysia to the braes of Scotland, Murray asked.
Because Norman looked like a man doing exactly what he'd like to be
doing—having the time of his life.

"They don't make a golf hole that can scare Greg Norman," penned Murray, "or a lie that fazes him. He hits a bad shot, he laughs at it. Win or lose,
he doesn't come into the press interview as if he's the chief suspect in a child
kidnapping case . . . but as if he's the star. He's as unself-conscious as a puppy
with a ball of yarn. He's flashy. He's got a shock of platinum hair that makes
him look like Jean Harlow from a distance. When he smiles, which is a lot,

his teeth light up like a keyboard. He could give Liberace lessons in glitz. Best of all, he looks like what you think a world-class athlete should look like. The way you'd like to look if you made your living in sports."

Murray continued, "If you wanted to be a golfer, this is the one you'd want to be. Like a lot of great athletes, energy just seems to radiate out of him just sitting still. He doesn't take this nice, slow feathery loop at the ball like a mechanical player. He lashes at it as if it were something he caught coming through his bedroom window at two in the morning."

The French have a saying that the style betrays the man. Norman's go-for-broke swings are certainly mirrored off the course where a wide variety of business interests have occupied every moment of his time. We are reminded of fast cars with his fleet of Ferraris and Jaguars. Reminded, too, that he has flown in a "Top Gun" F-16 fighter and harbors a burning ambition to land a jet on an aircraft carrier. "That would be a hell of a buzz," he is quoted as saying. He boasts he once raced in his car against a helicopter from the golf course back to his hotel—and won!

Wife Laura says danger is Norman's constant companion and he will never change. "I've learned to live with it," she says.

If you assess the game's leading players through their success in majors and their mountains of prize money, then Norman does not exactly leap out. Two British Open titles are the sum total of more than two decades of passionate hope and endeavor. His many defeats have been well documented with the underlying theme that good fortune has rarely touched him on the shoulder.

Beaten in majors by a freakish chip-in and a bull's-eye sand explosion highlight the scars that have wounded his golfing soul. But he is a person who never looks back, and he is acknowledged far and wide as a good sport and a desperately unlucky loser.

His outlook and psyche emerge from quotes from myriad visits to the media interview rooms over the years, for he is a fearless speaker, never backward in volunteering a strong opinion or supporting a cause.

- **On philosophy:** "I don't live in the past. My year starts today. I live in the present, and I think about the future."
- **On pressure:** "I don't feel it. Pressure's only what you put on yourself, and if you keep enjoying the game and can keep the whole thing in perspective, then it won't worry you."

- **On winning:** "To me every victory is special regardless of prize money or bonuses. I love to win; winning is the whole idea."
- **On motivation:** "I can motivate myself, but golf is a difficult game. Sometimes the harder you try, the worse you score. And when you try to relax, sometimes you don't play well either. So where's the middle?"
- **On celebration:** "I find victory gives very little reason to whoop it up, because I go into every tournament with the object of winning. If I am successful, then I have achieved what I set out to do. The players who indulge in elaborate winning celebrations are really the players who don't expect to win but find that somehow they have."
- **On improving:** "We're all victims of our own stupidity. When you putt great, why change it? When you swing great, why change it? But we do. Every single one of us in the history of the game has tinkered around with our golf swing and fiddled around with our putting stroke. It's human nature—to want to improve, even if it is only that 1 percent."

While Greg Norman plans to stay on the tournament scene until he is fifty, the inroads of his business interests continue to dominate his time. The free-spirited youngster who ran the beachfronts Down Under with the tail of his shirt hanging out is very much comfortable in a business suit these days.

A rare anecdote goes back to the summer of 1975 when he traveled by coach with a party of amateur colleagues from the Virginia Club in Brisbane down the coast to the town of Grafton across the border. He boasted to the amusement of his companions that by the age of thirty he would be a millionaire. He easily achieved his mark and upon return to his native Queensland telephoned each of the coach passengers to remind them of his prediction.

From his headquarters in Florida he is very much a hands-on boss of his Medalist Holdings company and with his course designing and construction spanning a dozen countries. His vineyard promotion is the latest in a long list of roller-coaster investments that establish him as top international business executive and developer. But there will always be room for tournament appearances along the way. Let's hope so, because the Great White Shark has played a dazzling role in taking golf to today's unbelievable heights.

GREG NORMAN

	Total New Money	Wins	Top10s	Top25s
Majors	$11,949,664	2	29	46
Other Official Tournaments (and International Wins)	51,089,604	72	209	278
TOTALS	$63,039,268	74	238	324

MAJOR CHAMPIONSHIPS

	New Money	Wins
Masters	$3,498,240	0
U.S. Open	1,844,551	0
British Open	4,179,063	2
PGA	2,427,810	0

BEST OTHER EVENTS

	New Money	Wins
Doral	$3,437,267	3
World Series of Golf	3,327,723	2
Memorial Tournament	3,000,375	2
Canadian Open	2,732,800	2

Year	New Money	Total Wins	Top10s	Top25s	Majors	Other Events
1976	$ 10,800	1	1	1	$ 0	$ 10,800
1977	789,149	2	5	7	0	789,149
1978	539,971	4	8	12	0	539,971
1979	938,828	3	6	8	113,248	825,581
1980	2,258,784	4	16	18	0	2,258,784
1981	2,243,687	3	9	13	460,907	1,782,780
1982	1,701,011	3	8	11	200,750	1,500,261
1983	1,777,551	6	10	14	57,113	1,720,438
1984	3,496,795	5	12	15	834,106	2,662,689
1985	1,732,753	2	8	14	151,241	1,581,512
1986	6,228,594	9	17	19	2,304,815	3,923,779
1987	2,965,848	2	14	18	492,800	2,473,048
1988	2,952,227	6	13	17	336,400	2,615,827
1989	4,135,468	5	12	19	954,066	3,181,402
1990	4,407,009	3	14	18	456,340	3,950,669
1991	1,198,616	0	7	8	126,416	1,072,200
1992	2,609,893	1	9	13	326,629	2,283,264
1993	5,614,359	3	15	16	1,700,140	3,914,219
1994	4,262,527	2	13	17	550,179	3,712,348
1995	4,789,635	4	12	18	1,048,856	3,740,779
1996	2,374,130	3	7	13	954,134	1,419,996
1997	3,639,306	2	11	14	85,910	3,553,396
1998	253,762	1	2	2	0	253,762
1999	836,128	0	2	6	602,028	234,100
2000	646,233	0	3	5	128,800	517,433
2001	234,197	0	2	3	0	234,197
2002	402,007	0	2	5	64,788	337,219

Indomitable Enigma

Ben Hogan

Jaime Diaz

In the engaging book *Golf in the Kingdom*, the mythical protagonist, Shivas Irons, leaves a journal that contains a section entitled, simply, "A List of People Who Knew."

It's a succession of nearly 130 names in apparently random order, as well known as Plato, Beethoven, and James Joyce, as obscure as Bishop Isadore Balls, and Jalal Rumi. All reside somewhere in the world of ideas. Near the end, after Picasso, Maimonides, and Typhus Magee, is the only golfer on the list. Ben Hogan.

Somehow, Hogan, who died in July of 1997 at age eighty-four, is a perfect fit. If ever a golfer carried himself as if he had learned something important, something timeless, hard-earned and true, then played with the nobility and conviction that proved the point, it was Hogan.

When he marched to dominating victories at Riviera and Oakland Hills and Oakmont and Carnoustie, Hogan, above all golfers, seemed to understand something others didn't. He knew. If golf's cognoscenti were asked to make a list of the three greatest players of all time, the names mentioned most often would surely be Jack Nicklaus, Bobby Jones, and Ben Hogan. Hogan won sixty-three times on the PGA Tour, surpassed by only Sam Snead and Nicklaus, and captured nine major championships, the most behind Nicklaus, Jones, and Walter Hagen.

Significantly, Hogan's record was compiled almost entirely in an incredible nine-year run from 1946 to 1953 that came to be known as the "Age of Hogan." Beyond his victories, it was the way Hogan gave every fiber of his being to making himself the supreme golfer that is his true legacy. His unrelentingly dedicated, confoundingly complicated, and utterly self-sufficient persona made Hogan the most distinct golfer who ever lived and gives him a singular place in the game's history.

To start with, Hogan's swing was different from that of other golfers of his time or before—more honed, more purposeful, more effective. "When I stood directly behind Hogan," wrote Charles Price, "I had the feeling that the shot was nine-tenths over with. He just had to go through the formality of swinging the club, so perfect was his alignment and so poised the promise of what was coming."

Once the action began, it was a fast-paced, seamless movement that suggested something mechanized—"stamping out bottle caps," as once described in *Time* magazine. But it was in still photos that Hogan's swing was most thrilling: the position he achieved at the beginning of his downswing, the shaft of the club nearly touching his right shoulder, the extreme angle of his wrists, and the "lateness" of the stored-up hit, so palpably the definition of golf power that it never ceases to shock the mind.

It followed that Hogan's shots were considered to have unique properties. "If it were possible to track the height of every shot ever hit," wrote Al Barkow, "I have the feeling that we would find that all were at particular levels of high or low except Hogan's. The man had his own exclusive channel in the sky."

Then there was Hogan's stoicism, which contained a keen intelligence and hinted at secret knowledge. As lifetime rival Sam Snead once said, "Hogan gave away less about himself than any man I ever met." His icy reticence embodied a "never complain, never explain" code. But when he did speak, it was with more penetration and pith than the more voluble. Hoganisms are part of the golf zeitgeist, from "I don't play jolly golf" to "You have to dig it out of the ground" to "Watch out for buses."

Hogan also had a career code all his own. His dismal beginnings, followed by bootstrapping success, followed by disaster, followed by true greatness, made him a classic example of the aphorism "It's not what a man achieves but what he overcomes."

Hogan achieved that ultimate measure of a great man: he became a concept. The word *Hogan* has come to symbolize a heroic, quixotic, loving attempt to master an unmasterable sport. "I know that I have had greater satisfaction than anyone who ever lived out of hitting golf shots," he once said. "I liked to win, but, more than anything, I loved to play the way I wanted to play." His golf carried extra conviction, as if it were more valid, more part of a grand design, more earned. When Hogan won, it was completely deserved. When he lost, it was more poignant, because no golfer ever gave so much. He was the game's ultimate warrior, seemingly under a sacred vow to endure everything golf could dish out. In that way, in providing light to the hardest, darkest, most forbidding parts of the game, he had more impact than any player who ever lived. As Dan Jenkins wrote, "Hogan was, Hogan is, Hogan always will be."

It was why the Scots immediately connected with Hogan as he made his one and only assault on the Open championship at Carnoustie in 1953. It's why his fellow pros went out to watch Hogan play. In fact, the better the player, the greater the influence Hogan seemed to have. Billy Casper so admired Hogan's aura that he suppressed his naturally loose, wise-guy bent in favor of a taciturn on-course persona reliant on a form of self-hypnosis he believed Hogan subscribed to.

Gary Player, who among the game's best most closely resembled Hogan in size, work ethic, and skill, dedicated his early professional years to duplicating every facet of his idol's swing, until even he finally gave up, concluding that Hogan's talent was that of a physical freak.

Under the tutelage of old Hogan contemporary Jack Grout, teenage Jack Nicklaus committed himself to sound course management and the more controllable left-to-right ball flight that had turned Hogan's career around in the mid-1940s. When the fledgling pro Lee Trevino witnessed "The Hawk" hitting soft cuts with a four-wood on Hogan's now legendary private practice hole at Shady Oaks in Ft. Worth, he junked his own low hook for a fade and four years later won the U.S. Open.

Johnny Miller admits that "the way I wore my hat and squinted my eyes, all that was from Ben Hogan." Nick Price carried a card of a Hogan photo with all his swing keys noted on it. Nick Faldo, proud to be called Hoganesque in his approach to the game, spent many hours watching videos of Hogan's action. So has Tiger Woods, whose teacher, Butch Harmon, used to sit at the family dinner table enraptured as his father, Claude, and Hogan discussed the game. "There is," says Harmon, "a lot of Ben Hogan in Tiger Woods."

Of course, for every emulator who made a mark, there have been thousands of deluded, hard-practicing, flat-swinging, pronating and supinating, white-cap-wearing, no-talking perfectionists whose identification with all things Hogan allowed them to believe their failures were simply necessary steps on an inevitable but rocky path to success. Hogan's methods and habits were such common knowledge, the jagged curve of his journey such an inspirational blueprint, it obscured the fact that, like any genius, he was one of a kind.

"So many things about Hogan were special," says Nicklaus. "He was the greatest shot maker I ever saw. He was more determined and could totally outfocus anyone else in his time of playing. No one seemed to know him very well, which made him that much more feared as a competitor. He probably worked harder than anyone to reach the top, and it took him a long time. Then, when he got there, his body was all but destroyed by the car accident. All he did was start over again at nearly forty and got even better.

"Nobody was like Hogan."

William Ben Hogan was born August 13, 1912, in a hospital in Stephenville, near his family home in Dublin, Texas, the same year, in golf's greatest harmonic convergence, as Byron Nelson and Sam Snead were born. He was the youngest child of Chester and Clara Hogan, having a brother, Royal Dean, and a sister, Clara Princess. Early photos show Ben sitting on a horse, his blacksmith father standing nearby.

"Ben sat perfectly on a horse," said his wife, Valerie Hogan shortly before she died in 1999. "Horses were the way he could be around his father, and he rode beautifully. When we first met, he would try to get me to ride. He'd say, 'Now, just don't let that horse know you're afraid of him.' I told him, 'Honey, I can't help it. I am afraid, and I can't pretend I'm not.' But my husband never showed fear."

When Hogan was nine years old, Chester shot himself in the family home and died several hours later on Valentine's Day. The effect on his youngest child has long been a subject of speculation. Psychologists say the suicide of a father can leave a son feeling responsible, angry, and carrying a lifelong distrust of males. Hogan, was indeed, insular around men but courtly with women. According to Hogan biographer Curt Sampson, he once said that if he ever did an autobiography, it would only be with a woman writer.

Valerie Hogan is certain the suicide had an incalculable effect on her husband. "I always got the feeling that Ben had been his father's favorite and that he had felt very close to his father," she said. "I'm sure the way he died had a lot to do with the way Ben's personality was. I don't think he ever got over it." Asked if she ever talked to her husband about it, Mrs. Hogan said, "I never did, and he never brought it up. I thought it would be too painful for him."

The hardship undoubtedly helped shape Hogan into an intense, watchful youth. To help support his mother, he began hawking the *Fort Worth Star Telegram* in that rough-and-tumble town's railroad station. At age eleven he began making the seven-mile hike from his home to the Glen Garden Country Club, then a nine-hole course where he could make sixty-five cents caddying an eighteen-hole round.

In the caddie yard, the undersized Hogan was initially bullied, sometimes rolled down a hill in a barrel, and generally made to run a gauntlet of a dozen other caddies. Finally "Bantam Ben" picked out one of the larger caddies and began a fight. That first important victory earned him a full-time place in the yard.

"I feel sorry for rich kids now. I really do," Hogan once said. "Because they're never going to have the opportunity I had. Because I knew tough things. I've had a tough day all my life, and I can handle tough things. They can't. And every day that I progressed was a joy to me, and I recognized it every day. I don't think I could have done what I've done if I hadn't had the tough days to begin with."

When Hogan was thirteen, a new caddie entered the yard. Byron Nelson vividly recalls that first glimpse of his future rival. "Though he was short, he had big hands and arms for his size," Nelson wrote in his autobiography. "He was quiet, serious, and mostly kept to himself. Ben liked to box, and so did another caddie we called Joe Boy. [At a boxing match put on for the members' entertainment] they boxed for about 15 minutes. I was just watching, because I never did like to box or fight."

Nelson liked to play golf, and he and Hogan became the best players in the yard. But Hogan couldn't quite beat Nelson. In the club's caddie championship in 1927, the two tied with a 39 for nine holes when Nelson made a long putt on the final hole. Nelson then took the second nine, 41 to 42. They each won a club, Nelson a five-iron and Hogan a two-iron, which they immediately traded.

Nelson set a daunting standard for Hogan for the next twenty years. By 1940, when both had been professionals for nearly a decade, Nelson had won the Masters and the U.S. Open and eight other tournaments. Hogan had won the Hershey Four-Ball with Vic Ghezzi and nothing else. At the 1942 Masters, Nelson beat Hogan in an eighteen-hole play-off by a stroke, just as he had at Glen Garden. By 1946, when Hogan was having his first great season, Nelson was in his last as a regular player. In fact Hogan's beginnings as a professional would have broken most men.

He turned pro at age seventeen at the onset of the Depression and actually withdrew from his first two tournaments—the Texas Open after a 78-75 start and a Houston event in which he started 77-76. "I found out that first day that I shouldn't have even been out there," he said years later. By the time he married Valerie Fox in 1935, his attempts to play the circuit had twice left him busted. As well as teaching golf without much success, he worked in the oil fields, in a bank, and as a mechanic. At one point he even dealt cards in a Fort Worth gambling house. Hindered by an extremely long backswing, his violent action through the ball too often produced low, hard-running hooks that he could not control. Later he'd describe such shots as "a rattlesnake in your pocket."

But Ben Hogan practiced—on off days, before rounds, even, to the absolute astonishment of his peers, after rounds. As Jenkins wrote, "Ben Hogan invented practice." He improved, but not enough to win. During the 1938 Oakland Open, Hogan's last desperate effort to make a living playing full-time golf, with no more than pocket change left, the tires of his car were stolen. It was a truly desperate moment, but he was able to hitch a ride to the club, and under the circumstances a truly miraculous final-round 69 earned him a tie for third and $280. He would come to say, "I played harder that day than I ever played before or ever will again."

While his obsessive practice and solitary personality set him apart from his peers, his constant companion was Valerie, who believed her husband was destined for something special. "I never knew that much about golf, but you could just feel the dedication," she said. "I just had a strong feeling that, whatever he decided in life, he would end up doing something that mattered. He had so much energy. He just cared too much to not be very good."

The next year Hogan won his first event, the North and South at Pinehurst, then the next two tournaments in succession. After losing the 1942 Masters play-off, he won the Hale America, the substitute for the U.S. Open, which had been suspended because of the war by the United States Golf Association. It forever gave Hogan the strongest case—made by others, of course—for having won five, not just four, U.S. Opens.

His first prime postponed by three years of military service, Hogan emerged in 1945 to win five events, the same year Nelson won eighteen. At the age of thirty-three, Ben Hogan appeared to be a player who would have a good but hardly great career. In fact, the Age of Hogan was yet to unfold.

In 1946, Ben Hogan won thirteen tournaments, the most ever won in a season next to Nelson's epic 1945 total. Remarkably, it was also a year in which Hogan suffered two of his most devastating losses. At the Masters he came to the final green needing a birdie to win, put his approach eighteen feet above the cup, then three-putted, missing a four-footer for par. At the U.S. Open at Canterbury, he again needed a birdie on the final hole to win and again three-putted from eighteen feet. "Disappointing? Yes, but you get used to that in this game," he would say after the second loss. Valerie Hogan never ceased to be amazed at her husband's resiliency.

"I've often wondered how he handled those things so well," she said. "He had a strong heart. I don't think he got over things quickly, but he acted like he did."

In his last major event of 1946, the PGA Championship in Portland, Oregon (then a grueling six-day match-play event), Hogan got to the final by beating Jimmy Demaret ten and nine, then claimed his first major championship by defeating Porky Oliver six and four. The next year he won seven more times, by which time he was closing in on mastery of his golf swing. At his physical peak he was five feet, eight inches and 140 pounds of power and quickness. Ted Williams, who approached the art of hitting a baseball in much the same obsessive way that Hogan did the golf ball, was once introduced to Hogan and came away saying, "I just shook a hand that felt like five bands of steel."

But Hogan's mental strength was even tougher. Wrote Herbert Warren Wind, "It would not be amiss to add that the superlative game he ultimately developed depended at least as much on the tireless thinking he put in over the years as it did on his tireless practicing." Valerie would see his preoccupation and wonder, "Aren't you giving that brain a rest? He'd look at me and say, 'Valerie, if you don't use it, it will go to pot.'"

"I think anyone can do anything he wants to do if he wants to study and work hard enough," Hogan once said. "And that's one of the great rewards of golf, I think—learning. I've seen people play terrific golf, but they didn't know anything about it. You see their names in the paper for two years, then they drop out, because they weren't schooled in how to propel the club and what was happening all the time and why. I've gotten just great satisfaction, as much as or more than anybody, in learning how to swing a golf club and what is going to happen when you swing it this way or that way. There's nine jillion things to learn. I don't think anyone knows all there is to know about the golf swing, and I don't think anyone will ever know. It's a very complex thing. Everything changes."

Through painstaking trial and error, Hogan happened upon a method to prevent him from hitting his dreaded low hook while consistently producing a powerful but soft-landing fade. He weakened his grip, opened his stance, and rotated his left forearm clockwise on his take-away as much as he could, feeling that, from such a position, he could release the club as hard as he wanted on the downswing without worrying about the ball going left. "As far as applying power goes," he wrote in his bestseller, *Five Lessons: The Modern Fundamentals of Golf,* I wish that I had three right hands."

After Hogan settled on these keys, the game became much simpler for him, as he explained in his book: "I never felt genuinely confident about my game until 1946. Up to that year, while I knew once I was on the course and playing well that I had the stuff that day to make a good showing, before a round I had no idea whether I'd be 69 or 79. I felt my game might suddenly go south on any given morning. In 1946 my attitude suddenly changed. I honestly began to feel that I could count on playing fairly well each time I went out; there was no practical reason for me to feel I might suddenly 'lose it all.' I would guess that what lay behind my new confidence was this: I had stopped trying to do a great many difficult things perfectly because it had become clear in my mind that this ambitious overthoroughness was neither possible nor advisable—or even necessary.

All you needed to groove were the fundamental movements—and there weren't so many of them."

It was in this period that Hogan developed his aura of inevitability. Hogan became so dominating in the late 1940s that his peers began to suspect he had a "secret"—some magic move that made him better than anyone else. The theories were numerous, but Hogan never acknowledged any of them. Snead, who took pride in twice defeating Hogan in eighteen-hole play-offs, wouldn't go along with what he felt amounted to a psychological edge for his rival. "Anybody can say he's got a secret if he won't tell us what it is," he remarked. But Snead did allow that he believed Hogan became a better player as he accentuated right-arm extension through the ball.

Most probably the secret was mental. Said Valerie Hogan, "I think there was something that he felt was a secret. He never told me; I never asked. I didn't want to know, because I might have given it away. He wouldn't have discussed it with anyone. It was something he did that others didn't do."

The best Hogan ever played on a day-in and day-out basis came in 1948. He won eleven tournaments that year, including his first U.S. Open and the PGA Championship. When he won two of the first three events of 1949, it gave him eleven victories in the last sixteen events entered. Since returning from military service in 1945, he had won thirty-eight tournaments, the highest victory total over four straight years ever witnessed on the PGA Tour.

Then it was over.

After losing a play-off to Jimmy Demaret at the Phoenix Open, Ben and Valerie headed to Fort Worth, where they were going to settle into the first home that they owned in fourteen years of marriage. But on the foggy morning of February 2, 1949, a Greyhound bus attempting to pass a large truck crossed a center divider on Highway 80 near El Paso. Hogan saw the headlights coming at him but could not get off the right side of the road because of a concrete abutment. The bus slammed into the left front of his Cadillac, pushing the steering wheel into the backseat and the engine into the driver's area. Hogan survived only because he flung himself across his wife before impact.

His injuries were massive. His collarbone was broken where the steering wheel had hit it. His pelvis, a rib, and his left ankle were also fractured. At first he appeared to have recovered rapidly and was scheduled to leave the hospital on February 16. But when a blood clot from his left leg reached his right lung, Hogan's condition became grave. The world's leading vascular surgeon, Dr. Alton Oscher, was brought from New Orleans on emergency to tie off the vena cava so that no more blood clots would be carried to Hogan's heart or lungs. As a result, his circulation was permanently impaired. His legs would swell and ache for the rest of his life.

After returning to Fort Worth, Hogan began his recuperation by walking laps around his living room. Toward the end of 1949 he played eighteen holes of golf for the first time but needed a cart. Two weeks later he walked a full round, the effort sapping him so much he spent the rest of the day in bed. Nevertheless, he filed his entry to play in the Los Angeles Open in mid-January—less than two months away in a still uncertain future. At Riviera, Hogan shocked the world by tying for first place with Snead, then losing in a play-off. As Grantland Rice wrote, Hogan didn't lose; "his legs simply were not strong enough to carry around his heart."

Just five months later, at the U.S. Open, Hogan achieved his most memorable victory. At Merion, to relieve his swelling legs, Hogan soaked in a hot bath for an hour before every round but still suffered searing cramps walking to the twelfth tee during the second round. Even so, he limped in with a superb 69. The ultimate test for his uncertain legs, he knew, would be Saturday's double round. Sure enough, they seized up again on the thirteenth hole of the morning eighteen.

He nearly withdrew but struggled inward, hole by painful hole, for 72. In the afternoon the other contenders faltered, giving him a three-stroke lead, but after driving on the twelfth he again staggered from pain. By the time he reached the eighteenth tee, the lead was gone. But after a good drive on the 458-yard par-four finisher, he hit an epic two-iron forty feet from the pin and two-putted to tie Lloyd Mangrum and George Fazio.

The next day, Hogan forced his unwilling legs into action yet again and dominated the eighteen-hole play-off by four strokes. His victory remains one of the greatest comebacks in the entire history of sports.

Ben Hogan was not the same golfer he had been prior to the accident. His left shoulder hurt constantly, and the sight in his left eye was impaired, eventually leading to terrible putting problems. Tournament golf required so much effort that from then on he would never again play more than six events in a year. And he never again played in the PGA Championship, which until 1958 required thirty-six holes of daily match play.

But Hogan adapted. Although he was not as long a hitter as before or as good a putter, he made fewer mistakes than ever. Whereas the old Hogan had often gone low, the revised version almost never went high. It was a game made for the majors, where, on the toughest courses, he could reel off par after par, interspersed with timely birdies, to outlast the field.

In 1951, Hogan won his first Masters and his third U.S. Open, where he closed with a 67 at Oakland Hills in perhaps the finest round of his career. In 1953 he achieved his pinnacle: another victory at the Masters, his fourth U.S. Open with a dominating performance at brutal Oakmont, and finally, in his first and only try at the British Open, a nearly flawless performance at Carnoustie. When he returned to the United States, it was to a Broadway ticker-tape parade. The only other golfer to receive that honor had been Bobby Jones.

Hogan then was forty. The Herculean effort he had put forth to regain and sustain his game had taken a huge toll. He came excruciatingly close, but he never won another major championship. Playing an abbreviated schedule, he won his last event, and his fifth victory at the Colonial in his hometown, in 1959. He had continued to play superbly at the U.S. Open, suffering heartbreaking losses in 1955 and 1956. His near miss at the 1960 championship at Cherry Hills was the most poignant.

Immaculate in his ball striking, Hogan put himself in contention for the thirty-six-hole final and proceeded to hit the first thirty-four greens in regulation. Tied for the lead on the seventy-first hole, a par five, he laid up a four-iron second shot some fifty yards short of a creek that guarded the tiny green like a moat.

With the pin cut in front of the putting surface less than fifteen feet from the water, and knowing that a play-off would probably be too much for him physically, Hogan took out a wedge and rolled the dice.

"The way I was putting, I knew I had to get within two feet or I couldn't possibly make it," Hogan said later. "I had the most beautiful lie you could have. I tried to put as much stuff on the ball as I could to hold it on my side of the hole. I played what I thought was a good shot. It was hit exactly as I intended, but I just misjudged the shot." The ball hit on the green but, loaded with backspin, sucked back into the water. Hogan made a bogey, then, gambling to cut off the dogleg on the eighteenth, drove into the water again and finished with a triple bogey. "It was the saddest thing, and it devastated him," said Valerie Hogan. "It would have been such a wonderful ending."

Hogan continued to play the odd tournament, finally ending his competitive career at the 1971 Houston Champions International. He remained active as president of his club company and played what his friends say was his last eighteen-hole round in 1980 at one of his favorite courses, Seminole, in Juno Beach, Florida.

He continued to practice at Shady Oaks CC near his Fort Worth home, often picking up his own shag balls, until he stopped around 1990. In those later years he was rarely seen in public.

"Underneath everything, my husband was very emotional," said Valerie. "Although I believe he was happy in his later life, he missed hitting golf balls and trying to figure it all out. He loved his club company, and that gave him a lot of fulfillment. He was creating something, the same way he created something when he hit golf shots. Of course, I don't think anything could completely replace the satisfaction he got from that.

"When he was in too much pain to hit practice balls anymore, he would come into the living room with a club and swing it a little. My sister would say, 'Valerie, I've never seen a man who loved anything like Ben loves golf. It's hurting him that he can't do what he loves to do.' She was right. Ben was cheated out of years of golf by the accident. He always looked at it as how fortunate he was to play again, that God let him live. But, as he got older, there was a sense of loss. There was sadness. He would have loved to have played forever."

Of course, on every practice range and every golf course—wherever and forever—Ben Hogan lives on.

BEN HOGAN

	Total New Money	Wins	Top10s	Top25s
Majors	$18,101,870	9	40	47
Other Official Tournaments (and International Wins)	67,891,280	48	189	232
TOTALS	$84,943,150	57	229	279

MAJOR CHAMPIONSHIPS

	New Money	Wins
Masters	$6,918,287	2
U.S. Open	7,155,568	4
British Open	1,106,140	1
PGA	2,921,875	2

BEST OTHER EVENTS

	New Money	Wins
Colonial	$6,083,353	5
Los Angeles Open	3,313,936	3
Phoenix Open	2,947,200	2
North & South Open	2,897,663	3

Year	New Money	Total Wins	Top10s	Top25s	Majors	Other Events
1932	$ 171,673	0	0	3	$ 0	$ 171,673
1933	112,000	0	1	1	0	112,000
1934	157,500	0	1	2	0	157,500
1935	0	0	0	0	0	0
1936	0	0	0	0	0	0
1937	950,068	0	5	9	0	950,068
1938	2,151,629	0	14	17	56,000	2,095,629
1939	2,946,632	0	16	17	285,463	2,661,169
1940	6,535,999	4	18	22	519,383	6,016,616
1941	8,205,834	3	25	26	779,459	7,426,375
1942	6,866,933	6	15	18	797,988	6,068,946
1943	0	0	0	0	0	0
1944	516,400	0	2	2	0	516,400
1945	6,070,150	5	17	17	0	6,070,150
1946	12,566,337	11	25	30	1,830,765	10,735,572
1947	6,802,670	5	18	22	490,816	6,311,854
1948	9,593,500	9	20	22	2,184,600	7,408,900
1949	1,917,400	2	3	4	0	1,917,400
1950	2,671,316	2	5	9	1,246,400	1,424,916
1951	3,185,733	3	4	4	2,008,000	1,177,733
1952	1,316,866	1	3	3	542,866	774,000
1953	4,674,140	5	6	6	3,114,140	1,560,000
1954	895,470	0	3	3	768,170	127,300
1955	1,297,300	0	2	3	1,189,800	107,500
1956	947,339	0	3	5	654,116	293,223
1957	447,000	0	2	3	0	447,000
1958	586,597	0	3	4	231,559	355,038
1959	1,009,453	1	2	3	149,053	860,400
1960	804,353	0	4	4	336,653	467,700
1961	159,067	0	0	2	108,757	50,310
1962	282,050	0	1	2	0	282,050
1963	32,823	0	0	1	0	32,823
1964	666,310	0	4	4	288,600	377,710
1965	266,470	0	1	3	158,970	107,500
1966	479,939	0	2	4	231,514	248,425
1967	610,200	0	3	3	128,800	481,400
1970	96,000	0	1	1	0	96,000

Jack Nicklaus

Kaye Kessler

At age ten he didn't know Sam Snead from Sam Sausage and skipped right over the fabled Slammer to shake hands with Skip Alexander. Ten years later he beat Ben Hogan head-to-head over thirty-six holes the first time they ever met, still came out second, but learned a cool lesson from the "Wee Ice Mon." Two years after that he had the audacity to dethrone the king, Arnold Palmer, in his own castle, only to be vilified in the process and jeered later in King Arnie's private Augusta preserve, as well as virtually everywhere east of the Monongahela River. Yet the same man would become the unanimous choice as "Golfer of the Century."

That should have said it all about Jack William Nicklaus. But it didn't. That adornment was the sum of all the totals—after the Golden Bear ostensibly had written the final chapter to the greatest fifty-year stretch of golf in the game's history.

The sum of all those facts should be forever sealed in a timeless capsule over which earthlings of generations X, Y, and Z may exclaim incredulously. To summarize them for mind-boggling reference, consider:

- His 20 major victories (18 professional, 2 amateur), 19 second-place major finishes, 9 thirds, and 73 top tens in about half of the 154 consecutive majors he played.

- He is one of only five players to win all four majors—which he's done three times with six Masters, five PGA Championships, four U.S. Opens, and three British Opens.
- He has seventy-one official PGA Tour victories, fifty-eight second places, thirty-six thirds.
- His one hundred victories worldwide, six Australian Opens, five World Series of Golf titles, six Ryder Cup appearances, eight times low-scoring average for the season and six times second, eight times leading money winner, PGA Player of the Year five times, ad infinitum. As venerable old Casey put it, "You could look it up."
- His regular PGA Tour career earnings of $5,697,038 pale only in comparison to today's standards; revalued in New Money terms, it becomes a mind-boggling $128 million and small change.

Statistics are staggering, but also stifling playthings. Winning a major his first year as a professional, then winning his last twenty-four years later and other such baggage of legends. Nicklaus meant so much more to the game of golf than figures that it is stupefying. Purely and simply, Jack Nicklaus is a gem of and for the ages. He was discovered, rough-cut and unpolished, by Jack Grout, a Texas compadre of Hogan, Byron Nelson, and Jimmy Demaret, legends of earlier days, before the PGA Tour earned its place in the sports cash registers.

He was so impressive as a fifteen-year-old that the immortal Bobby Jones asked to meet him, not vice versa. Jones not too long thereafter would be moved to anoint young Nicklaus with these indelible words, "He plays a game with which I am totally unfamiliar."

When he was ten, that uncut diamond in Grout's first rough collection of juniors at Scioto Country Club in Columbus was taken into the locker room by Grout to meet some of the game's great contestants in the 1950 PGA. Nicklaus found Skip Alexander and Lloyd Mangrum considerably more interesting than defending champion Snead.

Six years later, meeting Snead for the first time in a special exhibition at the new Urbana (Ohio) Country Club, he would be unflappable, bowing in the Friday afternoon match 68–72 to the famed Slammer—a match Snead would have but vague recollections of. Nicklaus, however, was impressed enough that he returned to Marietta the following day to shoot 64–72 and become the youngest Ohio Open winner in history. While admitting to a bad case of nerves teeing it up with the great Snead, Jack confessed that watching Sam's every move in their match inspired his performance so much in the final thirty-six holes at Marietta that he even forgave Snead for calling him "Junior."

Dan Jenkins, the redoubtable pundit of infallible judgment and inexorable opinions who grew up flat-out knowing fellow Texan Hogan hung the moon, grudgingly conceded in saner later life that Nicklaus jumped over the moon *and* Hogan. And in a very wry twist, it would be some unforgettable words from Hogan when Nicklaus still was a twenty-year-old amateur that would reinforce in a most unusual manner the profound teachings of Grout.

As in real life its own self, there are dissenters, the holdouts who staunchly stand up for their idols, be they Hogan, Hagen, Jones, Palmer, or old Ad Infinitum. For half a century they have chipped away at Jack's image. He had an upright swing and flying right elbow that would never stand the test of time; he lacked charisma; he overswung; had a flawed wedge game; was even "wristy" playing out of water; didn't hold his thumbs correctly—whatever. Right, and the Rolls-Royce has dirty tires and full ashtrays.

There isn't a golfer born who didn't have a secret, or at least a principle on which he staked his career, and in that regard Jack Nicklaus may be no different from many other greats. He learned it when he was ten, had it reinforced by Hogan, as previously mentioned, when he was twenty, and has repeated it so many times since then that it's probably written on his forehead under his hat brim.

"The head is the *most important* thing in the golf swing." Jack learned this the very hardheaded way when his late beloved mentor Grout took him under his wing in Columbus. "I'll never forget it," Jack recalled so vividly this past summer as he had so many, many other times in discussing his game. "I was taking lessons from Grout, and an assistant, Larry Glosser, was the guy assigned by Mr. Grout to hold me by the hair to keep my head still. I really hated the guy because that was in the days when all young boys sported crew cuts.

"He had Larry come out in front of me and grab me tightly by my little bit of hair while I was addressing the ball. 'OK, Jackie boy, now just go ahead and hit that ball for me,' Mr. Grout would say. And I'd swing and keep yelling 'ouch' after every shot until I finally learned in a few weeks to keep my head steady, every time on every shot, until the ball was well on its way. There is no doubt in my mind that that has been my number-one fundamental in golf ever since."

If, indeed, Nicklaus had a leg up on the rest of the golf world in his day, it definitely was because of his head. Pay attention the next time you see Jack draw his driver back—when he's in the golden bearing of his waning career, precisely as he was in the beginning. An instant before he starts the backswing he cocks his head to the right—and *locks it.* Locks his head until the ball is airborne. Lordy, what a simple game! It's a swing key that has proven its worth for more than a half century.

For all his splendid talents, it's the inside of Nicklaus's head that has always has been the best part of his game, and many have acclaimed him to be the most focused, soundest thinker golf has ever known.

Ironically, and in an interesting twist, Hogan deserves an assist for watering Jack's head-seed in their first-ever confrontation. Cherry Hills, 1960 U.S. Open, Palmer was about to add another, if improbable, crown to his kingly head. Lost in perhaps the greatest charge of Arnie's splendid career was the transformation of Nicklaus from a budding phenom into the greatest the game had ever seen. Jack's career was ascending even as an amateur. Old pro Hogan's was descending. But they just happened to be paired together in the final thirty-six-hole Saturday rounds of that Open.

Nicklaus had made significant waves in national golf circles but never had come under the stern eye of the brilliant Hogan. Palmer's closing charge was one for the ages. But Nicklaus and Hogan staged a most memorable sideshow, matching 69s in the morning third round to get within a shot of leader Mike Souchak and then letting it slip away in the afternoon when Jack shot par 71 to finish second to Palmer and Hogan 73 that dropped him to a tie for ninth.

Ah, now for the rest of that story, which would become a defining moment in the meteoric rise of Nicklaus. Jack was awestruck by Hogan's demeanor and play and would later write: ". . . playing with Ben turned out to be, if not what you might call a highly social experience, a perfectly pleasant one . . . he meticulously observed all of the courtesies a golfer is expected to afford his fellows during competitive play, but without ever saying one more word to me than he regarded as essential . . . not out of discourtesy . . . or disinterest in a young amateur . . . but simply a side effect of his own depth of concentration. . . . Ben had long ago discovered that to play his best, he had to focus his mind 100 percent on his own game. . . ."

Ben's best dazzled Nicklaus. And his afterthought gave Jack pause and great pride. Jack remembered Ben opening with an "indifferent 75, only to follow with a second-round 67, hitting every green in regulation. In their Saturday morning round, Hogan again hit all eighteen greens in a 69, and in the afternoon round he hit sixteen in a row (making it fifty-two holes in a row without missing a green) before his wedge approach to the par-five seventeenth landed on the green, only to spin back into the creek, bringing a disastrous double-bogey, double-bogey finish for a 73."

Hogan's post-round words, however, may have had a greater impact on Nicklaus's future than he realized at the moment. Speaking to writers in the locker room, Hogan conceded, "I guess they'll say I lost it [two closing pars would have tied him with Palmer] . . . but I'll tell you something. I played thirty-six holes today with a kid who should have won this Open by ten shots if I had been thinking for him."

The six inches between Jack's ears that kept him from becoming only the sixth amateur in history to win the championship certainly gained invaluable knowledge from Hogan's comments, however. On the other hand, Nicklaus's response much later to Ben's remark was equally telling. Said Jack, "I played with a great man today who would have won the Open [his record fifth] if I had been putting for him."

Defining moments in a career replete with defining moments? You bet. There aren't enough pages in any book to recount all of the magical defining moments that molded Jack Nicklaus into the greatest the game has ever known. But for starters, try these:

- "Ouch"—Larry Glosser's constant yanks that forever taught Jack to keep his head still.
- A memorable first meeting with Bobby Jones in James River, Virginia, that would start a friendship that lasted until Jones's death.
- The stern admonition from his beloved dad, Charlie, "If you ever throw a club again, your golf days are over," after the one and only time "Jackie-boy" threw a club when they were having a friendly round at Scioto in Nicklaus's formative years.
- Watching and wondering in awe who that guy with the blacksmith arms was hammering quail-high shots on the practice range at Sylvania Country Club—fourteen-year-old Jack's first glimpse of Palmer at the 1954 Ohio Open, preparing to defend his title.

- His first confrontation with Snead in 1956, losing an exhibition 68–72 but leading to his victory in the Ohio Open.
- Jack's remarkable thirty-sixth-hole victory at the Broadmoor in Colorado Springs over all-time amateur standout Charlie Coe for his first of two U.S. Amateur titles, which for the first time brought Nicklaus to the attention of the entire world of golf.
- The marvelous pair-mix with Hogan at Cherry Hills when he finished second to Palmer in the 1960 U.S. Open.
- Jack's play-off victory over Palmer at Oakmont in 1962, when he won the first of his four U.S. Opens, in his first professional year, an event where he had but one three-putt green in ninety holes, on the most treacherous greens in golf.
- Missing the cut in defense of his title at the 1963 U.S. Open in Brookline, Massachusetts, where Nicklaus won a more important battle with the media—an episode to be visited later.
- Certainly not to forget Jack's last, stunning major bow at Augusta in 1986—"my most memorable victory"—when he captured a record sixth Masters at age forty-six with a closing round of 65 that included a 30 on the back nine.

Brookline 1963, strangely, was a huge victory for young Nicklaus. His triumph over Arnie the year before not only was unpopular; it brought derisive shouts from Arnie's Army calling Jack "Ohio Fats" and "Old Blobbo" and making other unflattering remarks. Nicklaus, who had obviously benefited from his experience with Hogan, claimed to be impervious to the catcalls, even if Dad Charlie was not. Arnie's Army and other fans continued to bedevil Jack at the Masters, if not directly against him, cheering lustily when a bogey was registered after his name on the course leader boards.

Nicklaus, chubby to say the least, stoically marching the fairways with imperturbable focus and dressed about as colorfully as a deckhand, was not widely embraced by the eastern press corps in those days either. And while wife Barbara, who would become Golf's All-Time First Lady, eventually took charge of Jack's diet and dress code, charming the powerful eastern media that was forever enamored with Palmer was another war to win.

Shooting 76-77 and missing the cut at Brookline did not dazzle the media, but Jack's appearances in the pressroom certainly did. This would herald the beginning of one of the great relationships between athlete and sportswriter in history.

Asked to the interview area after his opening 77, Nicklaus was non-plussed and wondered aloud, "Why in the world do you want to talk to a guy who shot 77?" After being told it was because he was the defending champion, he obliged. Did he ever—Jack talked to the media for an hour and left most of them scratching their heads instead of notepads. Jack was even more astounded when he was asked into the interview after his second-round 76 that would have him packing and this time answered question after question patiently, frankly, and pleasantly for an hour and fifteen minutes.

That did it. Crusty, hard-bitten eastern writers like Joe Looney, Lincoln Werden, Dana Mozley, Al Laney, Pat Ward-Thomas, and many others came out of the pressroom with lavish words of praise, saying things like (from my notebook) "the kid's amazing, shoots himself in the foot and talks up a storm" . . . "boy, did we misjudge him" . . . "what a great interview—he just kept talking and talking and made all kinds of sense." Ad nauseam.

That Jack in later life would acquire the nickname of Carnac the Munificent—slapped on him mostly by close friends—is understandable because over the years Nicklaus has emerged as the very best interview in all of golf, if not sports. Never does he decline an invitation to come to the media interview room. Never is he without an opinion; never ducks an issue. Better yet, he developed a most uncanny knack for remembering the names of virtually every member of the press corps. And his eternal willingness and remarkable endurance in signing autographs for fans outdoes even Palmer and Chi Chi Rodriguez.

It's easy to smile, be gracious and patient when you win, particularly as often as Nicklaus. But one of Jack's most endearing attributes is the way he handles setbacks. If he is the greatest winner the game has known, he's also recognized as the most gracious golfer in defeat, a man without an alibi, an unparalleled sportsman. Nothing illustrates this better than the 1977 Masters, when Tom Watson beat him and Jack said, "Tom played great and deserved to win." A writer asked Jack if losing was a disaster, to which Jack replied, "It is when it's a lovely spring day and you don't have anything else planned."

Not that Nicklaus doesn't take defeat to heart. "I do not like to lose; it's as simple as that. It is definitely my plan to win every time I tee it up," he has said. "Pride probably is my greatest motivation. The only thing that embarrasses me is not giving 100 percent."

Ask him his biggest losses and Nicklaus never would single out a golf defeat. Not the U.S. Open at Pebble Beach when Watson pitched from the rutabagas and into the cup for birdie on the seventy-first hole to thwart him in 1982. Not the 1972 British Open at Muirfield when Lee Trevino holed out a "flier" from a bunker, then chipped in on the seventy-first hole to turn a sure bogey into a par to beat him by a stroke. Jack congratulated Lee, told him he was a great champion, then added with a wink," Why don't you go back to Mexico? You've done this too many times." After laughs subsided, Lee in all seriousness told Jack how sorry he felt for him.

Ironically, the toughest moments in Jack's private life also came when he was on golf courses. His beloved dad, Charlie, who introduced him to the game, died at age fifty-six in 1970 when Jack was on the first tee of the Doral Open. His mother, Helen, died in August of 2000 when Jack was playing a PGA practice round at Valhalla. And his mentor, Jack Grout, died in May 1989 when Jack was on the first tee at his Memorial Tournament in Dublin, Ohio.

Jack underscored just how much Charlie meant to him at the 2001 Memorial when he was asked what tournament he most wished his father could have seen him play. "This one," Jack said somberly, "because then I'd have had him with me thirty more years." When his mother died, he played on in his final PGA Championship, "because she made me promise I would if she should ever die while I was in a tournament."

Nicklaus's deportment throughout his illustrious career has been incredible, so positive in every respect that it should be a model for all professional athletes. Blessed with great health and the most remarkable wife in all of sport, he has been able to balance a great golf career with a splendid family life and a sometimes too vast expansion into the business world.

Jack Nicklaus insists he does not look backward at the game: "I never reflect." Still, his steel-trap mind can recount virtually every shot of every important round of golf he has played from the thirty-six-hole U.S. Amateur final victory in 1959 over Charlie Coe to the 66-67-68-68, 269 at Merion in the 1960 World Amateur, which was eighteen shots under what Hogan needed when winning his second U.S. Open on the same course in 1950. And you know he can give you tee to tin cup on his incredible final major win in the 1986 Masters when he was a wavering forty-six. If you really want to test him, let him run through the play-off eighteen with Palmer or the earlier 72 he played winning that initial major at Oakmont forty years ago. Jack's words resound at every invitation or inquisition since the earliest days and are rarely tainted with foot-in-mouth. For instance:

- "Barbara [mother of Jack's five great kids, who watched him play Pine Valley and Merion on their 1960 honeymoon] is worth at least fifteen of my majors."
- "The U.S. Open to me is a complete examination of a golfer. The competition, what it does to you inside, how hard it is to work at it, how hard it is to make it happen. I enjoy the punishment. I suppose I must be a masochist of some kind, but I enjoy that."
- "I never made many long putts, but then I never missed very many short ones."

And so much more . . .

It's the words of others, who forever knew Nicklaus had a fire in his belly like no other and thrived on the challenges, that also ring the bell:

Tom Watson: *"I always felt Jack Nicklaus was the best player ever; but I always felt I could beat him."*

Nick Price: *"Jack's the greatest player ever to play the game, and I have the greatest respect for him because he's the first guy who ever treated me like an equal."*

Gene Sarazen: *"Nicklaus is the greatest tournament player we have ever had . . . the longest hitter under pressure and a fighter to the last putt. We never had anyone like him in my era."*

Lee Trevino: *"Nicklaus flat out is the best to ever play the game."*

Tony Jacklin: *"Jack is a sportsman for all time."* This after Nicklaus picked up Tony's ball on the eighteenth green at Royal Birkdale in 1969, conceding Tony's two-foot putt and bringing about the first tie in the forty-two-year history of the Ryder Cup. Nicklaus told Tony, *"I don't think you would have missed the putt, but under these circumstances, I would never give you the opportunity."*

Perhaps it all goes back to dad Charlie, who drilled respect into Jack's head all the early years he escorted him around the junior and amateur wars. "Dad always told me, 'When a guy beats you, you better give him a firm grip and a big smile and make him think he deserved to beat you. All you can do is your best, and if you've given it away, you can kick yourself afterwards. But be genuine."

There isn't a soul in the world of golf who'd ever deny Jack Nicklaus was and still is the absolutely genuine article.

JACK NICKLAUS

	Total New Money	Wins	Top10s	Top25s
Majors	$ 37,844,140	18	70	91
Other Official Tournaments (and International Wins)	90,210,828	68	252	337
TOTALS	$128,054,968	86	322	428

MAJOR CHAMPIONSHIPS

	New Money	Wins
Masters	$11,017,207	6
U.S. Open	7,618,651	4
British Open	9,906,731	3
PGA	9,301,551	5

BEST OTHER EVENTS

	New Money	Wins
Doral	$6,567,012	2
World Series of Golf	6,167,018	5
Tournament of Champions	5,236,800	5
Pebble Beach	4,489,610	3

Year	New Money	Total Wins	Top10s	Top25s	Majors	Other Events
1962	$6,627,905	4	17	23	$1,420,920	$5,206,985
1963	8,060,661	7	20	24	2,408,852	5,651,809
1964	8,119,136	6	20	28	1,664,689	6,454,447
1965	7,107,907	5	19	21	1,582,861	5,525,046
1966	5,645,179	3	13	18	2,541,106	3,104,073
1967	7,759,400	6	17	18	1,951,080	5,808,320
1968	5,219,363	3	15	21	1,319,266	3,900,097
1969	4,076,426	3	12	18	421,619	3,654,807
1970	5,804,094	4	14	18	1,470,865	4,333,229
1971	6,569,490	7	18	18	2,304,830	4,264,660
1972	8,094,150	7	15	17	2,750,080	5,344,070
1973	7,262,175	7	17	18	1,816,957	5,445,218
1974	4,900,922	2	13	18	1,363,673	3,537,249
1975	6,792,304	6	16	18	2,486,577	4,305,727
1976	5,032,846	3	13	17	1,182,037	3,850,809
1977	5,503,674	3	15	17	1,723,780	3,779,894
1978	5,547,308	5	12	14	1,445,104	4,102,204
1979	1,358,323	0	5	7	927,123	431,200
1980	3,148,707	2	4	9	2,274,436	874,271
1981	2,279,544	0	8	14	888,709	1,390,835
1982	3,134,376	1	8	12	875,665	2,258,711
1983	2,450,779	0	8	11	594,000	1,856,779
1984	2,578,427	1	6	12	181,786	2,396,641
1985	1,391,150	0	4	8	181,300	1,209,850
1986	1,621,451	1	4	7	1,228,703	392,748
1987	341,590	0	1	5	209,848	131,743
1988	148,113	0	0	3	110,916	37,197
1989	319,160	0	2	4	70,560	248,600
1990	203,676	0	1	2	201,600	2,076
1991	388,950	0	1	4	50,600	338,350
1993	104,183	0	1	1	0	104,183
1995	134,000	0	1	1	0	134,000
1997	135,000	0	1	1	0	135,000
1998	194,600	0	1	1	194,600	0

Lee Trevino

Marino Parascenzo

Tony Jacklin, the consummate British gentleman-golfer, was about to tee it up against Lee Trevino in the World Match Play in England. The money was good, the wind favorable, the gallery agreeable, and the breakfast substantial. All Jacklin wanted now was a little peace and quiet.

"Lee," he said, "is it all right if we don't talk today?"

"Sure, Tony," Trevino said. "You don't have to talk. Just listen."

This was 1972, a point made to illustrate that at the time Trevino had been at the top rung of the game for about four years. He had entered talking, he continued talking throughout his career, and to this day he talks and then some.

Poor "Jacko." It was neighborly of him to make the request. But if he wanted Trevino to be quiet, all he had to do was ask him about hustling. That stops him in his tracks.

Call Trevino anything, but don't call him a hustler.

This is not a chapter out of some morality play. It is simply a view into a man, as he sees and perceives himself. The man is Lee Trevino, one of the most remarkable people ever in the history of sport, much less of golf. Trevino will be remembered for one of the greatest careers in golf history. People don't start any lower at anything.

Arnold Palmer had to carry water for his mom to wash clothes and dishes. Gary Player was facing life down in a gold mine, like his dad. Well, Chi Chi Rodriguez and Carlos Franco had it bad. Chi Chi licked his milk off a fork to make it last. Franco came from humble-nothing in darkest Paraguay. But Trevino came out of poverty in Dallas, Texas, United States of America—a dirt-floor, no-electricity, no-running-water, no-anything poverty. "My family was so poor," he once said, "when somebody threw our dog a bone, he had to call for a fair catch."

He never knew his father. He worked the Texas cotton fields as a kid, in the heat and the dust. He caddied when he grew big enough to wrestle the bag, about age eight. He never got to the eighth grade. He learned his golf from himself, digging it out of the dirt, like Ben Hogan. He made a fortune and lost it—or was relieved of it—and made a comeback.

In his twenty-two years on the PGA Tour, including time off after being hit by lightning and suffering a bad back, and with a swing generously described as unorthodox, he won twenty-seven times, including two each of the U.S. Open, the British Open, and the PGA Championship. (The Masters is its own story.) He entered the 2003 season looking for his thirtieth win on the Senior PGA Tour. Wisecracking all the way.

This is the short version: Trevino will be remembered as the Tex-Mex urchin out of the Dallas gutters who saved himself and conquered the world with wit and wood shots. Trevino also will also be remembered as a world-class talker.

Golf is a solemn procession at best. Not for Trevino. He chatters with anyone about anything—the bouquet and volume of the local wine, a hot-dog shop, last night's ball game, the British idea of cuisine, Arnie Palmer, the graphite shaft.

Perhaps most of all, Trevino will be remembered as the rascal who spent his early years hustling unsuspecting souls on the golf course. At which assertion Trevino might be very happy to hand you your head.

That's the story of Lee Trevino as hustler. "The Portrait of the Golfer as a Young Dog." Or how Lee Trevino once got stuck in the first bathtub in the White House.

That's an exaggeration. But that's OK. Lee Trevino is an exaggeration.

Someone once noted that whatever gets into print passes into history. And it's an article of faith for advertising folk, propagandists, and the like that a story told with conviction becomes the truth, true or not. Which brings us to "Trevino and the White House bathtub."

In 1917, H. L. Mencken, a newspaper columnist famed for his acidic wit, wrote about the first bathtub in the White House. He described it in detail. He said it had been installed by President Millard Fillmore. It turned out that Mencken was just having a little fun. The piece was a total fabrication. When he realized that people believed the thing, he was appalled at their gullibility. "They swallowed it as gospel, gravely and horribly," Mencken noted. He wrote a retraction, trying to stop the spread of the fiction. It didn't take. The tale became fact. It even showed up in an encyclopedia or two. Chances are that Trevino never took a bath in the White House, but he did end up in that bathtub.

At the 1973 U.S. Open at Oakmont, a golf writer went to Trevino just before a practice round.

"Lee," he said, "I'd like to do a story on you that's never been written."

"Yeah?" Trevino said. "Like what?"

"Like," the writer said innocently, "your days as a hustler."

Trevino stiffened like the Marine he had once been. He clenched his jaw, like he was trying to crack a walnut with his teeth.

"Sir," Trevino said, "I have never been a hustler in my life." And he turned and tramped down the fairway. So much for the "Merry Mex."

There was the matter, however, of all those hustler stories. And then there was the Dr. Pepper bottle ploy. The same writer looked up Trevino a couple years later, at the 1975 Ryder Cup, and carefully reopened the subject, with the proviso that Trevino hear him out and not skull him with something. Trevino cackled. "I got that mad, huh?" he said. "But that's right—I've never been a hustler. It's just, you believed all them damn stories from sportswriters, that's what."

What it came down to was semantics. It may be semantics to some, but to Trevino it was a matter of honor. To some the word *hustler* means someone who works hard, who really keeps at it. To others a hustler is a cheater. Any decent dictionary will offer you the choice. Trevino knows hard work. Few have worked harder. But a hustler? In his mind, that's a cheater.

But how about playing guys with a big Dr Pepper bottle? He'd tape the neck, hit the ball like a fungo in baseball, and then putt with it. He'd play a par-three course and get a half-a-shot a hole. Wasn't that hustling?

"If I gave you that bet, do you think I could play with that bottle?" he asked.

Sure.

"Right," Trevino said. "But there was nothing hidden. It was just a crazy bet."

Trevino frequented other courses and did plenty of gambling, but he is best known for playing at Tenison Park, a municipal course in Dallas. "Hustle-heaven," some used to call it. It was home to the notorious "Titanic" Thompson, who was always inventing ways to pluck a pigeon. For example, betting $5 he could throw a peanut over the clubhouse. There's no way to throw a peanut over a clubhouse. Unless the shell's been emptied and filled with lead!

It's easy to see how Trevino, hanging out at Tenison, could get painted with the same brush. Thompson would beat a guy right-handed, then offer to play him left-handed, to let him get his money back. Thompson was a natural left-hander. "But I made him once, for $5—left-handed," Trevino said. "We were playing along, and we came to the last hole, and I said, 'Five dollars says I can beat you left-handed on this hole,' and he says, 'You got it.' I hit his driver and his nine-iron, and I made five and beat him. He said: 'You know what? You're a goddamn freak, that's what. . . .' "

Trevino got Seve Ballesteros once, only they didn't have a bet down. They were playing a TV exhibition in Scotland, and of course Ballesteros was outdriving Trevino all day. Then they came to the hole Trevino had been waiting for. Trevino dug at him. "OK, Seve, I've been letting you outdrive me all day," Trevino said. "Now take your best shot, and I'm going to outdrive you."

Ballesteros would silence the chattering Tex-Mex. He bombed a drive. He turned to Trevino and grinned. Try that. Trevino, who needed about a drive and a wedge to match Ballesteros, squinted down-range, then smashed one fifty, sixty yards past him. Ballesteros was silently beside himself. The TV crew was awestruck. "Seve didn't know it," Trevino said, "but on that hole the fairway slopes away over there. You catch the slope just right, the ball will roll forever."

So it's this simple: To Trevino, a gambler gambles, a hustler cheats. And he doesn't cheat. A short course in hustling: "You lie about your handicap," Trevino said. "If you're a five, you say you're a ten. I never lied about my handicap. I never established one. I'd say I don't have one. I'm scratch.

"You put Vaseline on your club faces. Takes the spin off the ball. And in the old days, when the smaller British ball was legal, guys would sneak it in on you. Easier to play. Then there's protective coloration. Some hustlers carefully rubbed cornstarch on their hands and face. With a golfer's tan a guy can hardly say he hasn't played in a month."

So Trevino spoke his piece. And then somewhere, maybe fifty years from now, some encyclopedia entry will start out, "Lee Trevino, who started his career as a hustler from Dallas. . . ."

Lee Trevino has had his share of tests. The first was just being born. Then there was the lightning—almost getting killed. Also seeing his fortune disappear in the dust of a New Mexico real estate adventure. And the crippling bad back, having to hang upside down . . .

The lightning hit at the 1975 Western Open. Trevino and Jerry Heard were waiting out a rain delay at the thirteenth green, near a lake. Trevino was sitting against his bag. He remembered a stupendous crack and being lifted off the ground. Then his ears ringing, his hands jerking, and not being able to breathe.

Trevino figured the lightning had skipped off the lake, then gone through the steel club shafts in his bag and up his back. He also figured he nearly died. He remembers the emergency room doctor practically apologizing for having almost no experience with lightning victims. "They normally go straight to the morgue," she explained. Later Trevino would say, "In case of lightning, walk down the middle of the fairway and hold your one-iron over your head. Because even God can't hit a one-iron." Or: "When God wants to play through, you let Him." That's deathbed humor. Trevino doesn't laugh at lightning.

Take, for instance, the time he was at Firestone, at the ninth tee. Lightning suddenly crackled in the distance. Trevino broke from a standing start and didn't stop running till he danced up the veranda steps at the clubhouse, spikes and all, and bolted through the glass door and into the grillroom. Firestone's ninth is a par four, about 470 yards. "You think Carl Lewis is fast?" Trevino cracked. "Lightning comes around, and he's gonna eat some dust."

The lightning left him with a damaged back that kept him from one of his true loves—hitting balls. He used to hit maybe five hundred a day. He escaped with his life, but there was the matter of his game turning to mush. "I'm retired from practicing," he'd crack. The doctor limited him to twenty-five, thirty warm-up balls before a round and maybe fifteen minutes of putting. If he pushed either one, his back would go into spasms. Part of his regimen was to hang upside down on the motel room door, in some kind of harness.

By the summer of 1982 he required more back surgery. It may have saved his career. "If I had to play in pain again, I would have retired this year," he said at the time.

"The pain was constant from May of 1981 until now. It took me two hours each morning before I could tie my shoes. I couldn't practice. I couldn't really play. All I could do was crawl off the golf course each day and go lie down."

Yet always the wisecracks. He told the British Open press corps once that the doctor told him not to practice. "I told him I had to," Trevino said. "And he said, 'How long you been playing golf?' And I told him, since I was a kid. And he said, 'Hell, you don't know how to do it yet?' " Trevino had more surgery and emerged triumphant. "Hell, I'm playing better than ever," he said, "now that I'm not allowed to lift anything heavier'n a can of beer."

He got a scare in March 2001, at the Senior Tour's Siebel Classic. He was among the leaders in the second round. At the thirteenth tee he was at the top of his backswing when his back went into spasm, dropping him to his knees. He had to withdraw. But he came back to play. Not only play, but make the most valuable single golf shot in history. In the ESPN Par-3 Shootout, a made-for-TV exercise with Phil Mickelson, Paul Azinger, and Raymond Floyd in the field, he canned a seven-iron for a hole in one worth $1 million dollars. He got an additional $10,000 for being closest to the pin. "That was my first spasm since the doctor straightened me out in 1982," Trevino said.

"Yeah, it was scary at first. I thought, oh, no. Then I thought maybe it was a kidney stone. I'd gone through that before. It turned out I had put on too much weight and I was laboring on my backswing, putting strain on my muscles getting the club back." The episode passed; Trevino took off the weight and went back to work.

Trevino arrived in golf at just the right time. There must have been a script somewhere. The game already had larger-than-life figures in the late 1960s. Jack Nicklaus and Arnie Palmer. Billy Casper and his buffalo diet. Doug Sanders and his renegade wardrobe. And Gary Player, totally improbable for his size.

And if Player was improbable, then Trevino was impossible. Not only poor, but a graduate of a driving range, handyman at a daily-fee dust track in West Texas, and a guy with a swing better suited to hitting a running cat in the behind with a mop. In a game that worships silence, here was a bright stream of happy talk and one-liners. And also a guy with a reputation for plucking pigeons.

Trevino first came to national attention at the 1967 U.S. Open at Baltusrol, in New Jersey. It was his first trip east of the Mississippi. He couldn't afford a rental car, so he had to walk to dinner along the road and got splashed by cars. He had to do Chinese most of the week. He didn't own a jacket or suit, and in this strange new world he found himself barred from the restaurants he could easily reach.

He was just three shots off the lead going into the final round, right behind Nicklaus, Palmer, and Casper. The U.S. Open is famous for no-names popping up, but they're usually up there only in the first round, maybe the second. They don't dare stay up there through the third, not once they realize where they are. But Trevino had the golf world wondering, Who is this guy?

He even made it to the leader board early on the back nine in the fourth round. Then he shook a little, shot a 70 for a 283 total, and finished eight strokes behind Nicklaus. Trevino won $6,000. He was stunned. It was more money than he'd ever had in his life. And now he knew he could play. He had wanted to join the PGA Tour. Now he had to.

It went from amazing to incredible in just one twelve-month cycle. Trevino won the Open the following year, 1968, at Oak Hill. It was his first victory on the Tour. The irrepressible Tex-Mex from Dallas was beginning to make the impossible look easy while stamping that oddball swing on the psyche of a nation increasingly fascinated by golf.

He won the U.S. Open again in 1971, at Merion, beating Nicklaus in a play-off. There he got tagged with the hustler thing again. The papers would say that he had tried to gain the edge by scaring Nicklaus with a rubber snake. Trevino and Nicklaus had tied and went to an eighteen-hole play-off the next day.

At the first tee Trevino, rummaging around in his bag for a fresh glove, found a rubber snake he had bought for his daughter and had left in the pocket. He held it up to the gallery for a gag, and everybody laughed. Nicklaus chuckled and asked Trevino to toss it over and let him see it. Trevino flipped it to him. Trevino went on to shoot 68 and beat Nicklaus by three. Some writers wrote that the snake was a psych job. Some still do.

In 1959, when Trevino was in the Marines and stationed on Okinawa, he played a match with a Taiwanese named Lu Liang Huan—none other than Mr. Lu, a little guy in a funny little hat. Mr. Lu whipped him, ten and eight. They next met in the 1971 British Open at Royal Birkdale. Mr. Lu was best known for wearing a silly little hat the Brits called a trilby and politely lifting it at every opportunity. He also was known as the guy who almost won the British Open. Trevino led him by five with only nine holes to play. He won by just one shot.

Trevino won the British Open again the next year, 1972, this time by beating Nicklaus by one, thereby killing Jack's chance for the Grand Slam. Nicklaus arrived at Scotland's Muirfield having won the Masters and the U.S. Open. This was Trevino the Jack-Killer.

They say no one remembers who finishes second. But Nicklaus can't forget—second in the 1968 U.S. Open by four shots, second in the '71 U.S. Open in a play-off, second in the '72 British Open by one, and second in the '74 PGA by one. Put this another way: Trevino has one of the greatest records in golf. He's won six majors, four of them over Nicklaus. Tom Watson is the only player close to him. Nicklaus has also been second to Watson four times but in eight majors.

"There's no mystery to it," Trevino said. "There was nothing psychological about it. There was no gamesmanship. I kept it in the fairway is all. I don't care if a guy hits it forty yards longer—if he's in the woods, I'm gonna win that hole. If you hit every fairway, eventually you're gonna beat a guy."

But a Grand Slam over Nicklaus or anyone else was out of the question. Trevino could not win the Masters. Sometimes he wouldn't even play in it, and when he did, he'd avoid the stately old mansion of a clubhouse and change his shoes in the parking lot, coming and going. Some said this showed that Trevino, who had been in many exclusive golf clubs, was a little Tex-Mex kid who felt he'd got too far north of the border at stately and imperial old Augusta. Or that he was mad at Augusta National. Nonsense, Trevino has said many times. But the golf world has never been completely convinced.

Trevino insisted it was simply the course itself that was unsuited to his game. He hit a low ball, left to right. Augusta National favors a high ball, left to right. Then completely without rough, Augusta also favored the long ball hitters. They didn't have to restrain themselves. Trevino was always moderately short, never long-long. His strength was deadly accuracy. Trevino also confessed at Augusta he'd talked too much. He has told the story often, of how talking to Charlie Sifford way back he'd said he had no chance to win at Augusta and so he probably wouldn't go back. Overheard by a reporter, who wrote the story, it became simply a matter of pride.

"I should have just swallowed pride and gone on and played," Trevino said in his book *They Call Me Super Mex.* "But I felt everyone was wondering if I was as good as my word. . . ." And so he passed up the Masters in 1970 and '71. "That was the greatest mistake I've made in my career," he said.

Then there were other issues. In 1986 he objected to having to pay $90 for a badge for his son, Richard. It wasn't the money, he said. It was the principle of not allowing family in. And so it went. God knows what the real answer is. Maybe the contradiction is Trevino himself, in a world that hardly understood him. It certainly became confusing. Indeed, it still is.

At the 1988 Masters, Trevino uttered the ultimate rejection. "I hope to God they don't send me an invitation," he said. "I'm going to pray they don't. I don't want to be here." In 1989, at about age fifty, he was in the final year of exemptions into the Masters. He received what was likely to be his final Masters invitation. He was among the first to accept.

Some critics insist that there's a dark side to Trevino. They say that what you see isn't really what you get. They say on the golf course he's the Merry Mex, yakking and laughing. Off the course he's a brush-off artist and a loner. His defenders—if he needs them—argue that nobody ever suggested that the two are mutually exclusive in anybody. Early in his career he'd pull practically all-nighters—golf all day, party far into the night. Soon enough he saw where that road was headed. Then at restaurants the autograph hounds made life miserable and put dinner out of the question. So he began leaving the course and holing up in his hotel, taking room service, watching TV, putting on the rug. Maybe it's not a dark side. Maybe just a private side. Who doesn't have one of those?

Trevino has an easy answer to all this.

"Once I'm off the stage, I'm totally a hermit," he's said.

Sixty-three during the 2003 season, Trevino will leave golf with a number of legacies. The first is simple: just because you're not born with a silver spoon in your mouth doesn't mean you're going to steal one. And an effervescence that is as serious as it is funny. Another is that talent and ambition can do wonders, but only if mixed with hard work. And then there's the old standby: the indomitable spirit. It got him there, and he intends to stay. "I'm never going to quit," Trevino said. And pity the slings and arrows that try to touch him. "How can they beat me?" he once quipped. "I've been struck by lightning, had two back operations, and been divorced twice."

LEE TREVINO

	Total New Money	Wins	Top10s	Top25s
Majors	$12,149,585	6	22	45
Other Official Tournaments (and International Wins)	53,693,973	29	166	278
TOTALS	$65,843,558	35	188	323

MAJOR CHAMPIONSHIPS

	New Money	Wins
Masters	$ 733,872	0
U.S. Open	3,458,304	2
British Open	4,356,193	2
PGA	3,601,216	2

BEST OTHER EVENTS

	New Money	Wins
Memphis	$3,333,460	3
Canadian Open	3,120,567	3
Tournament of Champions	3,018,200	1
Colonial	2,866,189	2

Year	New Money	Total Wins	Top10s	Top25s	Majors	Other Events
1967	$ 738,208	0	4	8	$ 211,154	$ 527,054
1968	4,107,630	2	12	21	1,052,800	3,054,830
1969	3,775,530	1	13	22	67,872	3,707,658
1970	4,193,064	2	13	21	501,649	3,691,415
1971	7,179,893	6	15	21	2,206,240	4,973,653
1972	6,091,727	4	14	20	1,474,105	4,617,622
1973	4,306,567	2	11	20	397,656	3,908,911
1974	5,253,663	3	14	20	990,000	4,263,663
1975	3,158,366	2	11	19	140,000	3,018,366
1976	2,499,921	1	8	14	0	2,499,921
1977	1,862,228	2	5	11	426,040	1,436,188
1978	4,462,905	2	13	20	380,690	4,082,215
1979	3,222,252	2	11	18	251,544	2,970,708
1980	5,941,793	3	16	19	922,003	5,019,790
1981	1,800,759	1	4	14	102,713	1,698,046
1982	376,526	0	1	6	0	376,526
1983	1,385,502	1	5	10	401,982	983,520
1984	2,419,990	1	6	10	1,198,559	1,221,431
1985	1,246,466	0	4	8	785,287	461,178
1986	770,948	0	3	8	352,565	418,383
1987	328,628	0	2	3	61,628	267,000
1988	131,560	0	1	3	0	131,560
1989	434,893	0	2	4	70,560	364,333
1990	94,316	0	0	2	94,316	0
1991	60,223	0	0	1	60,223	0

Gene Sarazen

Furman Bisher

He was the most engaging person I have ever known in golf. Born Eugenio Saraceni, son of a carpenter in Harrison, New York, his formal education ended in the sixth grade, but later the world would become his classroom. He carried his game to five continents, sometimes playing exhibitions, other times winning championships. He was the first to win what came to be known as the professional Grand Slam: the U.S. and British Opens, the PGA Championship, and, finally, in the most dramatic finish known to man, the Masters, in 1935.

He struck what is still generally regarded as the greatest shot in golf, the double eagle on the fifteenth hole at Augusta National, setting up a thirty-six-hole play-off the next day with the crestfallen Craig Wood, who had already been celebrated as the winner in the clubhouse. Sarazen won strolling.

He was an innovator. He created the sand wedge and became a master at bunker escape. Other than the ability to use it, he never profited from it. He was under contract to the Wilson Sporting Goods Company at the time, and the Wilson people considered it just a part of the deal. So did they when Sarazen recommended that Wilson sign an athletic young pro out of West Virginia, Sam Snead. Everything was company property.

His contract was for $8,000 a year, and at the age of ninety-two he signed a ten-year renewal at the same price. He never got a raise, though championships he won did gain him a bonus. At about the time of the renewal, Wilson signed John Daly to a contract for $5 million, an item that didn't escape Sarazen's attention. "The figure made me dizzy. I never really made any money with Wilson."

"I was looking down the list of players and the money they won on the Tour this year," he said at the time. "The player in 169th position earned more than I made playing tournaments in my whole lifetime."

He played the major championships, though they hadn't become known as "major" at the time, but he never played the professional tour, such as it was.

"I never played the Tour on a regular basis," he said. "There was nothing in it. I worked for a company that manufactured jet engines in World War II, then connected with Martin-Marietta for several years in public relations later on."

That was another of his gifts, his public appeal. Sarazen was good on his feet.

Farming was yet another of his interests. Yes, farming, which is how he came by the address of "Squire." He held one job as a club professional, a connection essential to other players who needed a guaranteed income to underwrite life on the Tour.

"It was at Fresh Meadow on Long Island," he said, "but it didn't last long. I'd just won the PGA Championship in 1932, and a banker friend wanted me to switch to a new club a friend of his had built nearby named Lakeville. So they made me a deal, and I moved.

"They had a big dinner celebrating my PGA Championship, and lots of entertainment stars were there—Bert Lahr, Eddie Cantor, people like that. At a closing ceremony the club president presented me a check. I looked at it, and there was nothing on it. I looked at him, and he looked at me and said, 'I'm sorry, but the club is in bad shape and we can't give you anything right now.'

"They never did. These actors thought the club should be honored to have them as members, and they never paid their bills. The club went broke, and I was never a club pro again."

He got his first taste of golf as a caddie at the Apawamis Club, near his home in Harrison, in the company of Ed Sullivan, who would later become a major television figure. One day, as their numbers were called out for bag duty, Sullivan seized the flashy bag on the rack and Sarazen picked up "one of those little canvas Saturday bags," whose owner turned out to be Grantland Rice, the famed sportswriter. Thus a longtime friendship was begun.

It was, coincidentally, that day that he heard Francis Ouimet, then a mere caddie, had won the U.S. Open at Brookline, defeating England's two greatest golfing figures in a play-off. Moreover, upon learning that Ouimet had used the interlocking grip, Sarazen adopted it and used it from that day to the last swing of his life.

He later landed his first job as an apprentice professional at Brooklawn Country Club in Fairfield, Connecticut, and it was there that Saraceni became Sarazen.

This was his story: "I had a hole in one one day, playing in a little tournament, and my name appeared in the local paper the next day," he said. "When I saw my name in print, I thought it looked like a violin player. I wanted something that sounded more like a golfer, so I became Gene Sarazen. My father didn't approve of it, but I told him I was still proud of my Italian heritage, and I still am."

When he passed away in 1999, buried by the side of his beloved wife, Mary, Sarazen had reached the age of ninety-seven. We reach a point here in trying to determine how one compresses the ninety-seven exciting years of Gene Sarazen into these few pages.

There was never a day I spent with him, and I spent many, that some new chapter in his life wasn't revealed. Such as the day he was haying in the field at his farm near Germantown, New York, and he saw a car coming down the road in a cloud of dust.

"It was Mary. She said some fellow named Herbert Warren Wind was calling from New York. He said the Shell Oil Company was interested in doing this golf show with me," he said.

"I drove into the city the next day"—Germantown is north of New York, near Poughkeepsie—"and we made a deal, $50,000 and expenses. I thought it was going to be for one year. It lasted for nine and led to a lot of other good connections. What a treat it was, working with Jimmy Demaret."

It became the most rewarding affiliation of his career. He made more money and was seen by more people—well, let him tell you: "It was the greatest thing that ever happened to me in golf. It made me known all over the world. More people saw me on one Shell show than saw me play golf in fifty years."

Reruns of the series are still on some sports channels, and testifying to its international appeal, "Shell's Wonderful World of Golf" has been resumed with fresh matches filmed of present-day players.

As a competitive player Sarazen exploded on the scene in 1922, a fresh kid just twenty years old. Grantland Rice described him as "a cocky twenty-year-old" when he won the U.S. Open at Skokie in 1922. Then, a month later, he won the PGA Championship at Oakmont, four and three winner over Emmett French in the final, and "the cocky kid" was on his way.

Down through the years Sarazen spoke of only one fellow professional for whom he had a deep-seated dislike, and it began that year of 1922. He had been paired with Long Jim Barnes, an Englishman from Cornwall who had migrated to America, at the Southern Open in New Orleans.

Sarazen went out in 32, Barnes in 38 and having a rough time of it. At the turn Sarazen made a gesture in an attempt to be friendly, but it didn't come off that way. "You'll do better coming in, Mr. Barnes," Gene said. "You'll probably get the 32 on this side." Barnes's cold response was, "Listen, kid, you just play your own game. I'll take care of mine."

The rift carried over to the week of the Open at Skokie, when Sarazen showed up looking to play a practice round one day. Seeing Francis Ouimet, Chick Evans, and Barnes lined up to go out as a threesome, he asked if he might join in. Ouimet and Evans welcomed him, but when they told Barnes they had a fourth, he said, "I wouldn't like that. I'd rather play a threesome."

It cut Sarazen deeply, and he never forgot it. Years later, though, when he and I were working on some elaborate tee markers on a new course at Marco Island, each named for a great player of his era, he did include Barnes in the group, and he is thus enshrined by Gene Sarazen himself.

The young Sarazen was a dapper fellow who dressed stylishly and oozed personality. He became united with plus-fours, known to most as "knickers," and was still identified with them until the last days of his life. He also had an eye for stylish women and once spoke of a lovely young lady he often saw waiting to catch the train into New York. He learned she was a dancer in the Ziegfeld Follies, but all attempts he made to get to know her were to no avail.

Many years later on the West Coast, a lovely woman of dowager age approached him and said, "Do you remember that girl you tried to pick up on the train into New York several years ago?"

When he said, he did, she said, "I'm that woman. I'm Dolores Hope, Bob Hope's wife." Gene Sarazen was not shy about telling the story on himself.

The love of his life, though, developed out of an approach that worked, during the winter of 1923 in Miami Beach. Sarazen noticed a pretty blond across the dining room one evening and asked the hostess if she might arrange an introduction.

"Be sure to tell her that I just won the U.S. Open Championship," he told her.

"You might add that I would be happy to autograph a golf ball for her."

Her name was Mary Henry, then attending the Miss Harris School for Young Ladies. She came to watch him play an exhibition at Miami Country Club, and they began a regular correspondence. After winning the PGA Championship, he proposed and they were married at Briarcliff Manor in June 1924. There were no children by the marriage but two by adoption, a boy and a girl, named Gene Jr. and Mary Anne.

Mary Sarazen began to take an interest in golf with serious intent, leading to another story the amused Sarazen likes to tell on himself. In 1934, as Mary's intensity for the game increased, Gene lost the Open to Olin Dutra at Merion Cricket Club. As she met him at the train in Pennsylvania Station, the depressed Sarazen was greeted by an exhilarated Mary.

"Gene, Gene," she cried as they met, "guess what I did yesterday? I shot an 84!"

A downcast Sarazen looked at Mary and said, "Do you know what I did yesterday? I lost the U.S. Open by a stroke, and it's more important to you that you shot an 84?"

One special ingredient came with the marriage. Gene had always felt a degree of insecurity in nongolfing company, and Mary was able to help fill the void in his educational life. She was quite intelligent and moved with ease in any class or function and soon added polish to Gene's conversational skills. Another of her special touches was learning to speak Italian and learning to cook Gene's favorites Italian dishes, which endeared her to Sarazen's parents.

"I married a walking encyclopedia and gradually completed an education that had stopped at the sixth grade," he said in his book *Thirty Years of Championship Golf,* co-authored with Herbert Warren Wind.

On the other hand, Sarazen educated himself in the field of agriculture. What he had taken up as an avocation became a serious matter of business.

Sarazen the golfer became Sarazen the farmer between playing appearances, hence the popular name "Squire."

They first held acreage in Connecticut, a dairy farm near Brookfield. It was later sold to Gabriel Heatter, the World War II newscaster. They bought another near Darien, later sold it, and went in search of another.

"I'll never forget driving up the road to that farm near Germantown," he said. "It was just what we wanted, and we bought it from the man on the spot. I think he manufactured neckties or something like that."

They lived there for twenty-three years, and to illustrate how serious a farmer he was, annually Gene and his hands produced twelve to fifteen thousand bushels of apples and fifteen tons of grapes and maintained a herd of beef cattle.

"I used to drive the tractor, but I wasn't much for manual labor," he said. "I had a fine farm manger, Al Marchisio, who looked after the place when I was off on my golf travels."

Occasional trips to the islands off the southwest coast of Florida led to the Sarazens' final location on Marco Island. Earlier in life, Sarazen had landed in Florida not as a celebrity, but as a worker in a brickyard at Sebring, earning $3 a day. That was to tide him over until the tournament season began, far back in 1919. After marriage to Mary, her interest in seashell collecting led them to Marco Island, and they bought a condominium there, migrating between a home they owned in New London, New Hampshire, with the change of seasons. They eventually settled permanently on Marco Island, and there Gene became a fixture. He still played an occasional round into the nineties and shot his age with regularity.

It was a casual meeting with another man of Italian extraction that led to a connection that capped off his career. Dr. Don Panoz, a capitalist of many ventures, had made his fortune in the pharmaceutical business. Panoz is a native of West Virginia who transferred his interests to Ireland, where he established the Elan Corporation, then later returned to the United States and created the wondrous resort facility, Chateau Elan, north of Atlanta. In the process he decided to construct a golf course called the Legends, honoring three of the game's great players, Gene Sarazen, Kathryn Whitworth, and Sam Snead.

Sarazen was the main contributor to the design of the course, then later, when Dr. Panoz went a step further, Sarazen became the central figure of a world-class tournament played there. It was called the Sarazen World

Open, inviting national Open champions from around the world. It was an attractive new tournament concept, with every open champion invited, from the British and the American to those from the tiniest nations on the globe. It raised golf to a new standard in many an area where it had been in a retarded state. Open champions came from such distant points as New Guinea, Slovenia, Vanuatu, Pakistan, and even the Russians initiated a national championship.

The Sarazen World Open was first played in 1994, won by Ernie Els of South Africa, a champion who gave the event definition. Such international champions as Frank Nobilo of New Zealand, who won it twice, and Mark Calcavecchia, onetime British Open winner; and Sarazen always there to present the trophy, his once robust frame diminished by age, but not his personality. When the World Tour brashly moved in, it ran roughshod over the Sarazen event, and though the European Tour picked it up for a year on a minor basis, it expired. There is no doubt that the Sarazen World Open added years to Gene's life, but once it was gone, soon was he. He passed away in May 2000, and he and Mary lie side by side in a cemetery on Marco Island.

While a cherished highlight of his life—he even once suggested a marker for the spot from which he struck the four-wood—-the historic double eagle at Augusta National sometimes became rankling. On an exhibition tour in the Orient, he was often referred to as "Mr. Double Eagle."

"You'd think that's all I'd ever done in golf," he said.

His harvest of major championships began in 1922, at barely twenty years of age. He won both the U.S. Open and the PGA Championship that year. He was the repeat PGA Championship winner the next year. He came close several times in the U.S. Open and PGA, and in 1928 lost the British Open to his friend and rival Walter Hagen, by two strokes. A long dry spell came after his early splurge of championships—oh, he won the Western Open (then a major) the Metropolitan Open, the Southern Open, Miami Four-Ball with Johnny Farrell, but the nowadays-majors eluded him until the breakthrough year of 1932. He finally won the British Open at Prince's in southern England, with the caddie Hagen had lent him, Skip Daniels, now sixty-five years old, on the bag. He had won the U.S. Open at Fresh Meadow earlier, and 1932 is remembered as a kind of resurrection year. He would win his third PGA Championship in 1933, and by this time Sarazen had become the dominating American professional, a status reaffirmed when he struck the shot that led to winning the Masters, completing the "major foursome" in 1936.

His most resounding shot in British Open championship play would not come until he reached the age of seventy. The year was 1973. He had been invited to Royal Troon on the fiftieth anniversary of his first Open there, not a pleasant memory.

Though he was the reigning U.S. Open and PGA Champion in 1923, he was still required to qualify. He was sent out early the first day, late the second day, and caught foul weather both times. To his death he felt that he had been the victim of jaundiced scheduling.

Some measure of revenge came with his return in '73, when he aced the renowned "Postage Stamp" hole the first round, then birdied it out of the bunker the second day, playing in the same pairing as Arnold Palmer. The King bogeyed and parred the hole those two days—a Sarazen three against a Palmer seven.

Knickers were as much a part of his personality as his swing, and throughout most of his life he kept and displayed a complete wardrobe of knickers supplied by a personal tailor on Fifth Avenue. His cheerful smile and engaging manner opened many doors, and he associated with royalty, nations' presidents, movie stars, corporate executives, songwriters, politicians, war heroes, and of course, the athletic greats of his day. But of all the people of his acquaintance, he would say later in life, the "finest man" he ever knew was Archie Wheeler, an elder member at the Brooklawn Club, who had shown confidence in and gave responsibility to Sarazen as a teenaged apprentice.

Mr. Gene lived the good life, he gave as well as he received, witnessed by a scholarship he established at Siena College in Loudon, New York, and the various charity events he involved himself in around Marco Island. No professional athlete ever commanded more respect.

GENE SARAZEN

	Total New Money	Wins	Top10s	Top25s
Majors	$17,842,980	7	42	61
Other Official Tournaments (and International Wins)	48,411,156	33	146	194
TOTALS	$66,254,136	40	188	255

MAJOR CHAMPIONSHIPS

	New Money	Wins
Masters	$2,231,740	1
U.S. Open	5,986,745	2
British Open	3,069,801	1
PGA	6,554,694	3

BEST OTHER EVENTS

	New Money	Wins
Miami Open	$4,653,480	5
Florida West Coast Open	2,971,125	3
Metropolitan Open	2,617,092	1
Long Island Open	2,447,200	2

Year	New Money	Total Wins	Top10s	Top25s	Majors	Other Events
1920	$ 204,650	0	1	2	$ 0	$ 204,650
1921	593,508	0	3	4	295,708	297,800
1922	5,249,600	3	12	14	1,990,000	3,259,600
1923	2,104,831	2	7	9	1,095,551	1,009,280
1924	1,131,971	0	4	8	217,071	914,900
1925	1,571,168	1	3	5	372,368	1,198,800
1926	3,621,797	1	11	13	480,837	3,140,960
1927	4,023,454	4	9	11	567,354	3,456,100
1928	5,083,975	5	12	14	1,123,595	3,960,380
1929	4,401,614	2	14	16	822,889	3,578,725
1930	7,858,862	7	17	17	594,000	7,264,862
1931	4,798,929	3	14	15	902,163	3,896,766
1932	5,271,440	4	11	11	2,106,140	3,165,300
1933	2,047,875	1	7	7	1,316,575	731,300
1934	1,156,800	0	4	7	764,950	391,850
1935	3,211,787	4	8	12	1,226,267	1,985,520
1936	1,924,653	0	9	9	602,028	1,322,625
1937	2,491,806	2	7	11	249,606	2,242,200
1938	2,014,236	1	5	10	436,649	1,577,587
1939	1,379,281	0	7	10	224,000	1,155,281
1940	1,597,252	0	6	9	843,427	753,825
1941	1,481,219	0	7	8	535,319	945,900
1942	269,540	0	1	4	0	269,540
1943	36,480	0	0	1	0	36,480
1944	645,929	0	3	6	0	645,929
1945	693,397	0	2	4	54,897	638,500
1946	50,310	0	0	1	0	50,310
1947	167,163	0	1	2	123,063	44,100
1948	237,723	0	1	3	183,543	54,180
1949	87,075	0	0	1	0	87,075
1950	247,423	0	1	3	145,600	101,823
1951	178,097	0	0	2	178,097	0
1952	69,529	0	0	1	69,529	0
1953	29,007	0	0	1	0	29,007
1954	72,689	0	0	1	72,689	0
1955	54,897	0	0	1	54,897	0
1956	123,063	0	1	1	123,063	0
1958	71,109	0	0	1	71,109	0

Above and Beyond

Tiger Woods

Tom Auclair

With additional contributions by Jim Huber,
John Strawn, Jeff Rude, Jeff Shain, Lorne Rubenstein,
David Mackintosh, and Dick Mudry

Impressions of a Tiger—*David Mackintosh*

Arnold Palmer won his last PGA Tour title at age forty-three. Jack Nicklaus astonished the world when he won the Masters aged forty-six. Sam Snead was the world's rarest bird, capturing a PGA Tour event in his fifty-third year. Assuming competitive appetite and sound health, Tiger Woods has another twenty, maybe twenty-five, winning years ahead. Unless, of course, one of those life goals he's reticent to discuss is to depart center stage aged twenty-eight in the grand style of Bobby Jones.

My favorite measure of the heart-bumping joy the game of golf has provided millions over the past century is a close look at those background faces in the enthusiastic galleries great players have always attracted. In the oddest of ways, throughout the differing ages and differing fashions of the years, the intensity of their expressions remains constant, everlastingly frozen in the ecstasy of the moment.

Tiger Woods has given golf fans plenty of these thrilling moments during his brief professional career. By age twenty-seven he had already rewritten a huge section of the record book, but it is without doubt that special ability to produce spectacular seconds of palpable exhilaration that is his most impressive gift to golf's overall story.

Hogan's legacy is immortalized as a two-iron to the eighteenth green at Oakland Hills. A plaque marks the spot where Palmer's massive swipe from Royal Birkdale's deep rough won the 1961 Open. Watson's seventeenth-hole chip-in at Pebble Beach made more than one photographer's fortune. Sarazen's Augusta double-eagle echoed around the world.

But Woods! Has there been a major championship in recent years—indeed has there been a single tournament—without some extraordinary feat? Sometimes it is pure awesome and unadulterated power, frequently an exquisitely struck ball, flighted so pure and true the golfing heart veritably soars. Occasionally it is one of these delicate little inventions that defies gravity, logic, or reason but finishes beside the flagpole, to the bewitchment and amazement of millions.

The most terrifying part for his rivals: Tiger is just beginning to discover there are no limits in golf. Ben Hogan used to dream of the perfect round with eighteen single putts. Tiger is as likely to do that as he is to shoot 58. Maybe next week . . . maybe any week! Without the slightest doubt Eldrich Woods is the most remarkable player of his time. Tiger's place in history is yet to come. All we can do right now is marvel on the sidelines, thankful to be part of it.

Unquenchable Thirst for History—*Jim Huber**

The warmth of the Kentucky summer day was grudgingly giving way to dusk. If you really squinted, you could make out the flags at the end of the driving range, and a mist was beginning to turn the green gray. Three men stood, silently, at the far left. Three more stood just as far to the right. Farther to the right, I was preparing to do a commentary for a half-hour show that would wrap up that day's third round of the PGA Championship. A cameraman and his sound technician were my only partners.

On the left, Tiger Woods continued a furious attempt at deflating every single range ball left in the Valhalla barrel. His coach, Butch Harmon, stood

---

****Jim Huber** is an essayist, commentator for Turner Sports, and author of *A Thousand Goodbyes: A Son's Reflection on Living, Dying and the Things That Matter Most.*

behind him. His caddy, Steve Williams, was to his left. Though he would take the overnight lead to Sunday, as he had at Pebble Beach and St. Andrews thirty and sixty days previous, he beat those golf balls as though he trailed by a dozen, as if seeking his first victory somehow, some way. When the remaining sunlight became too faint for any definition, my cameraman focused a light behind me on the tiny chipping green. With a light on me and another backlighting, we became a target.

Thump!

I could no longer see Tiger from my position, but I suddenly heard his intent. Because he couldn't see into the range itself, he had begun lobbing wedges over our heads onto the chipping green.

Thump! Thump!

It felt a bit like what my news colleagues must go through in a war zone, their camera lights attracting stray or intended incoming shots. Somehow I felt a bit more comfortable than they must but could not help shaking my head in amazement.

It was nearly 9:00 p.m., and yet here he remained, in the closing stages of arguably the greatest summer in the history of professional golf, still at work. When we extinguished our lights, our job finally done, Tiger and his men packed their bag and moved to the lighted putting green behind the range bleachers. More work to be done.

There were dozens chasing him into Sunday, that many with a chance to overtake him and finally derail this runaway train, and yet all of them were elsewhere, relaxing, their day long, long-ago done.

I don't know if Tiger Woods is the greatest golfer of all time. That remains for someone who has seen them all, to be able to somehow judge. Would they throw him a ticker-tape parade down Broadway in honor of a Grand Slam? They had their chance, in a convoluted way, and chose to save their tape. If, then, that is the criterion, it must be Jones instead. Has he won nineteen majors yet? Not by the kindest of counts, and so it must be Nicklaus. Has he won out of a hospital bed? It must be Hogan then. Has he won a hundred tournaments yet? It is surely Snead then. Who can say? Who would presume to put hickory against steel, pastures against landscapes, round rocks against two-piece darts? All I can say is that I have seen a work ethic that would certainly stand up against anyone who has ever challenged the game. Dark doesn't faze him, for he finds his light in the strangest of places.

We talk of the summer of '00 as some kind of magical mystery tour, but there was neither magic nor mystery involved. Well, perhaps a bit of magic when balls happen to bounce in the most provincial of ways . . . and perhaps a wee bit of mystery the next evening at Valhalla and a few weeks later from a Canadian bunker. But hard work makes both of those happen. Combine that with remarkable, God-given talent and an unquenchable thirst for history, and it would be very difficult to find anyone in the game's history any better.

Thunk!

Graceful Predator—*John Strawn**

Tiger Woods stalks the links with predatory grace. In India, where maneaters still lurk, the last man in the parade of villagers walking home from the fields at dusk wears a mask on the back of his head in hopes that the tiger, who pounces from the rear, will falter at the sight of the staring eyes, mistaking to for fro.

But no such subterfuge will work on the golf course, where Tiger attacks from the tee, from the rough, from the fairway, from the bunker, from the front and the side and the rear, from all imaginable realms. Prey species, the biologists say, will freeze in a kind of painless ecstasy in the clutches of a predator. Tiger's rivals, too, succumb to a superior force, but with the pained realization that nothing can protect them. Tiger's opponents have the look of refugees, the hopeless gaze of the displaced. Tiger's dominance has the force of nature.

Focused to a Trance—*Jeff Rude***

After decades of wondering if we'd ever see "a next Nicklaus," we now try to envision the improbability of someone coming along who is more talented than Tiger Woods. In the process of winning four consecutive major championships in 2000–2001, Woods proved himself as golf's most dominant player ever, something Jack Nicklaus himself implied.

*John Strawn is author of the bestseller *Driving the Green*.
**Jeff Rude is a senior writer for *Golfweek*.

It has come to this: Woods won five PGA Tour titles in 2001—something only one other man has done the last twenty-one years—and was considered by many to have had an off year, punctuated by so-called slumps at start and finish.

At his professional rate of winning 1.2 majors a year, this freakish blend of power and touch would win seventeen more Grand Slam titles by the time he turned forty in December 2015, giving him a total of twenty-three. And given he bagged five of six majors during a stretch in 1999–2001, that total might be low. Moreover, if he continues to win five tournaments annually, his total will hit ninety-nine by age forty.

In sum, his potential and attributes are scary. He's the longest and best driver among the game's elite, a major reason he has led the PGA Tour in par-five birdie percentage in each of his first five full seasons. In his three-major 2000 he had what might have been the best putting year ever. And in 2001 he not only won his third consecutive Vardon Trophy but led the Tour in scrambling, saving par 69.8 percent of the time he missed greens in regulation. Oh, and did we mention he's physically and mentally stronger than any of his contemporaries? If he were more focused, he'd be in a trance.

So what's he missing? Nothing, except more staggering numbers to be compiled over the next two decades.

Across All Barriers—*Jeff Shain**

Beyond his dominance inside the ropes, Tiger Woods redefined golf's status in the eye of the sports public. No longer the domain largely of rich white guys, galleries and TV audiences took on a younger, more diverse look.

"He's getting the nongolf world involved with golf. The game is cool to play," said Tom Watson, winner of eight major championships. At a time of declining TV sports viewership almost across the board, Woods's presence allowed golf to buck the trend. Ratings for PGA Tour telecasts rose 11 percent in 2000, when he won the year's final three majors, and 7 percent again the following season.

Jeff Shain is golf writer for the *Miami Herald*.

"A lot of people are watching golf that never watched the game before in their lives," said Charlie DeLucca, longtime director of Miami's Dade Amateur Golf Association.

Woods's charisma cut across age and racial barriers, granting him acceptance from both the country-club set and the hip-hop generation.

"There's no ring in his nose, no ring in his ear, no gold in his mouth," said Renny Roker, whose Teens on the Green minorities golf program went from three cities to twenty-eight in its first year. "He's an athlete that not only has pride and dignity, but ethics and a way about him."

Passing Every Test—*Lorne Rubenstein**

Tiger Woods is powerful. Tiger Woods can hit the ball miles. Tiger Woods holes putts seemingly at will. But the most impressive thing about Tiger Woods is that he has, so far anyway, come up with an excellence beyond excellence when that has been required. He looks forward to the supreme moments when a golfer is most tested, then passes the test. Surpasses it.

Think of this choice moment that occurred during the 2000 NEC Invitational at the Firestone Club in Akron, Ohio. Woods had a 256-yard shot on the par-five, 625-yard sixteenth hole. The hole is meant to play driver, lay-up second, and short iron in. Woods set up over the ball with an iron; a television announcer said that he was laying up short of the water in front of the green. But Woods ripped at a two-iron, nearly coming off his feet at the end. His shot soared over the water, the flag, and just over the green. Woods got up and down for birdie and went on to win by eleven shots.

More than any golfer, Woods conveys the possibility of creating a moment when he makes an unforgettable shot. It's so rewarding to watch Woods because of the tension that golf, a slow game, generates while one waits for what could be an explosive moment. By explosive one need not mean loud. Think of Woods at the back-of-the-island seventeenth green during the 2001 Players Championship in Sawgrass, Florida. This was during the third round, when Woods was trying to make a run at Jerry Kelly, then the leader. His tee shot nearly went into the water behind the green but settled. He had a sixty-footer.

*****Lorne Rubenstein** is a golf writer, TV broadcaster, and author of *A Season in Dornoch*.

Woods made his stroke. The ball crept down the fast green, picked up speed, took this break and that break, then fell into the hole. Woods, of course, won the tournament.

Or think of the six-iron that Woods hit from a fairway bunker on the last hole of the 2000 Canadian Open. He had some 216 yards to the hole, across a lake. He was a shot ahead of Grant Waite, with whom he was playing. Waite was on the green in two and looked certain of making a birdie. Woods, over the ball. Woods, taking the club back. Woods, maintaining his balance. Woods, coming through impact, the ball tearing away, high and easily over the water, and now, over the flag. He made birdie. He won the tournament. He'd created another memorable moment. There is a deep pleasure in watching Woods. It consists of watching him construct an edifice of memorable, timely shots. He has made so many. And, surely, he will make many more.

Inside the Ropes with Tiger—*Tom Auclair*

In 1995 seventy-nine year-old Bob Robertson went the Scottish Open at Carnoustie, where he's a long-standing member. Entering the clubhouse he noticed a young man sitting quietly at a table.

"I saw this wee lad, who I didn't even think was a golfer, sitting alone," recalled Robertson. "I didn't know why he was there. There are very few black people in Carnoustie, fewer still on the Scottish circuit," Robertson said. "I was surprised to see this youngish, boyish-looking person perhaps left alone, perhaps because of his color. Some people call me a compulsive talker, and I guess that's what led me to go over and offer to buy him a coffee." The young man declined the offer but gave Robertson a wide smile. The smile made a huge impact on Robertson. "He gave you the impression of being sort of a loner, but when he smiled, he changed completely."

At Royal Lytham and St. Annes, July 2001, Robertson was stunned by the similarity between that chance encounter six years earlier at Carnoustie and another young man, one about to collect his first major championship trophy, the Open Championship. "When he took off those glasses and his hat, smiled, and gave that speech, he changed completely," Robertson marveled, watching along with the world as David Duval shed his shades and opened his heart to the public. When Robertson introduced himself to that "wee dark laddie" a few years earlier, there was no way of telling he was speaking to someone who would become one of the greatest players the game has ever seen. He had no idea that player was Tiger Woods, he said, and even if he had, it wouldn't have made a scrap of difference.

"It was his first effort in our country, where very few people would have been conscious of his potential," Robertson reflected. It even took him a while to figure out that Tiger was actually a competitor in the Scottish Open. Now Robinson often chats with his grandchildren about his meeting Tiger that day, a story they enjoy. He also has a very strong opinion of the man Tiger has become. "I think he's a great player," he said. "I was saying to my wife, 'He carries himself very well. He's very sensible, not bigheaded. I like people who can take success and not show signs of being blown up by it. He appears to be what my wife, Mary, likes to call a gentleman and handles himself in a gentlemanly fashion."

The clubhouse where Robertson met Tiger has since been demolished. In a twist of irony, so has Tiger's anonymity.

In light of the superlatives that have been lavished on Eldrich "Tiger" Woods, it is sometimes difficult to comprehend what he has been able to accomplish by his midtwenties. The world has seen great athletes, but how many of these have totally dominated their respective sports as intensely as Woods? Cassius Clay was a talented boxer, but for a long time he was the only person to consider himself the greatest. Michael Jordan may have been destined for greatness at twenty-five but had a long journey still in front of him before realizing it. A goodly number of players have been labeled and promoted as destined for greatness. A much lesser few have ever realized it.

In a game dominated by history and tradition, Woods has lifted himself to a zone of rarefied air. His success has reached such enormous proportions that searching for the right words to properly describe his numerous victories has also become a daunting task. In 1930 Bobby Jones won a clean sweep of the four major championships—the U.S. and British Opens, the U.S. and British Amateurs—a clean sweep his biographer and friend, Grantland Rice, would later come to term uniquely the Impregnable Quadrilateral. In time this would be simplified to the Grand Slam. When Tiger won the 2001 Masters, becoming the only player ever to hold all four professional major championships at the same time, most agreed it wasn't the Grand Slam. It was, however, the grandest slam modern-day followers of the game have ever seen.

In May of 2001, Woods repeated as champion of the Memorial Tournament, his third consecutive win, an event close to the prestige of any major, at Jack Nicklaus's own course and his very own PGA Tour event. The "Golden Bear," just a year earlier dubbed the "Golfer of the Twentieth Century," had the highest praise for Woods. "Name anybody who isn't amazed by what he has accomplished," Nicklaus said after Tiger's latest conquest. "Week after week, he just keeps continuing and continuing to do more." Woods effectively clinched the title early in Sunday's final round with a majestic eagle-three, his perfectly judged 247-yard two-iron across a lake coming to rest just six feet from the flagstick.

"He knew where he was and what position he was in, and the tournament was his to win at that point," Nicklaus added. "He had to make the shot to turn the thing around, and he made it. And he's been able to make that shot with a fair amount of regularity over the last few years. So not too much amazes me anymore, but it's still amazing."

When the 2001 Memorial Tournament was over and the postwin press conference was complete, a journalist and his son did an interview with Woods as he was surrounded by security and accompanied by another player through the media workroom, to and up an elevator, down a short passageway, and finally into a reception. While the journalist and his working son returned to their work area in the pressroom, the father asked, "Do you realize what just happened?"

"Well, for starters," said the cub reporter, "I just rode in an elevator with my dad, and two golfing legends." That was true, the veteran told his son, but the symbolism was what most struck the father. While he was conducting his interview with Woods, arguably the greatest player the game has ever seen, another icon of the trade was standing, hands joined to each other, quietly to the back of the elevator. He wasn't speaking. He wasn't being interviewed. He was going along for the ride up the elevator nestled into the back right-hand corner. Alone. That other passenger was Jack Nicklaus.

Woods's career is significantly different from that of his predecessors. While golf's greats honed their crafts for loyal followers around the world, none of them ever had to play their best while at the same time living in a realm usually reserved for rock stars. Such is the daily routine for Woods although his playing ability is definitely not bigger than the game, as suggested by Hal Sutton at the 2000 Players Championship. At the time Sutton, who went on to beat Tiger in a head-to-head battle, was concerned that the media had built Woods's image to a level that might suggest he was bigger than the game. But in truth by defeating Woods all Sutton did was reconfirm the truism that golf is an imperfect game. No matter how good an individual player is, no matter the press clippings that follow him, no matter what he has accomplished in the weeks and months leading up to an event, in golf, practically any player can win in any given week. Sometimes a player just hits better, crisper shots, or breaks don't go for one player or another, and the unexpected victor emerges. Therein lies the true beauty and what makes golf the greatest game in the world. There are no standings; no prior records help seeding. "Tee 'em up Thursday and add 'em up when you finish on Sunday afternoon. If yours is the lowest number, you win." And if you are fortunate enough to do so, enjoy it. It doesn't happen very often. Not in golf. Not for anyone. Except Woods, who has been able to win an amazing percentage of starts compared to the great men who have played the game before him.

To call Tiger Woods a sporting superstar is an understatement. He is an internationally famous athlete, yes, but his star quality, as Ernie Els commented after losing in a play-off to Woods at Kapalua at the start of the 2000 season, "is bigger than Elvis." That perspective helps us understand what Woods needs deal with every day, even the days he goes on to serve up some of the greatest performances in the history of the game. Woods cannot practice in anonymity. Woods cannot do anything in anonymity. While walking through a crowd of autograph seekers and engaging Woods in an interview, a journalist got jammed in the crowd, which was held at bay by security and ropes at both sides of the pair. In the madness Woods accidentally stepped on the journalist's foot. He stopped in the middle of the frenzy to ask if the scribe was hurt. Amid the hype and tension Tiger showed yet another aspect of his rich personality. He cares.

At the Western Open in July 2001, the final pairing of the third day's play, Davis Love III and Brandel Chamblee approached the first tee. At the same moment as they prepared to tee off, Tiger was across a practice green and standing on the tenth tee. He had just finished an uncomfortable run of eagle, double-bogey, birdie, double-bogey, birdie. He had slipped from minus five through the fifth hole to minus three. Tiger had double-bogeyed twice in three holes. At this point Love and Chamblee, two of the game's true gentlemen, led the world's top player by eight and five, respectively. It made little difference. The fans still wanted to watch Woods. A small polite gathering followed the tournament leaders; a gallery of at least twenty times that size followed back-marker Tiger. Such is the appeal of Woods. No matter how compelling the story is regarding the leaders, the story of a tournament that has Tiger in the field is always Tiger. That, of course, is good and bad. For the widespread appeal of the game it's great. For the new people brought to the game it's wonderful. For the increased purses players now vie for it's rewarding. But for those in the hunt on a Saturday afternoon it can be lonely. For those playing with and around Tiger it can be distracting. For all those players who have tremendous stories to tell as they weave their way to victory, it somehow means less when Tiger plays.

That said, you'd be hard-pressed to find many who would complain about Tiger and what he means to the Tour. Paul Azinger commented on Tiger's appeal following a round at the 2000 World Golf Championships–NEC Invitational by saying "He needs more protection. I mean it. I'm going to call Commissioner Finchem and tell him this guy needs more protection." Protection. Only ten letters, but they carry so much weight. The weight they carry is synonymous with the weight Tiger carries everywhere he goes.

Protection. Something Tiger has earned. Protection. Something we should all be willing to give. Tiger lives in a world no one else knows. He can almost never move freely around a golf course; he has demands for interviews, appearances, autographs, and much more than any human could ever handle in an entire lifetime. And his demands are all for now. Do this interview now, sign this autograph now, do that now, satisfy this sponsor now. Now, now, now! It is amazing he does what he does.

For those who play with Tiger for the first time it can be quite an adventure. Such as when Joel Edwards, who had won for the first time in his career the week before at the 2001 Air Canada Championship, received immediate benefit playing with Tiger for the first two rounds the following week in the Canadian Open. Edwards admitted he felt like he had been thrown into the deep end of the pool. Local security didn't make him feel much better when he approached the tenth tee. They stopped him and told him he couldn't go there. He showed his player badge, it made no difference, and he had to sneak under the ropes to hit first, as he had the honors. He shot 74. Edwards said later if he had to deal with a lifestyle and demands similar to Tiger Woods' he would simply go back home and sell golf balls. He would want no part of such a grueling lifestyle.

During that round Edwards told Tiger he had a friend named Strick who wasn't a fan. He just didn't like Tiger. He didn't know him, but he didn't like him. Admitting his sense of humor might seem a little weird, Edwards asked Tiger to sign something for Strick, something that indicated he was a friend of Strick. On the Canadian Open program, which had his picture on it as the defending champion, Tiger wrote: "To Strick, Thanks for all the wonderful support over the years!! Your friend, Tiger Woods." Tiger's not afraid to have fun, even if it means being part of the joke.

Eldrich "Tiger" Woods is a perfectionist in an imperfect game. He is a superstar on a plane all by himself. He has a smile that could light a room and talent that goes beyond description. He is a young man performing astonishingly well on a world stage that wants to gobble him up. And through it all he still manages to win at an amazing pace. He wins and he loses, all with the same intensity and graciousness, destined to become the greatest of all time.

When he won his third straight World Golf Championships–NEC Invitational in August of 2001, Tiger went past the $25 million mark in career earnings. He was asked if he had imagined his victories would come as frequently as they had in his first five years as a professional. "I never really looked at it that way," Tiger said. "I looked at it, first of all, getting on the Tour. That was the main objective in '96. From there, keep myself out here with a few victories and by winning the Masters, ten-year exemption, the grandfather clause. Then I had a place to play. From there what I really wanted to do was give myself a lot of chances to win. That's what all the great players in the history of our sport have done. They don't win every time, but at least they are there. If you put yourself there enough times, the victories will happen. I'm proud of the way I've been able to do that so far. I've put myself there quite a few times, and I've won my share, but I've been beat a few times, too; that's going to be part of the game."

Such is the level that he is judged, it seems amazing that one single mind can manage it all. Early in the 2001 season people spoke of a Tiger slump. His line for the first five starts of the year read: T8 at Mercedes, T5 at Phoenix, T13 at Pebble, fourth at Buick Invitational, and T13 at the Los Angeles Open. He may not have appreciated the talk of slump, but it didn't hurt his game as he won his next three starts at the Bay Hill Invitational, the Players Championship, and the Masters. Following his three-in-a-row at the Memorial, five top-thirty finishes rekindled the slump talk. Tiger then won the NEC Invitational, also for the third consecutive time. He continues to tweak his game, believing in his heart he can improve. He doesn't rest on past accomplishments. That may well be his greatest attribute and ultimately his greatest gift to the game.

He wants more!

Not Even Tiger—*Dick Mudry**

No one alive knows for certain what the future brings. Not even Tiger Woods. But the high-talented superstar has always known what challenges history has put in his path. He knows intimately the records of Robert Tyre Jones, Jr., and he recognizes the major championship marks Jack Nicklaus has given him to chase. And he knows what it takes to remain a Supreme Champion.

"The great man," the Chinese scholar Mencius wrote in the third century B.C., "is he who does not lose his child's heart."

Woods has always maintained the exuberance of youth. Despite the pressures, the game still is fun. If that childlike quality remains in his heart, he will rewrite records and continue to have a major impact on the game as long as he wants to. In the end his motivation to be the best ever comes from within, and that is his most powerful—or destructive—weapon. The lack of a challenge, you see, will not interest him.

---

*For more than thirty years **Dick Mudry** has traveled the world, covering golf at the national and international level.

TIGER WOODS

	Total New Money	Wins	Top10s	Top25s
Majors	$10,531,084	8	15	21
Other Official Tournaments (and International Wins)	34,676,840	33	77	99
TOTALS	$45,207,924	41	92	120

MAJOR CHAMPIONSHIPS

	New Money	Wins
Masters	$3,477,824	3
U.S. Open	2,569,830	2
British Open	1,771,930	1
PGA	2,711,500	2

BEST OTHER EVENTS

	New Money	Wins
WGC-NEC Invitational	$3,266,667	3
Memorial Tournament	2,473,200	3
Bay Hill Invitational	2,347,000	3
WGC-American Express	2,195,139	2

Year	New Money	Total Wins	Top10s	Top25s	Majors	Other Events
1996	$ 2,224,175	2	5	7	$ 0	$2,224,175
1997	4,822,571	5	10	15	1,122,131	3,700,440
1998	3,805,764	2	14	18	782,742	3,023,022
1999	9,084,846	10	18	20	1,543,783	7,541,063
2000	11,085,436	9	19	22	3,320,140	7,765,296
2001	6,796,175	7	12	21	1,160,289	5,635,886
2002	7,388,958	6	14	17	2,602,000	4,786,958

PART THREE

Nineteenth Hole

NEW MONEY BEST-YEAR RANKINGS

Byron Nelson	1945	$15,556,092
Ben Hogan	1946	12,566,337
Tiger Woods	2000	11,085,436
Sam Snead	1950	10,818,810
Arnold Palmer	1960	9,000,004
Tom Watson	1980	8,464,727
Jack Nicklaus	1964	8,119,136
Gene Sarazen	1930	7,858,862
Lee Trevino	1971	7,179,893
Billy Casper	1958	6,549,544
Greg Norman	1986	6,228,594
Gary Player	1961	5,963,872
Walter Hagen	1923	5,874,589
Ray Floyd	1981	5,361,065
Nick Faldo	1992	5,120,945
Seve Ballesteros	1988	4,602,934
Hale Irwin	1975	4,363,576
Bobby Jones	1926 & 1930	2,106,140

Footnote for those who consider the title of "Greatest Golfer Ever" to be between Tiger Woods and Jack Nicklaus—here is how the New Money race stands at the 2002 season's end.

NICKLAUS VERSUS WOODS

Professional Appearance	Jack Nicklaus	Tiger Woods
First Year	$ 6,627,905	$ 2,224,175
First 2 Years	14,688,566	7,046,746
First 3 Years	22,807,701	10,852,510
First 4 Years	29,915,609	19,937,356
First 5 Years	35,560,788	31,022,792
First 6 Years	43,320,188	37,818,966
First 7 Years	48,539,551	45,207,924

The Money Game

David Mackintosh

In the autumn of 2001, ninety-three years after Old Tom Morris was peacefully laid to rest in a small corner of his native St. Andrews, the world's best professional golfers returned to the Kingdom of Fife.

The purse for four days' work? A massive prize of $5 million, the winner banking an astonishing $800,000. When old Tom won the Open championship for the fourth time in 1867, he received just five pounds, $26. His first three wins carried no prize money at all.

In time, no doubt, that $5 million will itself diminish into faded green and gray, and our golfing grandchildren will have to delve deep in some ancient tome to solve the puzzle of what such a sum might be worth in the twenty-second century's new world currency.

The seven hundred years since man's earliest golfing steps have seen more than a few changes. Yet the lands where the game began, the breezy estuaries and sharp, craggy headlands, remain largely unaltered by man or time. An apt reminder that, even if during the passing centuries golf has donned a more sophisticated set of clothes, the core challenge remains as enduring as the motivation of all who play. Seven hundred years, a mere footstep in eternity. Fortunate indeed are we who are a tiny part of this extraordinary legacy.

1300–1900

Golf has ever been a game about money and sometimes of sheep. Back in the 1300s, when two Scottish shepherds turned their crooks "tuther wey roond" and took their new game—"tha gouf"—to Carnoustie's links land, it is easy to imagine after a few matches for the simple pleasure of winning, the idea of a gentle wager captured the mind of at least one canny lad.

Sensing his deftness at firing stones into rabbit holes in the fewest number of strokes and hearing clansmen speak almost warily of his ever-growing prowess, did he of the most silken swing not then wager his penny, silver shilling, or perhaps even a black-faced ewe to prove beyond dispute he was the best player on these short-grass sandy shores?

Unlikely it stopped there. When word went round the local communities and Thursday's town-market whiskey-quaffing sessions that MacPherson was about to wager his best sheep on his skill at this newfangled game, did not MacLennan and MacDougal and Frazer and Maxwell, along with a whole army of MacDonalds and MacKays, gather to watch the proceedings, perhaps even risking a Scottish shilling or two in side bets during the afternoon tussle?

And perhaps Chisholm or MacCloory or MacCloud left the proceedings with an itch to own a golfing crook, practice day and night to win an entire farm—whilst perhaps MacInvish was thinking, if such a game was beginning to attract such interest, surely he could come up with a way to charge an entry fee for the spectacle.

Golf survived the next seven centuries despite being "cried down" and run out of town by the king and by having its first golfing queen beheaded. Men were encouraged to take archery seriously but preferred a weekend match and a healthy side bet. Many were jailed for playing on Sundays or generously fined forty Scottish shillings—a good deal more than a week's wage. Despite bread-and-water or pillory, the game was destined to be stronger than procurator-fiscal indictment, than the magistrate's heavy-handed punishment.

James VI—"James of the Iron Belt"—was the first Scottish Royal to take a serious personal interest in golf. Later to die fighting with his men on foot at dreadful Flodden Field, James demanded the lord high treasurer settle his regular accounts for clubs, balls, even his bets. In February 1503 the official treasury records declared: "To the King to play at the Golf with the

Erle of Bothuile, iij Franch crowns." Certainly unlikely to have been a green fee—expect any king now or then to be comped—and unless the "Iron Belt" even more improbably paid for a round of John Barleycorn, this six-hundred-year-old account is the first written record of the cost of losing a five-way Nassau. Sadly the conversion value of "iij Franch Crowns" is lost in history, but it is nevertheless probable the Earl of Bothwell went home to his castle well satisfied with the day.

Things golf improved radically a century later under Iron Belt's great-grandson, James VI of Scotland, a fervent player and patron of the ever-more-popular sport. When his new job as James I—omnipotent ruler of the newly created United Kingdom—took him to London in 1603, the decision to treat his golf club-maker and "featherie" ball maker as essential members of his inner circle and expatriate them at his side was to have the profoundest effect on the worldwide expansion of golf. Not only had King James elevated the erstwhile pastime of shepherds and fisherfolk to highly accepted social status but as a result the world's first inland golf course appeared, tucked around the king's Eltham Palace in southeast London. Subsequently a more testing challenge would be constructed on nearby Blackheath Common.

More royal golf money changed hands in 1682. The duke of York, later to become James II, had been sent north of Hadrian's Wall by his brother, ruler of the now United Kingdom, as commissioner to the Scottish Parliament. On the links surrounding Edinburgh the duke took to the game of golf with passion, his fiery temperament producing one of the explosive wagers of the age.

An incredible, white-heated dispute over the origins of golf angered the duke to the extent he proposed the argument be settled by playing a golf match. The winners would have the right to declare whether the game of golf had originated in Scotland or England!

As his partner the duke chose a local cobbler, a commoner, but one with a strong swing, a trusty putting iron, and a vast amount of local artisan knowledge. Victory at the Leith links was an almost foregone conclusion thanks to the duke's astute but socially scandalous decision.

The House of Stuart duly accepted the winner's large bag of gold coin and declared Scotland the Home of Golf. John Pattersone greeted his wife later that day with half the wager in his saddlebag. Sufficient money to pay for the construction of a stout stone house in the grandest part of Edinburgh, and enough left over to commission the splendid personal crest of arms that adorned that new home for the rest of his lifetime.

That golf matches for money had been played from the game's earliest days is certain, and artisans such as John Pattersone probably made a handsome living from their part-time skills. Golf clubs, with their red coats and military-derived traditions, would not arrive on the scene until the mid–eighteenth century, along with which came the now-traditional silver trophies, winner boards, and, of course, the noble concept of "golf for honor." The largely U.S. tradition of honor boards seems neatly to captivate this message.

First newspaper coverage of a game of golf for money appeared in Edinburgh almost half a century later, 1724 to be precise, announcing "a solemn match at golf for the sum of 20 guineas" between Alexander Elphinstone, the younger son of Lord Balmerino and Captain John Porteous, commander in chief of the Edinburgh City Guard. The subsequent press report stated that the match—won by Elphinstone—had been witnessed by the duke of Hamilton, the earl of Morton, and a large concourse of spectators.

The beginning of the game where everyone played in separate groups for the same prize is not, as one might suspect, the 1860 Open championship. Presented in 1744 by the city of Edinburgh, the original "Open-to-All" golf trophy was a silver golf club, later to become the outright property of the Honorable Company of Edinburgh Golfers. The first and subsequent tournaments were "Open to all Golfers from any part of Great Britain and Ireland," but in 1764 the Leith club golfers successfully petitioned the city of Edinburgh to restrict the competition to their own members. Oddly this Quaich tournament would continue uninterrupted not only during the brief civil war instigated by Bonnie Prince Charlie in 1745 but during the aftermath of French-Charlie's bold but doomed venture—when England took its savage reprisal.

Here was an "open" competition certainly, but one with an ironic twist. The trophy was to be retained by the owners, there was no prize money, and the winner, at his own cost, was required to buy a gold or silver golf ball to add to the trophy.

A costly venture that perhaps gives us a clue as to that noble concept of playing golf for the pure honor of victory. Only men with money, nobles and financially secure esquires, might venture forth in such a competition without the fear of financial embarrassment. It would perhaps have been easier to explain how one lost an entire flock of sheep on a six-foot putt after a bad day on the links.

That first "open" was hardly a success. Despite plenty of publicity in Edinburgh and the surrounding lothians—the city's town crier and his drummers marched daily for almost two weeks announcing the forthcoming championship—only ten players took part, none from out of town.

There would be no more attempts at open-competition golf until 1857, when the Prestwick Club on Scotland's Ayrshire west coast, then the home club of Old Tom Morris, proposed a match between eight clubs, including St. Andrews in the north and Royal Blackheath as the only English representative, each club to present four players.

Foursome teams would be blind-drawn, the winners determined by a form of "all-against-all" round-robin-style matches. The winning pair would then play a final singles match for the top prize, the victor entitled to the champion's medal.

Word got around, the idea so popular that by the time the program was finalized a further five clubs had been incorporated. Not entirely "open" of course, restricted to club-member amateurs, and no cash prizes, but a step in the right direction nevertheless.

The success of that first 1857 match encouraged Prestwick members, at the behest of Morris, to consider the inauguration of a similar event for professional players. The timing was propitious. The recent death of Allan Robertson—acknowledged by his peers as the greatest player of the times—had left the champion's dais vacant.

In May 1860 Prestwick Club members quickly raised five guineas for a medal, later to be substituted for a thirty-guinea red morocco leather belt with handsome solid-silver side plates and clasp-buckle. As no other club wished to become involved in the organization of the championship, Prestwick took sole charge.

Three rounds of the quirky twelve-hole course gave Musselburgh's Willie Park the open title and one year's use of the resplendent belt. There was no prize money. Thus the venerable Park, Sr., won the first championship. But not the first "Open" as is now commonly perceived. The 1860 event was a purely professional affair. That omission was soon to be rectified, with one small blip. First came a club member's proposal that the 1861 title be opened to "gentlemen-players" (that's amateurs in today-speak) from a mere eight clubs. The resolution was passed unanimously.

On the eve of the 1861 competition, however, the championship committee declared the second contest for the Championship Belt would in future be open to the entire world.

Just eight professionals made up the 1860 field played for the honor of the title—"Champion Golfer of the Year"—the same words the R&A use today at their investiture of the new Open champion. There was no prize money at all, also the case in 1861, '62, and '63. In 1864, the fourth year of the competition, prize money was offered, a paltry five pounds for the runner-up, three pounds for third, two pounds for coming in fourth. The winner: still nothing at all!

Things would not get much better over the next few years, although when young Tom Morris won his first of four consecutive titles in 1868, he received six pounds plus use of the championship belt. After his third successive win in 1871, Morris took outright ownership of the belt, causing that two-year championship hiatus in the history books.

When the current championship Claret Jug appeared on the scene, and once again Morris emerged triumphant, the winner was now also entitled to a massive eight pounds. Professional golf for cash was emerging, if still ever so slowly, from a five-hundred-year incubation period.

The nineteenth century drew to a close on a vociferous note, a resonant clarion call to the future. In a rapidly industrializing Great Britain that still sent small boys up factory flues and stately-home chimneys to scour away choking coal dust for penny wages, professional golf was not even a latent gleam in the minds of the later-to-be-powerful trades union movement.

Yet the 1899 Open Championship, played over the links of St. George's, Sandwich, for just the second time, which had attracted a record entry of 101 competitors, almost collapsed as a result of the first concerted effort by professional golfers to better their condition. They called a strike!

Just days before the tournament where the R&A would crown the last "Champion Golfer of the Year" of the nineteenth century, a majority of the field threatened to withdraw from competition—unless prize money was increased substantially. The first prize of forty pounds had remained unchanged for eight years, despite sufficient public interest in the game that the organizers could now charge gate money for the spectacle. Poor MacInvish, alas born a few centuries before his time!

Looking at the many millions of dollars the game now offers, it is easy to side with competitors whose changing areas were frequently rank stables, entry by the servants' entrance to a clubhouse kitchen where stand-up leftovers might or might not be served, the front door forbidden by members who had recently applauded their skills in public.

Yet in these same closing moments of the nineteenth century, the annual rent of a good croft (small Scottish farm)—those to be had with the incursion of sheep and enforced depopulation of the Highlands—was still considerably less than the first prize of forty pounds sterling.

Which is possibly why the three top players of the era, Harry Vardon, John Henry (J. H.) Taylor, and James Braid—"The Great Triumvirate"— decided to forgo the pleasure of leading or even participating in the dissent. A different slant is equally probable.

Vardon and Taylor were Englishmen; Braid, then twenty-nine, although born in north-of-the-border Earls Ferry, was an adopted Englishman who would spend forty-five years of life as the professional at London's rich Walton Heath Club.

This 1899 Open was being played in these Englishmen's backyard, the St. George's Club, Sandwich (later to become Royal St. George's), huddled around Pegwell Bay, the white cliffs of Dover a small kiss to the south. And while the major championship of the British Isles annually garnered the best players, this did not necessarily produce the hand-shaking camaraderie we'd like to believe is an age-old tradition. Moreover, the majority of that week's invading Scots, to put it bluntly, were as uncouth as they were ragged and were more than unlikely to strike up instant friendships with their smoother southern cocompetitors.

A fly on the wall at meetings that blustery summer week would have observed a small piece of golf's history in the making. Here a plotting huddle of fairly ragged men in a lowly outhouse, there the illustrious and aloof Triumvirate, in all probability comfortably ensconced at the Bell pub-hotel on Sandwich harbor. And worried R&A officials, in the palatial surrounds of the long since demolished Guildford Hotel, were fearful a flawed decision could end the championship forever.

The second Open championship to be played in England (the first venture south of the border was in 1894) thus got under way in the midst of acrimonious and unresolved polemic. With the four rounds to decide the championship then played over two days, the canny northern professionals planned a skillful coup.

So many players withdrew after the first round the resulting chaos required the entire afternoon round to be entirely reorganized. The same evening the organizers announced an increase in the top prize, from forty to fifty pounds, the second place from twenty to twenty-five.

The winner might now pay annual rent on an additional fifty acres of good grazing with the difference, but it's equally probable the repositories of any new funds would be a series of public houses on the long route north.

When much-the-favorite and well-educated Englishman Harry Vardon claimed the title, and accepted the trophy with a polite thank-you, the organizers were probably spared some embarrassment.

If the suggestion that nineteenth-century golf professionals spent most of their free time in barroom pursuits appears excessively critical, although golf was less than a decade old in the United States, the darker side of the John Barleycorn–induced antics of this mostly disheveled band was already public concern on the western side of the Atlantic. For instance, in 1898 Scotsman Fred Herd won the U.S. Open, whereupon the relatively newly formed United States Golf Association required Herd pay a security fee were he to take the winner's trophy off the premises, fearing he'd pawn the cup for drinking money.

To give the R&A their due, in line with awakening public interest in the sport the prize purse had been boosted from the miserly 20 pounds of 1891 to 110 pounds the following year. On the other side of the equation, those 20 pounds had been static for more than two decades.

The 1896 edition of the Open at the Honorable Company of Edinburgh Golfers Muirfield links perhaps best exemplifies the value placed on the championship by the players themselves; an important title, yes, but far and away less significant than earning a living by "playing for money."

After seventy-two holes Harry Vardon and J. H. Taylor were tied, and an eighteen-hole play-off the following day was dictated by competition rules. "Sorry," they responded. "Tomorrow we have an important money game down the road at North Berwick." A small but important victory for players' rights, the play-off was postponed until later that week, when Vardon claimed his first of six Open titles.

O'er the Waves—Bright Beginnings

The standard version of how golf finally took hold in the USA is an 1887 Christmas gift of six Tom Morris hickory sticks among Yonkers, New York, friends. Rather more inexplicable is why the game failed to take root much earlier—although various American towns now lay claim to early golf venues, subsequently abandoned from lack of interest.

In the period between the mid-1800s and the latter part of the nineteenth century, some *350,000* Highland men and their families made the perilous journey to the New World, initially settling for the main in North Carolina, subsequently around the Cape Fear region, and, after Wolfe gained the upper hand over the French in Quebec, around the eastern seaboards of Canada, including Nova Scotia.

Later immigrants were impoverished, sad, disenfranchised Highlanders, erstwhile tenants of English landlords put in place by a London government that, after the 1745 rampages of Bonnie Prince Charlie, determined northern rebellions would never again destabilize an ostensibly United Kingdom.

Anxious to increase lands revenues, first from seashore kelp harvesting and later by sheep grazing, the new masters of northern Scotland forced a significant proportion of the mostly agrarian population to flee to wherever refuge and food could be found. Many landlords simply dispatched their problems across the Atlantic as cheap westward ballast of the transatlantic wood-freight trade, a despicable albeit economical solution.

Before these unfortunate souls, however, a solid proportion of Scottish emigrants derived from a separate Celtic vein. Many families of certain wealth—tacksmen, the middle to upper echelons of the clan system—arrived with adequate funds to join the land-owning classes of the Carolinas and Cape Fear region. Yet it would appear not one single Highlander brought with him, in addition to a well-moistened bag of pipes, a sackcloth bundle containing a cleek or a long-nosed spoon with which to while away a sun-soft evening in the Carolina meadows—even although by all contemporary accounts they'd fled a Scotland already caught up in the excited clamor of golf.

On the face of it, that not a single Scots immigrant was a golf addict seems quite extraordinary. The superficial and perhaps logical explanation appears to be that almost without exception these early settlers were clansmen from the west and the high-north Sutherland end of the country, whereas early golf in Scotland was limited to the mideastern seaboard of the country.

Even that seems a flimsy and less than wholly satisfactory explanation, but the facts are incontrovertible, more astonishing when one considers that for close to one hundred years up to the mid-1800s, the principal language of the Cape Fear region was Scotland's own Gaelic.

For whatever reason, golf lay dormant in the Land of Opportunity until a huge groundswell of desire was awakened by two school chums originally from Dunfermline, Scotland, but in adult life, expatriate businessmen based in Yonkers, New York.

Robert Lockhart, a traveling linen merchant, often brought travel gifts for his friend John Reed, the local steelworks manager. A visit by generous Lockhart to Old Tom Morris's shop in St. Andrews during 1887, where he bought the clubs and balls to be shipped to his friend as a Christmas gift, would soon reshape sporting recreation throughout the entire North American continent.

The immediate popularity of the game in the United States of America was truly formidable, as if a pent-up dam had exploded at the seams. In 1888 just six men formed the St. Andrews Club in Yonkers; come 1894 there were fifteen clubs dotted around New York: two on Long Island, four in Westchester, one in Connecticut, and six in New Jersey, including Baltusrol. And of course, St. Andrews remained strong, now with a new home on the outskirts of Yonkers.

A mere seven years later, at the dawn of a new century, there wasn't a state in the entire United States of America that did not boast at least one golf course. More than one thousand all told—a number that amazingly would double yet again over the next decade—virtually every club teeming with aspirants. The Golden Years they certainly were, and the Scots, although hardly pioneers in the field, were now quick to take advantage.

One estimate of the period suggests no fewer than 250 men from the then-small Scottish fishing village of Carnoustie emigrated to the United States over a stretch of ten years, their sole purpose to teach the game of golf to their American cousins.

An early arrival on U.S. shores, Willie Dunn, had met W. E. Vanderbilt while teaching the game in France. A man of immense wealth, Vanderbilt contracted Dunn to construct the Shinnecock Hills Club on Long Island in 1891. Three years later Dunn won the first U.S. Open, subsequently considered unofficial—a "championship" that would lead to the formation of the USGA that same year.

In the following year, 1895, Dunn was able to bring the famed money matches of his homeland to the attention of the American fan. Willie Park, Jr., son of the first Open champion, was brought from Scotland to challenge Dunn in a three-match series at the princely sum of $200 per match. The purchasing power of this $600 purse is possibly best compared with the $50 paid two years earlier by the Country Club of Boston to establish their first six-hole golf course. In the same year Horace Rawlins won the first "official" U.S. Open, his earnings—one gold medal and $150 in cash.

Park's tour would be the forerunner of many more exhibitions and sponsored money matches during the next five years, none more important than Harry Vardon's famed nine-month tour of the country in 1900. Sponsored by the burgeoning sports empire of A. G. Spalding, the reigning Open champion received the staggering sum of 900 pounds ($4350) as recompense for playing exhibitions that featured the new Spalding gutty ball, the "Vardon Flier." In addition, Vardon's lucrative contract allowed him to retain all monies won during the tour.

There were now more than a quarter of a million golfers in the United States, most of whom had started playing with the imported Eclipse at thirty-five cents apiece, later graduating to a fifty-cent ball. Golf had rapidly become corporate business, and a new era was coming into sight.

Henceforth, big business would seek out golfers to publicize its products. Exhibition matches would offer rewards vastly in excess of tournament prize money. Players could frequently add to their wealth by a significant share of gate money. In the space of a decade, the top professional golfers had evolved from mere tradesmen of the lower orders to stars of a bright new firmament. When Vardon's tour reached New York, even the Stock Exchange closed for his visit.

Money, the onetime villain that had not so long before been considered a threat to the integrity and honor of golf, would thenceforth and forever after play a dominant part in its spectacular evolution.

Contributor Biographies

Tom Auclair

Golfweek's senior writer Jeff Rude wrote of Auclair, "The iron man of the PGA Tour is not a player but an entrepreneurial multimedia golf junkie. His name is Tom Auclair, and he is the game's ultimate road warrior. Just hearing the details of his 2001 Road Odyssey can make one tired." That "Road Odyssey" continued through 2002 as he made it three consecutive years of covering every stop on the PGA Tour, with the exception of those weeks when there were two events and he could be at only one. He has the distinction of having covered more events than any other journalist ever has over such a short period. Rude said, "He doesn't just cover it; he smothers it." Auclair started covering golf at the 1989 U.S. Open at Oak Hill and is married to long-suffering Karin, and they have three children, T.J., Kyle, and Katelyn. T.J. and Kyle are part of the "Inside the Ropes" team, an Internet venture founded by Auclair and now one of the most respected sites in the business.

Al Barkow

Barkow has been writing on golf for over forty years. He was the golf writer and associate producer of the original "Shell's Wonderful World of Golf" television series. He was also the editor in chief of *Golf* and *Golf Illustrated* and the author of numerous books on the history of American golf, including *Golf's Golden Grind: The History of the Tour, Gettin' to the Dance Floor: An Oral History of American Golf*, and most recently, *The Golden Era of Golf: How America Rose to Dominate the Old Scotsgame*. Barkow continues to write on golf as a freelancer, with articles appearing in such publications as the *New York Times* and *Sports Illustrated*. He lives in Albany, California.

Furman Bisher

Bisher is the doyen of American golf writers, a man whose credentials and achievements could fill this entire book. Briefly, as a sportswriter Bisher knew Gene Sarazen not only for a large portion of the first Grand Slammer's illustrious career but in later years as a friend and occasional golfing companion. Apart from this specific and unique credential, "The Bish" has honed a unique place in the hearts of many, not least his regular, some might say fanatical, following at the *Atlanta Constitution*, where he's penned a regular column for more years than he'd probably care to count. A past president of the Golf Writers of America, his other achievements, accolades, personal recognition, and honors are about as innumerable as the quantity and quality of his writing over the past six decades. Wisdom, wit, and outright openness have made Bisher an idol to most, not least the humble compiler of this anthology.

Jaime Diaz

Diaz is a senior writer for *Golf Digest* and *Golf World* magazines. Since 1983 he has also covered golf at *Sports Illustrated* and the *New York Times* and contributed articles to other periodicals, including *Travel & Leisure, Golf*, and *Golf Magazine*. He is the author of four books on the game, including *The Elements of Scoring* with Raymond Floyd, *Hallowed Ground*, and a history entitled *An Enduring Passion*. A graduate of the University of San Francisco, he lives with his wife, Stephanie, in Temecula, California.

James Dodson

Dodson is a regular monthly columnist for *Golf* magazine and the author of *Final Rounds: A Golfer's Life* and *The Dewsweepers*. He is currently working on the first authorized biography of Ben Hogan.

John Garrity

Garrity is a senior writer at *Sports Illustrated* and author of more than a dozen books. His writings on golf and other subjects have been anthologized in numerous volumes, and he has contributed to many magazines, including *Rolling Stone, Connoisseur, The Village Voice, Smithsonian, The Saturday Evening Post, TV Guide, Texas Monthly, The National Catholic Reporter*, and *Alfred Hitchcock's Mystery Magazine*. In addition to his many writing awards from the Golf Writers Association of America, he has twice been honored by the Herbert Hoover Presidential Library Association for articles on the former president in *Smithsonian* and *Sports Illustrated*. His golf books are *America's Worst Golf Courses* (1994), *Making the Turn* (with Frank Beard, 1992), *Golf: A Three-Dimensional Exploration of the Game* (1996), and *Tiger Woods: The Making of a Champion* (editor and original text, 1997). He has also written the historical text for *The Ultimate Golf Book* (edited by Chip McGrath and David McCormick), published in 2002. Mr. Garrity graduated from Stanford University in 1971 and worked in New York as an editor at Simon & Schuster before turning to writing full-time. He lives in Kansas City, Missouri, with his wife Pat, a church liturgist.

Ron Green, Sr.

Green is a sportswriter with the *Charlotte Observer* and has won numerous national sportswriting prizes, including several Golf Writer's Association of America top awards.

Dave Hackenberg

Hackenberg is the golf writer, pro football writer, and a sports columnist for *The Blade* newspaper in Toledo, Ohio. He is the author of a centennial history book of Toledo's Inverness Club, where Byron Nelson served as head professional in the early 1940s. For many years Hackenberg was a regular contributor to PGA of America Magazine and has also had stories published in most major golf publications as well as numerous Internet sites. He was Ohio's sportswriter of the year in 1999 and a member of the board of directors of the Golf Writers of America Association since the same year. He and his wife, Sue, have two daughters.

John Hopkins

Hopkins is the principal golf correspondent for the *Times* of London and frequently appears as a distinguished guest on TV golf programs on both sides of the Atlantic. Hopkins is president of the British Golf Writers Guild.

John Huggan

Huggan is a freelance golf journalist based in North Berwick, Scotland. He is a contributing editor to *Golf Digest* and a contributing writer to *Golf World* in the United States. In the United Kingdom he is a regular contributor to *Golf International* magazine and is the golf columnist for the *Scotland on Sunday* newspaper. In a former life Huggan was the senior editor in charge of instruction at *Golf Digest*. He has coauthored books with David Leadbetter, Hank Haney, and Gary McCord. He is also the author of *Golf Digest's Cure Your Slice Forever*. In a former-former life Huggan was a good enough player to represent Scotland as an amateur from 1981 to 1984, during which time one of his teammates was a young lad by the name of Colin Montgomerie.

Joey Kaney

Kaney is founder and president of Mr. Stat, Inc., a business based in Warrenton, Georgia, specializing in maintaining statistics and records for golf tournaments large and small—from the PGA Tour's BellSouth Classic in Atlanta to the Dan L. Lanier Invitational in Metter, Georgia. Tour clients include the Celebrity Players Tour and the NGA/Hooters Tour. A decent golfer since the late 1980s, Kaney still grinds away at giving par a run for its money, sometimes taking it! Kaney has a daughter, Heather, and a son, Hogan.

Kaye Kessler

Kessler writes about himself: "Older than snow, dumber than dirt, Kessler spent forty-five years as sportswriter/columnist with Columbus, Ohio, newspapers—with four years out for good behavior winning the war of Piccadilly Circus and other European ports during World War II. Along with covering all twenty-eight years of Woody Hayes's antics as Ohio State football coach and the entire fifty-plus years of Jack Nicklaus's career starting when Jack first took club in hand age ten, Kessler has covered more than one hundred majors on the golf circuit, World Series, Super Bowls, Olympics, frog-jumping contests, and sled dog races. He served two terms as president of the Golf Writers Association of America, three as president of the Colorado Golf Hall of Fame, and has been on more sports association boards than you can count. Ohio Sportswriter of the Year in 1984, recipient of the PGA of America Lifetime Achievement Award in Journalism in 2001. After putting two newspapers out of business, he moved to Colorado in 1985 to help get the International Tournament off the ground at Castle Rock, serving seven years as player relations and media director before becoming semiretired and turning to freelance writing in 1993. Daughter Kris is a counselor in the Department of Defense (DODs) system in Aviano, Italy, son Rodney vice president of Stowe Mountain Ski Resort in Vermont. His lovely wife Rosemary, responsible for the success of the children, died in 1995."

Stephen R. Lowe

Lowe is a professor of history at Olivet Nazarene University. His most recent book, *Sir Walter and Mr. Jones: Walter Hagen, Bobby Jones, and the Rise of American Golf,* won the 2000 USGA International Book Award.

Lowe is also the author of *The Kid on the Sandlot: Congress and Professional Sports*. His articles have appeared in a variety of periodicals, including *Golf World*, *Golf Magazine*, *Pebble Beach Magazine*, *Journal of Sport History*, and the *Georgia Historical Quarterly*.

David Mackintosh

Mackintosh is senior golf writer for the *Buenos Aires Herald* and media relations manager for the PGA de las Americas, an organization operating a large calendar of national championships in Latin America and the Caribbean. Close on two decades of uninterrupted major championship reporting has given him a magnificent overview of the astounding changes in the game—and the money! Mackintosh has written on golf for many major national and international publications and appeared on various television and radio programs, including ESPN and the Golf Channel. In a former life he worked for the Reuters news agency and was based in Buenos Aires for two decades. In an earlier incarnation he played golf for Kent, England, and remains a fervent member of the Royal Blackheath Club. A native of Scotland, he and wife, Susana, now reside in Florida.

Sidney Matthew

Matthew is a trial lawyer practicing in Tallahassee, Florida. He has several books on Jones to his credit: *The History of Bobby Jones Clubs* (1992); *Life & Times of Bobby Jones* (1995) (winner of Benjamin Franklin Award by the Printing Industries of America), *Secrets of the Master—The Best of Bobby Jones* (1996), *Bobby Jones on Golf* (1997), *Champions of East Lake—Bobby Jones & Friends* (1999), *Bobby Jones Golf Tips—Secrets of the Master* (1999), *Bobby Jones Extra!* (2001). He also penned *Wry Stories on the Road Hole* (2000) and *History of the Tallahassee Bar* (2000). The author's films include *The History and Tradition of Golf in Scotland* (1989) and the universally acclaimed *Life & Times of Bobby Jones*, narrated by actor Sean Connery and broadcast nationally on CBS television preceding the 1996, 1997, 1998, and 2000 Masters Tournaments. He wrote and helped produce *Citizen Smith*—the biography of famous Floridian Chesterfield Smith (in 1997). Matthew is married to Linda and has three children and three grandchildren.

Marino Parascenzo

Parascenzo, former golf writer with the *Pittsburgh Post-Gazette*, has won more than twenty national writing awards with the Golf Writers Association of America and the Associated Press Sports Editors. Parascenzo is now a freelancer, writing for magazines and the Internet. He is a former president of the Golf Writers Association and founder and chairman of the GWAA's Journalism Scholarship Program, a source of aid for needy journalism students. His work has appeared in *Golf Digest, Golf Magazine, Sports Illustrated*, the *Sporting News*, the U.S. Golf Association's *Golf Journal*, and other American and foreign publications.

Mike Purkey

Purkey is a Senior Writer at *GOLF* Magazine, where he has been employed since 1990. He is president of the Golf Writers Association of America and and has served terms as vice president and as a member of that organization's board of directors. He has been an award winner in writing contests for both the GWAA and the North Carolina Press Association.

Dan Reardon

Since 1985 Reardon has been the voice of golf in St. Louis on radio station KMOX, one of the most acclaimed broadcast outlets in the United States. Over the years he has provided reports from more than fifty major championships and dozens of additional professional events. In his tenure at the station he has conducted one-on-one interviews with virtually every major and minor figure in the game, ranging from a sixteen-year-old youngster named Tiger Woods to an eighty-plus Byron Nelson. In addition to his duties with KMOX he has written on golf dating back to 1970 and continuing today. He was a part of the nationally syndicated golf program "Golf Plus" reporting on the Senior and LPGA Tours as well as anchoring the program occasionally. A native St. Louisan, he has made transplanted St. Louisan Hale Irwin a part of his beat starting at the U.S. Open at Oakland Hills in 1985. Since that time the geographic proximity of the two has enabled him to visit regularly with Irwin on mike, perhaps more than any other member of the golfing press.

Phil Tresidder

Tresidder, based in Sydney, is Australia's best-known senior golf scribe. As a youthful reporter he cut his teeth in Britain sending back stories to his newspapers on the achievements of trailblazer Norman von Nida. In the years that followed, he was assigned to produce articles for Jack Nicklaus, Gary Player, and Arnold Palmer on their regular visits "Down Under," and he witnessed the famous triumvirate winning their total fourteen Australian Open Championships. His most memorable day occurred at Augusta, when he played the morning after with the little South African, Gary Player, fresh from his sensational Masters victory. Tresidder is the author of books on Greg Norman and Karrie Webb and a bestselling fun book, *The Golfer Who Laughed*. He is a member of the leading Sydney Golf Clubs, the Australian and the Lakes.

Ben Wright

Wright broadcast golf and other sports for CBS-TV for twenty-three years. He has been the golf correspondent for the Sunday *Times*, the *Observer*, and the *Daily Mirror*, and was the *Financial Times'* first golf columnist. He has also announced golf for BBC, ITV, Australian TV, and NZTV and has written columns for *Links Magazine*, *Western Links*, and *Southern Links* and is the author of the highly acclaimed *The Spirit of Golf, Good Bounces and Bad Lies*, and *Speak Wright*.

Afterword

An idea evolving over a decade produces an army of allies, some of whom actively put a hand to the directional tiller, but beyond the friends, acquaintances, colleagues, and professional experts who at some time or other were willing to offer an ear or advice there are some people whom I have never met, and never will, who deserve more than a modicum of credit.

When the reader begins to delve into the past, examining and wondering just how on earth Joey Kaney produced the statistical miracle that makes up the entirely new comparison analysis tables in this book, truthfully we need go back as far as the tail end of World War II and those few extraordinary men who organized millions upon millions of pieces of data, ran them cautiously through an experimental, electro-mechanical sorting process in an attempt to break Axis intelligence codes. Before 1944 a computer was a human being. Then Alan Turing, by applied mathematical logic, made the major breakthrough that programs operating on numbers could represent themselves as numbers or as anything else. Half a century later a considerable slice of the world's population sit down at a personal computer as a part of normal daily life.

The ubiquitous PC that enabled Joey to process the vast amount of historic data into the form and structure presented in these pages has come a long way since its earliest bulky predecessor was at least partly responsible for Allied victory. Without the great-grandfather of the digital computer, Alan Turing, or the man who brought us simplified home computing, Bill Gates, none of what we've been able to do here would have been possible. Thank you, gentlemen.

To those wonderful writers who agreed to be part of this book it would be remiss not to give formal thanks for their constant support, open kindness, and most important, belief in the project. From Scotland to Australia the warmth of their friendship has nurtured this volume. Take a bow, Furman Bisher, Sidney Matthew, James Dodson, Dr. Steven Lowe, Dave Hackenberg, Jaime Diaz, Ben Wright, Mike Purkey, Al Barkow, Kaye Kessler, Marino Parascenzo, John Garrity, Tom Auclair, Jeff Shain, Jeff Rude, John Strawn, Jim Huber, Lorne Rubenstein, Dick Mudry, Dan Reardon, Phil Tresidder, Ron Green, Sr., John Hopkins, John Huggan.

Contributing writers are not the only people who have helped this book into covers. The names are in no particular order—I just hope I've been able to recall everyone who, at different times, gave valuable assistance, comment, or just simply good commonsense opinions. The PGA of America's Julius Mason, Jaime Roggero-Carbone, Rebecca Szmuckler, and particularly Bob Denney, a valued friend and memory man. The United States Golf Association's Craig Smith, Suzanne Colson, Pete Kowalski, USGA librarian Rand Jarris, Allison McClow and Denise Taylor at the PGA Tour, the Royal & Ancient Golf Club of St. Andrews' Angela Morrison, Sir Michael Bonnallack, R&A pressman Stewart MacDougal, the Western Open's Tim Cronin, Greenbriar historian Robert Conte, Royal Blackheath's Tony Dunlop, Royal Cape's Dick Lockley, Loren Smith, the late Alister Nicol, Bank of Scotland's Muriel Young, and of course my terrific team at McGraw-Hill Contemporary Books, Matthew Carnicelli, Mandy Huber, Katherine Dennis, and Brigid Brown.

So many others helped, just by being a sounding board for ideas or actively making suggestions. These include Romulo and Vicki Zemborain, Daniel Vizzolini, Ricardo Monchietti, Peter Miles, Alejandro Ronone, Gavin Lough, Gudren Noonan, Bob Sommers, Dan Jenkins, Carlos Grande, Robert Cowan, Jason Joly, Paul Schlegel, Peter Alliss, Jonna Wiley, Jeff Williams, Eduardo Payovich, Art McCafferty, Brian Docherty, Craig Stadler, Ben Crenshaw, Scott Tolley, Henrique Lavie, Tom O'Callahan, Jay Townsend, Larry Dennis, Mike Biggs, Nancy McSorley, Paul Trow, Donald Panoz, Randy Hasty, Rhod McEwan, J. R. Steinbauer, and to anyone I inadvertently omitted, please be considered included in spirit. Special big-time thanks to John Marshall for his eagle-eye overview of the entire script and, of course, a hug of gratitude to my agent Nancy Crossman, a calm and patient lady whose confidence allowed me to sleep at nights.

All errors are mine. Credit is to everyone who helped make this book a reality, most particularly Joey Kaney and my wife, Susana.